EXTRAORDINARY
WOMEN
of CHRISTIAN HISTORY

EXTRAORDINARY
WOMEN
of CHRISTIAN HISTORY

WHAT WE CAN LEARN FROM
THEIR STRUGGLES AND TRIUMPHS

RUTH A. TUCKER

BakerBooks

a division of Baker Publishing Group
Grand Rapids, Michigan

Published by Baker Books
a division of Baker Publishing Group
P.O. Box 6287, Grand Rapids, MI 49516-6287
www.bakerbooks.com

Printed in the United States of America

Library of Congress Cataloging-in-Publication Data

Tucker, Ruth, 1945–
    Extraordinary women of Christian history : what we can learn from their struggles
and triumphs / Ruth A. Tucker.
        pages cm
    Includes bibliographical references and index.
    ISBN 978-0-8010-1672-1 (pbk.)
    1. Christian women—Biography. 2. Women in Christianity—History. I. Title.
BR1713.T828 2016
270.092′52—dc23   2015026964
    [B]

Unless otherwise indicated, Scripture quotations are from the Holy Bible, New International Version®. NIV®. Copyright © 1973, 1978, 1984, 2011 by Biblica, Inc.™ Used by permission of Zondervan. All rights reserved worldwide. www.zondervan.com

Scripture quotations labeled KJV are from the King James Version of the Bible.

Baker Publishing Group publications use paper produced from sustainable forestry practices and post-consumer waste whenever possible.

Contents

Introduction

I invite you on a pilgrimage, dear Reader. Come along with me . . . to places
we have never seen before and to people we could otherwise never have expected to know. . . . And we shall meet sundry folk even more exotic than
ourselves. "By adventure"—by happenstance—we have fallen into fellowship.

Thomas Cahill, *Mysteries of the Middle Ages*

The setting is the Mediterranean world of the first century. She wears
men's clothing to disguise her gender. A coworker and companion of the
apostle Paul, Thecla is a miracle worker, missionary, and desert holy woman.
Church fathers revere her, and today she is recognized as a saint. Another
desert saint is Mary of Egypt. Leaving behind a life of depravity and sex
addiction, she denies herself basic necessities to follow God's call. She dies
on April 1. More than fifteen hundred years later, Pulitzer Prize winner John
Berryman writes a poem titled "April Fool's Day, or, St Mary of Egypt."

Springtime in the Italian Apennine Mountains, 1212. Young, beautiful, and highborn, Clare runs away with Francis only to be cloistered in
a convent for the remainder of her life. Later they both are canonized as
saints, the great duo from Assisi. Generations after Clare, in another Italian village, Catherine of Siena is thought by many to be mentally ill. To
show her identity with plague victims, she drinks pus from the sores of
the one to whom she is ministering. Seventeenth-century French mystic
Jeanne Guyon takes her spirituality a step further. She pulls out healthy

teeth and rolls in prickly nettles in her imagined service to God. But she's also capable of offering timeless advice:

> I entreat you, give no place to despondency. This is a dangerous temptation . . . of the adversary. Melancholy contracts and withers the heart, and renders it unfit to receive the impressions of grace. It magnifies and gives a false coloring to objects, and thus renders your burdens too heavy to bear. God's designs regarding you, and His methods of bringing about these designs, are infinitely wise.[1]

Argula von Stauffer stands up to Catholic prelates in defense of Martin Luther. To them, she is no more than a daughter of Eve. Anne Hutchinson, another such daughter—and the mother of fifteen children—is banished from Boston by Puritan preachers. Deemed a heretic, she is justly killed by Native Americans, so say the Puritan divines. In 1865 Catherine Booth, with her husband William, cofounds the Salvation Army and is a popular preacher among the affluent of London's West End.

Carry Nation, in her Kansas campaign against alcohol, wields a hatchet to smash saloons. Pandita Ramabai, across the globe, establishes a mission society and sets in motion a great religious revival in India. Popular evangelist and founder of the Foursquare Church, Aimee Semple McPherson captures the headlines in the spring of 1926. Missing in action. Speculation. Rumors. A drowning? A kidnapping? Appointment with a plastic surgeon? Hiding out with her handsome music director? Except for her not having drowned, the verdict is still out. Eliza Davis George fights racism to serve as a Baptist missionary to Africa. After toiling some six decades, she dies in 1979 at age one hundred.

One after another these extraordinary women grab our attention, sometimes for all the wrong reasons. They form a dizzying and disparate array of personalities and lifestyles. Imagine them today as headliners for a grand conference, the *mother* of all women's retreats. Impossible, some would say. Imagine them all fitting into the same heaven. Impossible? Their enormous differences and flaws are not easily swept under the carpet, but they all stand solidly on common ground. Amid their malfunctions and failures, they profess an undying faith in Christ and seek to serve him. We dare not dismiss them any more than we would their biblical counterparts.

We easily imagine that the demarcation between biblical history and church history is very clear, one stopping as suddenly as the other begins, one sacred the other secular. But the church fathers recognized a continual flow as a river from one century to the next. True, they stipulated certain writings as the canon of Scripture, but one generation of believers followed another with no assumption that those featured in the biblical text had an edge over those who followed after.

Jerome, in fact, rated his friend Marcella above the prophet Anna. Here is this celebrated theologian and Bible translator of the fourth century, concluding that Anna comes out on the short end:

> Let us then compare her case with that of Marcella and we shall see that the latter has every way the advantage. Anna lived with her husband seven years; Marcella seven months. Anna only hoped for Christ; Marcella held Him fast. Anna confessed him at His birth; Marcella believed in Him crucified. Anna did not deny the Child; Marcella rejoiced in the Man as king.[2]

Jerome might have added that Marcella demonstrates sacrificial ministry in action, forsaking her wealth to serve the poor and afflicted. He would not have made favorable remarks about Héloïse, who lived and died several centuries later. Except for her cloistered life as a nun, her story is easily situated in the twenty-first century, as the opening paragraph of a 2005 *New York Times* book review indicates:

> Almost a thousand years ago, a teacher fell in love with his student. Almost a thousand years ago, they began a torrid affair. They made love in the kitchens of convents and in the boudoir of the girl's uncle. They wrote hundreds of love letters. When the girl bore a child, they were secretly married, but the teacher was castrated by henchmen of the enraged uncle. At her lover's bidding, the girl took religious orders. He took the habit of a monk. They retreated into separate monasteries and wrote to each other until parted by death.[3]

The account of Héloïse illustrates the wide-ranging popularity of historical biography. And her case is not unusual. The lives of Hildegard of Bingen, Teresa of Ávila, Susanna Wesley, Aimee Semple McPherson, Corrie ten Boom, Mother Teresa, and others have been written multiple times. This introductory volume, with issue-oriented questions at the end of each chapter, will hopefully stimulate more writers and more readers to dig into their fascinating stories. And may this book also spur similar overviews featuring Asian, African, and Hispanic women.

So how does an author even attempt to write some sort of two-thousand-year overview of Christian women from around the world? It's an impossible assignment. Indeed, had my publisher permitted me more space, I might have titled this book *777 Extraordinary Christian Women*. Truly hundreds of such women have been left out, and the reader can only sigh and scribble additional names in the table of contents. Needless to say, my pleasure in choosing the tastiest candy from this sampler box of chocolates turned into a very subjective task. In the end, weight gain was the biggest consideration, thus a lean and shapely volume.

But aren't there already enough sampler-box books of women in Christian history? And aren't there profiles of these women online? Perhaps. But in many cases the candy is too sweet for the palate—sugarcoated heroines. Flaws and failures are frosted over, without a hint of the bitter cocoa that gives chocolates that singular gourmet tastiness. In fact, as I reread and edited the manuscript, I was struck by how many failed marriages and failed ministries had become added ingredients of this volume. And I was loathe to leave them out. These women are anything but the super-saints of pious heroine tales. They are real people, and they are like us.

The greatest honor we can bestow on them is to present them as honestly as the sources allow. The Bible is our model. Beginning with Eve, the text is straightforward about sin and failures. Sarah's anger toward her husband and her foul attitude toward Hagar are not disguised, nor is the account of Lot's daughters, who carry out their conspiracy to commit incest with their father. Rebekah is a manipulative wife and mother. Rachel is an envious sister and a conniving thief of household idols. Tamar pretends to be a prostitute and seduces her father-in-law. And all this in Genesis alone.

No woman is well served when we transform her into a plaster saint. The words of Helen Taft Manning are fitting:

> I should hope that . . . she [M. Carey Thomas] may escape the fate of the many heroes and heroines of the past whose immortality is little more than

a name and a list of achievements, due to the misguided piety of their biographers. Those biographers have tried to erase from the record such qualities as seem to them uncomfortable or undignified . . . and have succeeded in making of their heroes plaster saints. . . . [Such biographers are] guilty of a criminal waste of rich and abundant material.[4]

Throughout the book I have used first names, in part to distinguish women from their husbands, but also because the use of a last name is a historical formality that does not seem appropriate. Although these women were often involved in significant public ministries, the private side of life was equally demanding. Married women in particular felt the burden of balancing ministry with obligations on the home front. Those women who were identified primarily by their positions of authority had often circumvented church polity and procedures to attain their status, their standing authenticated by their giftedness—or visionary claims—alone.

Here we take a round-the-world pilgrimage, encountering women from our colorful Christian heritage. Their voices rise out of the grave to challenge and inspire us to sacrificial service even as they warn us of sin and temptation. We are ever conscious that they inhabit their own historical and geographical settings and hold to religious values and worldviews that often seem utterly bewildering to the twenty-first-century mind. Nevertheless, they are part of that "cloud of witnesses," a long train of believers who first walk out of the pages of Genesis and continue on to the present day.

"By adventure"—by happenstance—we have fallen into fellowship.

1

Thecla and Early Martyrs, Monastics, and Saints

The apostle Paul. Love him or hate him. It's hard to be neutral. That certainly was true for Pearl S. Buck. Speaking of her missionary mother, she wrote: "Since those days when I saw all her nature dimmed I have hated Saint Paul with all my heart."[1] A missionary to China herself, Pearl later became a best-selling author and winner of both the Pulitzer and Nobel Prizes. I have just reread Peter Conn's biography of her and realized once again what a fascinating individual she was. She died in 1973 in her late seventies.

If her passing made the news, I was unaware. Some two decades later, however, I did take notice of her. While alone on a long road trip, I listened to her award-winning novel, *The Good Earth*. More than ten hours of audiocassettes left me spellbound. Since then I have been a fan. How I would love to time travel back to the late 1960s and have lunch with her. I would want to glean some writing tips and quiz her about her incredibly interesting life. But more than that I would like to talk about Paul. I would politely point out that he would have been the least likely person to dim the nature of a missionary—male or female—who had journeyed all the way to China to spread the gospel.

Pearl should have known better than to presume Paul was some sort of male chauvinist. He commended women associates as faithful coworkers, not the least of whom were Phoebe and Priscilla. He simply took women's public ministry for granted. For that alone I would tell her I love Paul. But besides his support for women in ministry, I love Paul because he was so honest, so straightforward. No feigning of phony spirituality. When he was furious with Barnabas or Peter or others who opposed him, he did not pretend otherwise. He was no super-saint. Indeed, he candidly disclosed his own struggles and spiritual failures.

So what's there not to love about Paul? There's plenty, if the only Paul one knows is the one who's been accused of dimming the natures of women. Such has too often been the case throughout history. If only there were a document that would prove once and for all how much he encouraged women in ministry.

Some would say there is: the *Acts of Paul and Thecla*. The central thesis of this ancient text is Paul's close collaboration with a female coworker. This writing, however, is apocryphal, not accepted as part of the biblical

Paul Speaks on Marriage and Celibacy

As we consider Thecla and other women who renounced marriage and sexual relations, it behooves us to consider how important Paul's writings on this subject were to many believers in the early church. They interpreted and applied his words in his first letter to the church in Corinth from a perspective that seems strange to most Christians today.

> Now for the matters you wrote about: "It is good for a man not to have sexual relations with a woman." But since sexual immorality is occurring, each man should have sexual relations with his own wife, and each woman with her own husband. The husband should fulfill his marital duty to his wife, and likewise the wife to her husband. The wife does not have authority over her own body but yields it to her husband. In

canon—and rightly so. It is widely regarded as little more than a fanciful romance. A reader seeking to find a realistic record of early Christian ministry will be seriously disappointed. In fact, once we step outside the pages of the Bible, biographical accounts are airbrushed, all blemishes removed. Personalities are flattened like pancakes and topped with syrupy spirituality. What a pity.

Beginning with Thecla, we move beyond sacred texts as our sources. The question we mull over in our minds, then, when we encounter what appears to be a fanciful story, is not could God have performed such a miracle but rather did God. Whether we are considering the martyrdom of Perpetua, the angelic life of Macrina, the self-sacrificing Marcella, the holy and venerable Paula, or the scandalous Mary of Egypt, we do well to understand the purpose behind the writing. Many of the early Christian texts, we must remember, were written primarily to inspire. What we sometimes sadly miss in these accounts is the forthright honesty of the Bible. From Eve and Sarah to Gomer and the woman at the well, Scripture exposes warts and all.

the same way, the husband does not have authority over his own body but yields it to his wife. Do not deprive each other except perhaps by mutual consent and for a time, so that you may devote yourselves to prayer. Then come together again so that Satan will not tempt you because of your lack of self-control. I say this as a concession, not as a command. I wish that all of you were as I am. But each of you has your own gift from God; one has this gift, another has that.

Now to the unmarried and the widows I say: It is good for them to stay unmarried, as I do. But if they cannot control themselves, they should marry, for it is better to marry than to burn with passion.

1 Corinthians 7:1–9

THECLA
Legendary Companion of Paul

A convert of Paul in Iconium, Thecla gave up a life of leisure to become a missionary on the run, disguising herself as a man to escape her pursuers. She is regarded "equal to the apostles" and a saint in Eastern Orthodoxy and was so considered by the Roman Catholic Church until 1969, when she was removed from the list. The claims for her sainthood were deemed spurious.

Although the *Acts of Paul and Thecla* was considered apocryphal even in the early church and was thus not included in the canon, the historicity of Thecla herself was rarely questioned. In fact, the church fathers, with the notable exception of Tertullian, commended her as a true follower of Christ—and Paul. St. Augustine cited her to bolster his support of what he regarded as Paul's view of marriage, and John Chrysostom commended her for giving up her priceless jewelry. Gregory of Nyssa testified that long after her death Thecla appeared to his mother as she was about to give birth to her first child.

By the fourth century the cult of Thecla was in full swing. She was revered for her commitment to virginity as the ultimate ideal of Christian virtue. But not virginity alone. She was heralded as a courageous missionary and an orthodox defender of Paul's teachings.

We first meet this young virgin sitting in the window of her upscale home in Iconium. She is transfixed by the sound of a man's voice, even more so by his words. The speaker is the apostle Paul, who has found lodging with her neighbors Onesiphorus and Lectra. But Thecla is not the only one who has come under his spell. She observes other women making their way to the meeting. She longs to join them and see for herself who this man is. "For three days and three nights Thecla does not rise from the window, neither to eat nor to drink."[2]

So distressed is her mother that she sends for Thamyris, Thecla's fiancé. Perhaps he can bring her to her senses. Her daughter, she tells him, is "tied to the window like a spider, lays hold of what is said by Paul with a strange eagerness and awful emotion." She is worried sick. Thamyris goes to the window and kisses Thecla, but she pays him no heed. She's obsessed—obsessed by a man who is preaching celibacy, depriving "young men of wives, and maidens of husbands."

An important aspect of this apocryphal treatise is its meticulous listing of names and places, many of which correspond with the biblical text, lending the work an aura of authenticity.

Thamyris, distraught by the turn of events, appeals to the local tribunal, demanding that Paul be held accountable for his contemptible teaching. When Paul defends his instruction as the very revelation of God, he is bound over to guards and locked in prison. Thecla sneaks away and searches him out. After arriving at the prison by night, she bribes the guards with costly bracelets, enters Paul's cell, and kisses the chains that bind him. When she is discovered "enchained by affection," both she and Paul are ordered to go before the tribunal. When she refuses to respond to questions or even acknowledge her fiancé, her mother cries out, "Burn the wicked wretch."

Paul is then cast out of the city, and Thecla is ordered burned at the stake. But "though a great fire was blazing, it did not touch her; for God, having compassion upon her, made an underground rumbling, and a cloud overshadowed them from above, full of water and hail." Having escaped the flames, Thecla, with the help of a young boy, is guided to a cave where Paul is hiding. There she hears him praying: "O Saviour Christ, let not the fire touch Thecla, but stand by her, for she is Yours."

We want them to run away together and live happily ever after as a celibate gospel-preaching team, but that is not about to happen. Soon back in Antioch, the beautiful young Thecla is sexually harassed by Alexander, a high-ranking official. "And taking hold of Alexander, she tore his cloak, and pulled off his crown, and made him a laughing-stock." Not to be made a fool, he brings her before the governor. As punishment, she is bound "to a fierce lioness. . . . But the lioness, with Thecla sitting upon her, licked her feet; and all the multitude was astonished."

The rulers, however, are determined to put her to death. They bring her to the arena to face wild beasts, only to witness another miracle: the lioness protecting her from all harm. Again she survives unscathed—and more than that. She sees a ditch full of water and throws herself in as an act of self-baptism. Alexander's wrath, however, is only intensified. He will defeat her with bulls "exceedingly terrible," and they "put red-hot irons under the privy parts of the bulls, so that they, being rendered more furious might kill her."

In the end, Alexander concedes defeat, and Thecla is brought before the governor, who issues an edict before the crowd: "I release to you the God-fearing Thecla." Soon after this she disguises herself in a man's attire and again meets with Paul and then spends the rest of her days either traveling with him or living in a cave where the sick and demon possessed are brought for healing. Despite opposition from "lawless ones," she lives to ninety, at which time she is miraculously entombed inside a rock.

> And there came a voice out of the heaven, saying: Fear not, Thecla, my true servant, for I am with you. Look and see where an opening has been made before you, for there shall be for you an everlasting house, and there you shall obtain shelter. And the blessed Thecla regarding it, saw the rock opened as far as to allow a man to enter, and did according to what had been said to her: and nobly fleeing from the lawless ones entered into the rock; and the rock was straightway shut together, so that not even a joining appeared.

PERPETUA
Early Christian Beheaded in the Arena

The account of Perpetua and her slave girl comes from an early source, *The Passion of Perpetua and Felicity*. It is the testimony of a death more than a biography or autobiography of a life. In fact, nothing is known of Perpetua's youth. We first meet her in 203, a young mother and a catechumen, still unbaptized. In early Christianity, most conversions, unlike Paul's or Thecla's, transpired over a period of time rather than as a response to a vision or an evangelistic invitation.

Hailing from Carthage in North Africa, Perpetua was a student of Saturus, a deacon who conducted catechism classes. She was twenty-two and the mother of an infant son, the father of whom is not mentioned. Her means of support or how she acquired a servant are not specified, but the account does identify her aged father as an esteemed nobleman.

The most startling aspect of Perpetua's story is that she seems almost to beg for martyrdom, and not only she but also her pregnant servant, Felicitas, and many others. In fact, the wish for holy martyrdom became so intense that one Roman official reportedly snarled: "You wretches, if you want to die, you have cliffs to leap from and ropes to hang by."[3] How can she be offering herself for execution when the emperor's edict targets only those "teaching or making converts"? She has not yet even been initiated into the believing community.

Her parents and her brother were beside themselves over the turn of events. Desperate to rescue their daughter, her father pleaded and threatened, while her mother sought to awaken her maternal instincts. But nothing they did lessened her resolve. Her testimony speaks of their mutual suffering: "I nursed my baby, who was faint from hunger. In my anxiety I spoke to my mother about the child, I tried to comfort my brother, and I gave the child in their charge. I was in pain because I saw them suffering out of pity for me." A later medieval version of her testimony does not permit such weakness: "But she threw the child aside, and repulsed her parents, saying: 'Be-gone from me, enemies of God, for I know you not!'"[4]

On the day of their execution, Perpetua and Felicitas were ordered to the arena, where they were gored by a "mad heifer." When the spectators shouted "Enough!" the young women were brought before a gladiator. When he failed to fully sever her neck, Perpetua, according to the *Passion*, took charge herself: "She screamed as she was struck on the bone; then she took the trembling hand of the young gladiator and guided it to her throat."

Both Perpetua and Felicitas, mistress and slave, are celebrated as saints in the Orthodox and Catholic Churches. Indeed, CatholicCulture.org informs the reader that the story of their martyrdom "has been loved and reverenced by the faithful for centuries." So also today: "What a wonderful story for children," for it "teaches a most beautiful lesson [not only] in modesty" but also of courage: they were "so brave, and so full of love." And, according to the site, it teaches us about race, that we should "not let our color be a stumbling block . . . for Perpetua was white and Felicitas was black."[5]

That the account of a mother leaving a child behind and offering herself to be martyred is a wonderful story for children is surely not a universal truism. Nor is the claim of their being a white master and black slave convincing. They were both North Africans.

MARCELLA
Biblical Scholar and Translator

If Thecla was regarded "chief of virgins" by certain church fathers, Marcella (325–410) ranked close behind. Virginity was truly the highest spiritual status a woman could attain. That men had come to this conclusion and heralded this heavenly way of life was beside the point. One of the leading proponents of women virgins was Methodius, a fourth-century bishop in Asia Minor whose very significant and only surviving work is his fictional *Banquet of the Ten Virgins*. Here the virgins are wined and dined at a festive banquet in the garden of Arete. Each virgin gives a discourse. Thecla opens the ceremony by leading a twenty-four-verse hymn praising the purity of virginity, with the nine other virgins joining on the chorus.

Marcella offers the first discourse, "since," according to Methodius, "she sits in the highest place, and is at the same time the eldest."[6] She lays out God's plan from the beginning, when "the men of old times thought it nothing unseemly to take their own sisters for wives, until the law coming separated them, and by forbidding that which at first had seemed to be right, declared it to be a sin." God allowed men and women "during the period of childhood, to amuse themselves like young animals," to practice polygamy and to populate the world. Marriage continued to be affirmed throughout the whole Old Testament period, but it was "Christ alone [who] taught virginity, openly preaching the Kingdom of Heaven. . . . For in old times man was not yet perfect, and for this reason was unable to receive perfection, which is virginity."

These words should not be confused with Marcella's own words. Her life exemplifies service far more than celibacy. Born into a wealthy aristocratic family in Rome, she enjoyed the privilege of education and culture and the finest fashion money could buy: fancy gowns, hairpieces, jewelry, and layers of makeup. Banquets and balls offered entertainment for both young and old. Soon a well-heeled aristocrat arranged to marry the beautiful maiden. When he died less than a year later, it was assumed that after her period of mourning she would be the most eligible young widow in town. But her life took a very different turn.

For Marcella, the call to Christian ministry was tugging at her heartstrings. There was no sudden conversion experience, no appeal from a traveling evangelist to transform her into another Thecla. Her call had been seeping into her psyche since early childhood, when her mother, Albina, had offered lodging to Athanasius, one of the greatest theologians of the early church. He was the patriarch of Alexandria who had been hounded out of the region by his theological enemies. He had fled to Rome, where he was warmly welcomed into her mother's palatial home.

Amid his busy schedule, the famous churchman found time to interact on theological matters with her mother while Marcella listened in. The memories she cherished most, however, were miracle stories associated with desert monks, particularly St. Anthony. When Athanasius departed to return to Constantinople, he presented Albina with his book, *Life of St. Anthony*, a treasured gift never to be forgotten.

Although a Christian herself, Albina years later would urge Marcella to remarry for money. Cerealis, an older man with close imperial ties and a vast estate, was most eager to wed her widowed daughter, and Albina had her eye on the inheritance. But Marcella was determined to move in a different direction—to give up her wealth and truly follow Jesus in ministry. There was no precedent, however, at least according to Jerome, for such a life of poverty. "In those days no highborn lady at Rome had made profession of the monastic life, or had ventured—so strange and ignominious and degrading did it then seem—publicly to call herself a nun."[7]

Nevertheless, Marcella vowed to forfeit wealth and serve the poor. Abandoning her costly finery, she donned a plain brown garment suited for a washerwoman. Though not seeking to stir controversy, her action was nothing short of shocking—and shameful. Had she gone to the desert and lived in a cave, she would have brought less disgrace to her family than living like a pauper in plain sight amid style-conscious Romans.

As time passed, other women joined her in ministry, and together they became known as the Brown Dress Society. Her Aventine Hill mansion served as a refuge for the poor—and for scholars. The most celebrated visitor was Jerome, who for three years was her houseguest. An attentive hostess, she was also an astute editor and critic of his Bible translation, putting to good use her knowledge of Greek and Latin. More than that, she was a constructive critic, not accepting his "explanation as satisfactory," as he later testified, "but she proposed questions from the opposite viewpoint, not for the sake

9

of being contentious, but so that by asking, she might learn solutions for points she perceived could be raised in objection. . . . What cleverness."[8]

When Jerome returned to his monastery in Jerusalem, Marcella became his spokesperson. "Thus after my departure, if an argument arose about some evidence from scripture, the question was pursued with her as the judge." Fully aware of criticism that might be flung her way due to her gender, Jerome insisted she discourse with her challengers "as if what she said was not her own, even if the views were her own," coming "from [Jerome] or from another man . . . lest she seem to inflict an injury on the male sex."[9]

Among those of the male sex she did not offend was Pope Anastasius I, bishop of Rome, who was contesting the teachings of Origen, a renowned scholar and theologian. Having never read Origen's treatise himself, the pope consulted Marcella (a renowned *anti-Origenist*) before condemning the work. Defenders of Origen would argue that his beliefs (relating to the creation of the world and other matters) were distorted by his critics and that Marcella contributed to that distortion, but her influence in high places was an accepted fact.

In 410, when Alaric and his hoodlum army of Visigoths sacked Rome, Marcella was one of the many casualties. Refusing to believe that she had no hidden jewels or money, they roughed her up and struck her to the ground. She died the following day at age eighty-five.

PAULA
Hebrew, Greek, and Latin Linguist

"If all the members of my body were to be converted into tongues," wrote Jerome, "and if each of my limbs were to be gifted with a human voice, I could still do no justice to the virtues of the holy and venerable Paula."[10] Sounds almost like the words of a lover.

A wealthy fourth-century Roman widow, Paula was converted to the monastic life through the influence of Marcella, who was more than twenty years older than she. Marcella welcomed Paula into her circle of prayer and service to the poor. Paula was thirty-five when she first met Jerome at Marcella's home. It might have been love at first sight considering all they had in common. Both were born in 347, educated in Rome, and interested in languages, translation, biblical studies, and theology.

Jerome was highly impressed with Paula's intellect and capabilities, particularly her knowledge of Hebrew, Greek, and Latin. Indeed, it is an interesting historical footnote that he conscripted her to help him with his great Bible translation. So close was their relationship that rumors of inappropriate conduct, perhaps spurred by Jerome's enemies, spread throughout the Mediterranean world. Jerome's sudden departure from Rome to the Holy Land and Paula's own departure sometime later only fueled such stories. In Palestine Paula established a monastery for women, but the gossip continued. "Before I knew the house of saintly Paula," wrote Jerome, "my praises were sung through the city." But an "evil report" quickly sullied his reputation. "The only fault found in me is my sex, and that only when Paula comes to Jerusalem."[11]

As a desert ascetic, Jerome was surely not free from sexual desires. "How often did I fancy myself among the pleasures of Rome!" he confessed. "I often found myself amid bevies of girls. . . . My mind was burning with desire, and the fires of lust kept bubbling up before me."[12] Whether or not there was any truth to the rumors about him and Paula, Jerome outwardly defended virginity. More than that, he glorified it: "I praise matrimony. But only because it produces virgins."[13] On a numeric scale, he assigned marriage a 30, widowhood a 60, and virginity a solid 100.

Bishop Palladius later lamented that Paula was under Jerome's spell. "For though she was able to surpass all, having great abilities, he hindered her by his jealousy, having induced her to serve his own plan."[14] She died in her midfifties and was buried in the Church of the Nativity in Bethlehem. When Jerome died some fifteen years later, his body was interred nearby.

MACRINA THE YOUNGER
"Angelic and Heavenly" Saint

Macrina was a genuine living saint, at least in the eyes of her brother Gregory of Nyssa (who was also regarded a saint by both the Orthodox and the Catholic Churches). She lived an "angelic and heavenly life," with "no anger or jealousy, no hatred or pride." He questioned whether "indeed she should be styled woman," explaining, "For I do not know whether it is fitting to designate her by her sex, who so surpassed her sex." As with many notable saints, her birth in 330 was accompanied by a miracle:

> At her [mother's] first confinement she [bore a daughter] Macrina. When the due time came for her pangs to be ended by delivery, she fell asleep and seemed to be carrying in her hands that which was still in her womb. And some one in form and raiment more splendid than a human being appeared and addressed the child she was carrying by the name of Thecla, that Thecla, I mean, who is so famous among the virgins.[15]

This Thecla was, of course, no other than Paul's convert and fellow missionary who wore a man's attire (thus truly not "styled a woman"). So Macrina at the very time of her birth was greeted by this great saint of centuries earlier. The mother in labor, Emmelia, would give birth to nine more children. Reared among servants and luxurious surroundings in Caesarea in Cappadocia, Macrina was homeschooled with an emphasis on Scripture. According to her brother Gregory, "the Psalter was her constant companion, like a good fellowtraveller that never deserted her."[16]

Barely in her teens, Macrina (the Younger, as opposed to Macrina the Elder, her saintly grandmother) vowed, upon learning of her fiancé's death, to devote her life entirely to God. Her most outstanding endowment, according to Gregory, was her profound influence on others, including her mother and brothers. In fact, when one of her beloved brothers died, she became the "prop of her mother's weakness" so that her mother did not "behave in any ignoble and womanish way, so as to cry out at the calamity." She also convinced her widowed mother to live a life of asceticism:

> And weaning her from all accustomed luxuries, Macrina drew her on to adopt her own standard of humility. She induced her to live on a footing of equality with the staff of maids, so as to share with them in the same food, the same kind of bed, and in all the necessaries of life, without any regard to differences of rank.[17]

Macrina followed this ascetic lifestyle until her mother's death and long after when she served as an abbess of her own monastery. As is true of all those who would become saints, her holy life needed authentication by a miracle. The testimony came from a soldier who had visited Macrina's monastery with his wife and little girl whose deformed eye was most "hideous and pitiable." Macrina sent a sister nun to the pharmacy for a drug "which [was] powerful to cure eye complaints." However, overwhelmed in the presence of this great saint, the parents forgot to take the drug when they returned home, only to subsequently discover that their daughter had been healed without it—a miracle that confirmed Macrina's sainthood.

Not that there were no other miracles. But Gregory summarizes them while at the same time insisting he is omitting them:

> Consequently I omit that extraordinary agricultural operation in the famine time, how that the corn for the relief of need, though constantly distributed, suffered no perceptible diminution, remaining always in bulk the same as before it was distributed to the needs of the suppliants. And after this there are happenings still more surprising, of which I might tell. Healings of diseases, and castings out of demons, and true predictions of the future. All are believed to be true, even though apparently incredible, by those who have investigated them accurately.[18]

Gregory of Nyssa, considered one of the great church fathers, wondered if Macrina should be "styled" a woman because she "so surpassed her sex." Such a perspective was not uncommon in the church and in civic life, and it colored the ministry of women in the centuries that followed, even to this present day.

MARY OF EGYPT
"A Fire of Public Debauchery"

If Macrina is remembered for her holy life, Mary of Egypt, born in the mid-fourth century, is not. Without her testimony of dissolute behavior, her story would be lost in the desert dust.

That Mary's confessions are not as widely read as Augustine's *Confessions* is surely not because hers are any less graphic—or pornograhic. Indeed, his story pales in comparison. She and Augustine were contemporaries, both North Africans. Apart from her tale of degradation, followed by years of penitence as a hermit in the desert, however, she accomplished little when compared with the celebrated bishop of Hippo. Her story of "insatiable and an irrepressible [sexual] passion" was passed along for two centuries before it was written down. As such it surely must have offered titillation for sex-starved desert monks. It is best told in her own words as purportedly related during a chance meeting with Father Zosimas, a desert pilgrim.

> I am ashamed. . . . But as you have already seen my naked body I shall likewise lay bare before you my work, so that you may know with what shame and obscenity my soul is filled. . . . Already during the lifetime of my parents, when I was twelve years old, I renounced their love and went to Alexandria. . . . For about seventeen years . . . I was like a fire of public debauchery. . . . Then one summer I saw a large crowd of Lybians and Egyptians running towards the sea. I asked one of them, . . . "Will they take me with them if I wish to go?" [He said], "No one will hinder you if you have money to pay for the journey and for food." And I said to him, "To tell you truth, I have no money, neither have I food. But I . . . have a body." . . . Seeing some young men standing on the shore, about ten or more of them, full of vigor and alert in their movements, I decided that they would do for my purpose. . . . I frequently forced those miserable youths even against their own will. There is no mentionable or unmentionable depravity of which I was not their teacher. . . . At last we arrived in Jerusalem. I spent the days before the festival in the town, living the same kind of life. . . . The holy day of the Exaltation of the Cross dawned while I was still flying about—hunting for youths. At daybreak I saw that everyone was hurrying to the church, so I ran with the rest. When the hour for the holy elevation approached, I was trying to make my way in with the crowd which was struggling to get through the church doors. . . . But when I trod on the doorstep which everyone passed, I was stopped by some force which prevented my entering.[19]

Stricken with remorse, Mary confessed her depravity before an "icon of the most holy Mother of God." She then retreated to the desert beyond the Jordan River and endured privation until her death nearly a half century later. She is today celebrated as a saint in both the Catholic and the Eastern Orthodox Churches.

CONCLUDING OBSERVATIONS

After graduating from college, I spent a summer as a counselor at Word of Life Island in the Adirondack Mountains of New York. Each week Jack Wyrtzen, founder and director, brought in special speakers to challenge the college-age campers. Invariably they had testimonies of sinking deep into sin before finding God. As counselors we always wondered if this week's speaker would be able to top the previous week in a shocking tale of depravity. In introducing these individuals, Jack promised us compelling accounts of their wallowing in the "garbage pails of sin."

Mary of Egypt would have rated high as a Word of Life speaker, though we never heard a testimony of sex addiction per se. One might wonder if her story had been embellished for effect—as we often wondered back then. Nevertheless, her story is a refreshing contrast to Thecla's wild and crazy miracle tales and Macrina's life of angelic holiness. These women mostly seem too good to be true and as such may seem out of place in the twenty-first century. Alongside these stories we see women who sacrificed their wealth to reach out to the marginalized while at the same time keeping their intellects well oiled. Marcella and Paula might today be ranked high among the church fathers but for their gender.

Like the celebrated church fathers, they were not scholars only. Separating spirituality from scholarship to them would have seemed absurd. Biblical translation and theological studies were not academic disciplines. The goal was perfection, whether sought for by the holy woman herself or imagined by the hagiographer. Today the accounts of these women teach us how deeply and earnestly individuals in another era strived for holiness.

QUESTIONS TO THINK ABOUT

How does Thecla fit into the narrative that flows from the New Testament into the early Christian church? If parts of her story seem fanciful, should we ignore her altogether? How do we relate to biblical stories that seem almost impossible to believe?

Does the story of Perpetua and Felicitas appear to be contrived? How would you regard someone today who volunteered to be martyred—a mother leaving an infant behind? Should Perpetua have had more regard for her aged father? Do you think she was obeying Jesus in leaving behind her family and taking up the cross to follow him?

What aspect of Marcella's life and ministry do you find most inspiring? How do you assess her alongside Paula? How would you feel if someone such as Jerome paid high tribute to your scholarship, faith, and holy living?

Would your brother (or any brother you know) sing your praises as Gregory did of his sister Macrina? Would her story be more believable if he were to disclose that she was sometimes cranky and critical?

Do you think leaders in the early church exaggerated the claim that both Jesus and Paul celebrated virginity and celibacy? How should we assess that claim today?

Do you think the testimony of Mary of Egypt rings true, or do you suspect that a desert monk with time on his hands may have begun an embellishment that after two centuries turned into a page-turner?

If you were assigned a roommate for a two-day women's retreat, which one of these women would you hope to spend time with? What questions would you ask her?

2

Hilda of Whitby and Medieval Nuns and Abbesses

Paris. Perhaps the most romantic and most written-about city in the world. Like many Americans I have memories. Perfect sunny summer weather. Shady boulevards. Notre-Dame. *Mona Lisa*. Eiffel Tower. Champs-Élysées. Arc de Triomphe. Nightfall on the Seine. The list goes on. We saw it all.

It was a last-minute Paris-on-the-cheap stop on our way home from Kijabe, Kenya, where I had been teaching. A nice little family holiday. But we were poor back then, and a two-star high-rise hotel and two days of hurried walking were all we could afford. Pinching pennies, we stopped for a quick lunch at a café only to be charged extra for butter. Imagine that. When we complained, the condescending waiter responded in French, leaving the impression that he didn't appreciate Americans.

Lying on a park bench at midnight is also filed in my memory bank. Backache so severe I was sure I couldn't walk the dozen blocks and up the stairs to our shabby quarters—no fire escape. I dreamed that night that we were trapped in the flames on the twelfth floor.

When I contemplate my mixed emotions and memories of that city, I am reminded that Paris is as shabby as it is chic and known for revolution and riots as much as for high fashion and culture. Crime and conspiracy fill the pages of its history alongside the high academic scholarship of the Sorbonne. So also in the twelfth century. Paris is where romance blossoms, even while terror and violence are lurking outside locked doors.

Abelard, one of the most celebrated teachers and philosophers of the medieval world, is tutoring Héloïse, his gifted and drop-dead-gorgeous pupil. What follows has all the earmarks of a twenty-first-century tabloid cover story. Romance, lust, exploitation, pregnancy, intrigue, violence—and religion—all filtered through the curtain of the medieval church. In the words of Henry Adams, "The twelfth century, with all its sparkle, would be dull without Abelard and Héloïse."[1]

Though often overlooked as a tabloid story, the relationship between Clare and Francis is also intriguing. That their names are prefaced by *saint*, however, places them in a different realm. But the story is similar: the lovely teenage Clare sneaks out in the dead of night to meet Francis, who, like Abelard, had been a popular singer—a dashing troubadour.

Jesus Speaking on Childhood

In medieval times many young girls were left at convents where they spent the rest of their lives, sometimes for spiritual reasons, often out of financial necessity. Today most Christians would be horrified by such treatment of a child. We wonder if parents in earlier times wrongly based their decisions to give up their children on the words and actions of Jesus.

Then people brought little children to Jesus for him to place his hands on them and pray for them. But the disciples rebuked them.

Jesus said, "Let the little children come to me, and do not hinder them, for the kingdom of heaven belongs to such as these." When he had placed his hands on them, he went on from there.

Matthew 19:13–15

The stories of Héloïse and Clare begin as fairy tales more than tabloid exposés. If not actually princesses, both are beautiful, young, and wealthy. Abelard and Francis each play the role of Prince Charming, luring the maiden away from the castle. Clare even gets her long, flowing hair shorn. How fairy tale is that! But this is where any resemblance ends. Cloistered nuns simply don't fit the script except that Clare seems to live happily ever after. Not so Héloïse.

Many medieval women who devoted their lives to monastic ministry had a noble heritage. Growing up in a castle, if not a convent, was almost a requisite, and the decision to enter the convent was often made when they were very young. Hilda of Whitby and Lioba, both celebrated abbesses, rose from the ranks of English nobility; Hrotsvitha, a playwright and poet, from the ranks of German nobility.

We sometimes assume these saints are too good to be true, as their biographers, aka hagiographers, would lead us to believe. But scratch the surface and we find real women to whom we can relate.

HILDA OF WHITBY
Celebrated Snake-Stone Abbess

We would know virtually nothing about Hilda but for the seventh-century monk Bede, who wrote a history of the English nation and is credited as the first English historian. He praises her holy life and ministry that was foretold by a dream.

> All who knew Hild, the handmaiden of Christ and abbess, used to call her mother because of her outstanding devotion and grace. She was not only an example of holy life to all who were in the monastery but she also provided an opportunity for salvation and repentance to many who lived far away and who heard the happy story of her industry and virtue. This was bound to happen in fulfillment of the dream which her mother Breguswith had during the child's infancy. While her husband Hereric was living in exile under the British king Cerdic, where he was poisoned, Breguswith had a dream that he was suddenly taken away, and though she searched most earnestly for him, no trace of him could be found anywhere. But suddenly, in the midst of her search, she found a most precious necklace

under her garment and, as she gazed closely at it, it seemed to spread such a blaze of light that it filled all Britain with its gracious splendour. This dream was truly fulfilled in her daughter Hild; for her life was an example of the works of light, blessed not only to herself but to many who desired to live uprightly.[2]

Born in a castle in Northumberland in 614, she was reared in King Edwin's palace, her father having been poisoned by a political opponent. Later the king was baptized a Christian as were all those living in his court, including the then thirteen-year-old Hilda. For two decades her trail goes cold; then we learn that she had accepted an appointment from her bishop to serve as a nun and later an abbess. In 657, she was transferred to a monastery at Whitby, where she continued to practice Celtic monasticism, known among other things for its practice of housing monks and nuns in small cottages.

There she ruled over a double monastery of separately housed women and men, five of whom would later become bishops. Emphasizing Bible study and good deeds, she was a public servant though not likely wielding great political power. Nor did she, as some have claimed, call for the convening of the Synod of Whitby, though it was apparently held at her monastery. That synod was as political as it was ecclesiastical, and it brought the Celtic church under the control of Rome. Her role may have been little more than that of hostess. Had she actually wielded power, she might have moved the decisions of the synod in a different direction. In fact, loyal as she was to the Celtic church, it is entirely possible that she was very disappointed by the outcome.

There is no reason to doubt that Hilda was an energetic administrator and competent educator. Indeed, Whitby became known as a great center for learning under her leadership. She was quick to recognize the gifts of others, including Caedmon, whom later scholars would claim to be the first English poet. Although he was a mere herdsman on her monastic estate, Hilda recognized his talent and invited him to become a monk. Alongside the psalms and the Song of Songs, his only existing hymn is weak and unimaginative, but his influence on the development of the English language is widely recognized. Of him Bede wrote:

There was in the Monastery of this Abbess [Hilda] a certain brother particularly remarkable for the Grace of God, who was wont to make religious
verses, so that whatever was interpreted to him out of scripture, he soon
after put the same into poetical expressions of much sweetness and humility
in English, which was his native language. By his verse the minds of many
were often excited to despise the world, and to aspire to heaven.[3]

It is surely an exaggerated claim that Hilda, by recognizing Caedmon,
"came close to inventing English literature." Hardly. But she served as a
most competent abbess and is the heroine of the delightful serpent legend of the ammolite stones. These "snake stones" are observed today in
the region. Apart from a grand miracle, their origin is a mystery. As the
story goes, Hilda and her nuns were preparing to clear land to construct
an abbey. The completion of the work, however, was in jeopardy due to
a most exasperating infestation of snakes. It might have been spiders, but
snakes were bad enough. Hilda to the rescue. In a striking demonstration
of power, she confronted the hideous serpents and turned every one into
a stone. (If only Eve might have been so audacious!)

Despite a serious illness during the final six years of her life, Hilda
founded one more monastery some fourteen miles away at Hackness. On
the day she died (November 17, 680), it was reported that the bells there
mysteriously began to ring.

LIOBA
Evangelist and Miracle Worker

Described as "a great model of Christian perfection," Lioba grew up
in the early eighth century in a monastery in the English countryside and
would later become a noted missionary abbess in the heavily forested
and sparsely populated region of Bavaria. Boniface, her bishop, regarded
her highly and addressed her in later years as "the reverend handmaid in
Christ."[4]

Her birth was prefaced by a dream. When her elderly mother, said
to be of noble heritage, unexpectedly became pregnant, a voice revealed
that the child she was carrying was God's anointed servant. In a relationship reminiscent of Hannah and Samuel, she trained her young daughter

in acts of piety and then turned her over to Mother Tetta, abbess of the Benedictine convent of Winburn.

Here there was no time for leisure. Menial labor was interrupted only by strict hours of study, prayer, and daily rituals. Indeed, there was no childhood for this little girl, who might have easily wondered if she had been abandoned or orphaned. But she was not alone. She had companions whose situations were similar. Did she whisper at night and tell stories and secrets? Did she miss her mother and father and all those she had to leave behind? Did she shiver alone in the dark to the sound of the howling wind? Did she stifle romantic and maternal longings? We unconsciously imagine that these little saints in the making were devoid of emotions and as hardened as Hilda's snake stones.

Life outside the eighth-century convent was anything but idyllic. Villages were surrounded by small fields and dense forests where superstition smoldered under dank carpets of moss. Monsters were as real as the roving militias and prowling wolves. Mud-daubed wooden huts with thatched roofs were a summer breeding ground for insects; in winter they turned into smoke-filled dens. Scourges of every sort curbed fertility and family size. Even in the smallest village, it seems that someone was always dying. Every household, whether of noble or peasant stock, took its turn.

But the times were not entirely grim. There were feasts and festivals and games, often accompanied by loud, ribald laughter. There was teasing and romance and fighting and family togetherness that pushed one day into the next, while the rhythms of the seasons flowed into years and decades. In the convent, time almost stood still amid the silence except for the books and the daily cadence of the Benedictine rule.

The most overarching aspect of Lioba's youth in the convent was separation from the world. Her biographer describes the complex as being "surrounded by strong and lofty walls" where "no entrance should be allowed to a person of the other sex . . . except in the case of priests who had to celebrate Mass."[5] The description is that of a self-imposed imprisonment: "Any woman who wished to renounce the world and enter the cloister did so on the understanding that she would never leave it."[6] The world was outside the high walls where only fantasies took flight.

But for Lioba any fantasies would have been trumped by a real world of aging parents. In her early twenties, she expressed concern for her widowed mother in a letter to Boniface. A relative who had known her parents, he was not under the tight monastic restrictions placed on her. "I ask you also to remember my mother Aebbe," she pleaded. "She is still alive but suffers from ill health and for many years now has been afflicted with infirmity." Lioba perceived him as a brother, "for there is no other man in my family in whom I can put my trust as I can in you."[7]

Whether Boniface cared for her mother is not revealed. His real interest had been in Lioba herself. She had years earlier sent him a short sacred verse written to "exercise [her] budding talents" and expressed her desire to serve God. He remembered her when he was appealing for missionaries to serve with him in Germany. Unable to turn down the proposal, she

Hrotsvitha: Playwright with a Sense of Humor

If Caedmon was less than original in his creative efforts, the same could not be said for Hrotsvitha (c. 935–1002). She was a secular canoness (having taken no vow as a nun) attached to a German Benedictine convent. Known for her scholarship and writings, her interests were wide-ranging, though she is remembered primarily for her interest in mathematics and her work as a playwright. She wrote in a serious vein, but not without a clever sense of humor. In one of her plays, Governor Dulcitius enters the monastery in the dead of night and with evil intent ambushes three holy virgins. They escape to the convent kitchen and hide behind barrels while the delusional fool mistakes them in the dark for the hanging pots and pans. They watch and whisper, "Oh, look! He must be out of his senses! I believe he thinks that he is kissing us. . . . Now he presses the saucepans tenderly to his breast, now the kettles and frying-pans! He is kissing them hard! . . . His face, his hands, his clothes! They are all as black as soot."[a]

[a] Dulcitius, available at http://www.classics.ucsb.edu/classes/clas130-F08/week8/3 .DULCITUS.htm.

followed his call (and the call of God) to this desolate backwoods region where she served as an abbess, training nuns and commissioning them to form new communities.

Besides her administrative and charitable service, Lioba was by reputation an evangelist and miracle worker. In one spectacular incident, she calmed a raging storm. As a ruling abbess, she acted forcefully, unlike decades earlier when she had written to Boniface of her "lowly self" as the "lowest servant of those who bear the sweet yoke of Christ." She rose up "as if she had been challenged to a contest, flung off the cloak which she was wearing and boldly opened the doors of the church." With the sign of the cross, she stretched her hands to heaven praying to God through the Virgin Mary. At her command, the thunderclouds disappeared, giving way to sunshine.[8]

Another miracle credited to her may have had sinister implications. Even before her German mission had begun, she had learned from Boniface that there were grave dangers, including the persistent "seduction of nuns."

The miracle involved healing the nun Williswind, a woman "of excellent character and edifying conduct." The report is that she was "attacked" by hemorrhoids, causing "loss of blood from her privy parts" and "severe pains of the bowel." Indeed, so serious was this "grave illness" that "her strength ebbed away," and she could barely get out of bed. Her condition worsened to the point that she was taken to her nearby family home to die. In the end Lioba was called in for last rites. Williswind was "already enveloped in a linen cloth, as corpses usually were." Lioba healed her, and Williswind carried on her ministry at the convent.[9]

But what, we might ask, apart from childbirth, could have caused such a severe affliction? Was she one of the many nuns who was raped? Did she nearly lose her life due to a violent sexual assault? It is not difficult to imagine a vicious barbarian, hormones raging, dragging her into the tangled forest and brutalizing her almost to the point of death. All that is left of her psyche is shame and pain. Among her healing miracles, Lioba is also reported to have healed reputations. Any medieval nun who had been sexually assaulted would have needed healing: body, soul—and reputation.

HÉLOÏSE
A Woman Who Loved Too Much

Strong willed and highly educated, Héloïse speaks as a modern woman with whom we can easily identify. The Hollywood film version of her life, *Stealing Heaven* (1988), does not do justice to her multilayered personality. She was far more than a pretty face. But that she fell in love with Peter Abelard, the twelfth century's most astute and debonair scholar, only adds to her allure.

Unlike many educated medieval scholars who feigned humility, Abelard was as arrogant as he was articulate and good-looking. Students flocked to him, not only for his incisive reasoning and logic but also for his style. He was bold and brazen and dared them to think for themselves and question what other teachers were telling them. His attraction extended to the ladies as well. Héloïse later reminded him: "You left many love-songs and verses which won wide popularity for the charm of their words and tunes and kept your name continually on everyone's lips." He might be considered the Neil Diamond of his day, and his work made even his lover famous: "Your many songs put your Héloïse on everyone's lips, so that every street and house echoed with my name."[10]

She was still in her teens when their paths had crossed. Her brilliance was as appealing as her beauty. So spellbound was Abelard that he sought out her guardian, her uncle Fulbert, and offered to serve as her tutor, with an ulterior motive, as he later confessed: "I . . . decided she was the one to bring to my bed, confident that I should have an easy success." Why? "I had youth and exceptional good looks as well as my great reputation to recommend me." Héloïse would be putty in his hands: "Knowing the girl's knowledge and love of letters, I thought she would be all the more ready to consent."

As planned, soon there was "more kissing than teaching." They were silly in love. Rumors spread. He wrote songs. She swooned. Word was all over Paris. Everyone knew—except for Fulbert. Was he in denial or simply out of the loop? He was a cleric at the cathedral of Paris. He would find out soon enough. "No stage of love making [was left] untried." Héloïse became pregnant.

Fulbert was furious. He had been made the fool. Utterly humiliated. Abelard made an awkward attempt at amends. Yes, he would marry her, but the nuptials must be kept secret so as not to risk his reputation. Fulbert fumed. *That lying weasel!* Héloïse was whisked away to relatives. The baby was born. At the bidding of Abelard, she entered a convent. Now Fulbert was absolutely livid. It was his move. He retained two thugs. They entered Abelard's apartment in the dark of night. Confusion, terror, panic, excruciating pain. Abelard knew exactly what was happening. "They cut off the parts of my body whereby I had committed the wrong."

A remorseful Abelard entered the Abbey of Saint-Denis. After a time he resumed his lectures. Again students flocked to hear him. But church authorities were not impressed. He was accused of heresy. All the while he was deliberately out of touch with the mother of his child.

After more than a decade, Héloïse learned of Abelard's whereabouts. In a haunting letter she implored him: "Tell me one thing, if you can. Why . . . have I been so neglected and forgotten by you? . . . You are bound to me by an obligation which is all the greater for the further close tie of the marriage sacrament."

Why, why, why would he treat her so meanly, she wondered, pointing out to him, "particularly now when I have carried out all your orders so implicitly that when I was powerless to oppose you in anything, I found strength at your command to destroy myself." Here she reminded him that she had entered the convent for one reason alone: her love for him. She had destroyed herself for him. There was no joy in pretending to serve God. The other nuns "do not know the hypocrite I am." She went through the motions, but her heart was not in it. "Of all the wretched women, I am the most wretched, and amongst the unhappy I am the unhappiest."

It is difficult to fit this long chapter of her life into a contemporary setting. Where besides prison could a woman be so trapped as Héloïse was? Today any woman who takes a vow can walk away into secular life. I know women who have done just that. Some—like Betty, now with children and grandchildren—continue to be active in the church. For Héloïse, however, options were extremely limited. How we might wish she could have simply abandoned the convent and returned to Paris to start a day school for girls, escaping the painful circumstances that were contaminating her soul.

There at the monastery for years on end, she was obsessed with Abelard. "Lewd visions," she confessed, "take such a hold upon my unhappy soul."

And this even while the Mass was celebrated. "Everything we did and also the times and places are stamped on my heart along with your image, so that I live through it all again with you. Even in sleep I know no respite. Sometimes my thoughts are betrayed in a movement of my body, or they break out in an unguarded word."

She was a brilliant woman stripped of her dignity. What a pity that her legacy is largely a very sad love story. She would carry on for decades as a prioress at the Paraclete, a monastery established by Abelard himself, and she would be praised by church leaders. But in some sense she was ruined. Even her son was reared by others, though she apparently looked after him from a distance. Peter the Venerable, one of her admirers, responded to her request: "I will gladly do my best to obtain a prebend [stipend] in one of the great churches for your Astrolabe, who is also ours for your sake."

She had written to Abelard, "[I] would have had no hesitation, God knows, in following you or going ahead at your bidding to the flames of Hell." There is no indication that she ever renounced those words. She did, however, later resume correspondence with him, convincing him to interact with her on theological matters. But the love that she so longed for was not forthcoming. There was never closure for her—unless his death and burial at her convent eventually brought her solace. Here is how I years ago concluded an article on this fascinating duo:

> Legend tells us that when Heloise died, Abelard's grave was opened so she could be buried with him, and as they lowered her body, he opened his arms to draw her into his bosom. It is a touching climax, but not one that fits. For Heloise and Abelard, life was real. There was no place for sentimental legends.[11]

CLARE OF ASSISI
Kidnapped Teen, Canonized Saint

Just when it seems it would be impossible to surpass the story of Héloïse for sheer suspense and sex appeal, here comes Clare of Assisi (1194–1253). At first glance she is little more than one more medieval holy woman canonized a saint for a perfect life. But in many ways her story is every bit as fascinating as that of Héloïse, whose name seems incomplete unless paired with Abelard. So also Clare and Francis.

With the election of Pope Francis in 2013, there has been great interest in the original St. Francis of Assisi. Most people know him primarily as a garden statue who loves animals. He is surely more than that. After founding his order of preaching mendicant friars, he granted Clare's wish and permitted her to establish a monastic order for women. His motivation for ministry was simple: "Preach the gospel at all times, and when necessary, use words." This timeless maxim, though, did not apply to Clare's Poor Ladies, who were cloistered behind high walls.

In my church history courses, I used to include a little aside on St. Francis. He was married, I would tell my students. That always piqued their interest. He, by his own account, was married to "a fairer bride than any of you have ever seen." She was the absolute love of his life, and he remained faithful to the very end. As a *husband* he had no equal. Her name? Not Clare. Certainly not. Her name was *Lady Poverty*.

And without suggesting any sort of scandalous trio, it is fair to say that Clare was married to him and to her as well. Her absolute commitment to poverty and to Francis is what most differentiates Clare and her sisters from other medieval nuns. And Francis was committed to her in a romance that may have been more than merely a spiritual love.

Today there are some twenty thousand Poor Clares worldwide, though not necessarily following the same precise rules. Some are strictly cloistered in full habit; others seem to be pushing the envelope, as is true of the Poor Clares living on Shattuck Road in Saginaw, Michigan. Their website shows them in street clothes (including pants) working in the garden and interacting with one another. They sponsor a gift store selling items they make, including pet sympathy cards, most appropriate considering St. Francis and his love for animals.

It's been eight hundred years since the days of Clare herself, and not surprisingly the life of a nun has changed, as I learned when I spoke with one of the Saginaw sisters. They still consider themselves to be cloistered, not serving in the outside world as most nuns do. They do leave the monastery, however, for occasional retreats and family funerals. Likewise their code of silence is more lax, evidenced by this nun's willingness to chat with me briefly by phone. When I asked about the less restrictive lifestyle, she was quick to explain that in today's heterogeneous society it is necessary to go out occasionally and speak to groups explaining who they are.

Although committed to poverty, Clare's purpose in establishing a religious order was prayer. The Poor Clares were contemplatives who spent much of their day in meditation. But it is the matter of poverty that truly set them apart. Her fasting rule was strict. She and her sisters were expected to eat only once a day except for Sunday and Christmas and then no meat, eggs, or dairy products—a vegan diet. They lived on alms, but unlike the Franciscan friars, who begged for funds as they conducted ministry, Clare and her sisters never went outside the walls to beg. In fact, they were never to speak to outsiders, and talking among themselves was severely restricted. They rose to pray in silence in the middle of the night and again at dawn. A priest performed the daily Mass within hearing but out of sight.

The Saginaw Poor Clares welcome online prayer requests. For Clare supplication was an aspect of prayer, but her emphasis was contemplation, particularly meditating on every aspect of the life of Christ: his birth, his public ministry, his death, and his resurrected glory. Any spiritual oneness with Francis would have been trumped by Jesus, her true husband and lover:

> Draw me after you, heavenly Spouse, we
> shall run in the fragrance of your perfumes!
>
> I shall run and not grow weary until you
> bring me into the wine cellar
> until your left hand is under my head
> and your right arm blissfully embraces me;
> and you kiss me with the most blissful kiss of your mouth.[12]

Who would have thought that Clare would fashion such an erotic prayer? But how else, apart from such fantasy, could she and her sisters endure an almost impossible cloistered lifestyle devoted to prayer and poverty?

Clare, like Francis, hailed from Assisi. Today the town is a pilgrimage destination for those who wish to feel the presence of Francis in the cobblestones and cathedrals. When Clare was a young girl, she may have daydreamed about the dashing young man a dozen years her senior. "Francis was one of those people who are popular with everybody," writes G. K. Chesterton, "and his guileless swagger as a Troubadour and leader of French fashions made him a sort of romantic ringleader among the young men of the town."[13]

He was without a doubt the pop star of the day. But that was before his conversion.

Growing up in this walled Roman town of Assisi in the upper Tiber valley, Clare enjoyed the luxuries and social graces of the nobility: high fashion, priceless art and home furnishings, sumptuous feasts and extravagant entertainment. No surprise, she lived in a castle. Besides her wealth, she was considered a local beauty. Before she reached her late teens, she was betrothed to a man of the same social standing, a planned marriage she would rebuff, having come under the spell of Francis.

Clare was not your typical high-class rich girl. Prayer appealed to her more than parties. And then she became enthralled with Francis. He had come back to town as an evangelist calling for the rebuilding of God's house, badly in need of repair. In fact, he stole from his own father's lucrative textile business to pay for the work. When his father hauled him before the local bishop, Francis stripped naked and committed himself to God and a life of poverty. Soon after he stole again—this time, the heart of Clare. They talked together and fell in love.

Perhaps the term *fall in love* is less than accurate. But they did develop a bond of love that is rarely surpassed. A spiritual love, most devotees

Clare Elopes with Francis

A girl of seventeen, named Clare and belonging to one of the noble families of Assisi, was filled with an enthusiasm for the conventual life; and Francis helped her to escape from her home and . . . elope into the cloister, defying her parents as he had defied his father. Indeed the scene had many of the elements of a regular romantic elopement; for she escaped through a hole in the wall, fled through a wood and was received at midnight by the light of torches.

G. K. Chesterton, *St. Francis of Assisi*

insist, but it was likely more than that. She was a fair, nubile young maiden aglow in all her virgin loveliness; he, in his late twenties, hormones fully operational and easily fired up. There surely must have been sexual longings. But the poverty Francis preached required a repression of all such desires.

Yet their relationship had all the ingredients of a burgeoning romance. For months they conversed through clandestine rendezvous, going over every detail of his plans for her ultimate escape. After that, who knew what would happen? In formulating a plan for her celibate life of poverty beyond the city walls, Francis was flying by the seat of his pants. He was not known for caution, and his first priority was to rescue her. The family castle was in plain sight next door to the cathedral, the windows looking out onto Piazza San Rufino. Stealth was the key. Francis set the scheme in motion. On the day appointed, his comrades arrived in the dead of night.

Clare escaped through a window and under a breach in the wall. The first stop on this *underground railroad* was a makeshift forest chapel where Francis and his followers were holed up. Here before an altar to the Blessed Virgin, Francis ceremoniously sheered her of her long flowing hair, and then gave her his own coarse robe to wear instead of her fine gown and cloak. He then escorted her to a Benedictine convent for temporary lodging.

Whether the audacious deed is deemed an elopement or outright kidnapping depends on perspective. Today a teenage girl whisked away in the dark of night at the bidding of a cult leader twelve years her senior would be considered a kidnap victim. And so she was back then. But Francis had factored that into the equation. Church law trumped local law. So when the posse arrived to forcibly return her to her family, she clung to the altar as a safe haven. Indeed, so tenaciously did she hang onto the railing that her clothes were torn in the melee and her shorn head was exposed—proof positive that she had given her life to God.

The family realized they had met their match in Francis—and God. And no medieval nobleman would deny the incredible clout of the Catholic Church. Nor was the contest over, surely not for Francis and his uncommon power of persuasion. Soon Clare's younger sister joined her, as did her mother. The stay at the Benedictine monastery was brief, and within months they moved to their own quarters next to the church of Saint

St. Clare Goes to Church on Christmas Eve

St Clare was . . . so ill that she could not go to church with the other nuns to say the Office on the night of the Nativity of Christ. All the other sisters went to Matins; but she remained in bed, very sorrowful. . . . But Jesus Christ, her Spouse, unwilling to leave her comfortless, carried her miraculously to the church of St Francis, so that she was present at Matins, assisted at the Midnight Mass, and received the Holy Communion, after which she was carried back to her bed.

The Little Flowers of St. Francis of Assisi

Damiano. Here, joined by other women, Clare lived in seclusion until the end of her life.

CONCLUDING OBSERVATIONS

As we look back on these women in our Christian heritage, we are confronted by stark opposites. Life in general and human nature in particular during medieval times were both radically different from and amazingly similar to life in the twenty-first century. How do we compare and contrast our own situations and psyches with theirs? And who are *we*? Dare I assume we are all North American middle-class women as I am?

The similarities are significant. Although some historians insist that romantic love was not *invented* until after the Enlightenment, we see a serious case of romance and heartbreak with Héloïse and Abelard, every bit as intense as was Jacob's love for Rachel more than two thousand years earlier. Women today frequently share the same fascination with fashion and makeup and hairstyling that was common then. At the same time, we are able to comprehend the sacrifice of worldly pleasure to serve God. Mother Teresa does not stand alone as a contemporary example. Missionary women, both Protestant and Catholic, are in many instances equal to these women in their selfless service. And as religious websites indicate, claims of the miraculous today are no less spectacular than then.

Yet we dare not trivialize the differences. Women then had very few options in life and virtually no access to education apart from a monastery. Health care was primitive, life spans short, and death in childbirth common. We are sometimes tempted to imagine beautiful maidens, glamorous fashions, enchanting castles. It looks believable on the movie set, but it's not true to life. The glory of the Greek and Roman civilizations had long passed. Barbarians had overrun Europe. "Life was very primitive," writes Philip Hughes. "Life in this vast Western backwoods—on this vast frontier—was hard and cruel . . . filled with all the violent crime one cares to imagine."[14]

Life was dirty and disease ridden even in castles and convents. A vow of poverty only added to the misery. Imagine typical women's issues: menstrual cramps, heavy periods, vaginal or urinary tract infections, pregnancy, morning sickness, childbirth, hot flashes all lived out with virtually no amenities. Such was medieval life. Toilet tissue, sanitary napkins, and clean bedding play no part in the world of Hilda, Lioba, Héloïse, and Clare.

QUESTIONS TO THINK ABOUT

What in your life experience helps you comprehend the era referred to as the *Dark Ages*? Have you or anyone you've known lived in a situation without basic amenities that middle-class women take for granted?

Have you ever visited a medieval castle? How would you compare and contrast it with your own home for ease of heating, cooling, cleaning, cooking, eating, washing, bathing, and family activities? Do you ever think of yourself as living in luxury? Do you ever contemplate your *wealth* in comparison to those living in actual poverty?

How do you regard dreams? Have you ever had a dream that appeared to be a message or prophecy directly from God? How do you assess the dreams foretelling great ministry for Hilda and Lioba?

Imagine Lioba's thoughts as she was left behind at a convent as a small girl. Does her treatment appear now as child abuse? Do you know of situations today that are reminiscent of growing up in a convent? Do Jesus's words on children apply in such situations?

How do you assess the relationship between Héloïse and Abelard? Should he be considered a cad? An abuser? A handsome, pop-star lover? Héloïse is rightly categorized among women who love too much. Have you ever found yourself in their company?

Is it possible to have a spiritual love affair that rises above physical temptation, as Clare and Francis reportedly had? Have you experienced such a relationship yourself? How do you regard the practice of imagining Jesus as spouse and lover?

Which of the women featured in this chapter would you find the most suitable prayer partner at a women's retreat?

3

Hildegard of Bingen and Catholic Mystics and Scholars

Hyacinth Bucket (she always insists the pronunciation is "bouquet"), played by Patricia Routledge, was the star of *Keeping Up Appearances*, a popular British sitcom, still seen in reruns on PBS. She is a social climber always trying to impress those she encounters, whether car salesmen, realtors, or neighbors. Her husband, Richard, and her low-class brother-in-law and sisters, Daisy and Rose, play second fiddle but with clever lines of their own. It's a brainless, silly show, and I would never admit having watched it were it not for the fact that Routledge also played the part of Hildegard of Bingen in a 1994 docudrama. I showed portions of the film on more than one occasion to my seminary students. Those who, like me, knew Hyacinth found it difficult to see the actress as Hildegard.

But perhaps Hildegard was a lot more like Hyacinth than we imagine. Matters of pride and one-upmanship are certainly not unknown to people who devote their lives to religious vocations. Like many other religious women of her day, however, Hildegard was not above using self-deprecating terms to advance her cause—"poor little woman though [I am]." She was anything but a "poor little woman," and she is widely recognized today as a renaissance woman long before the Renaissance. Her music has never been more popular. In fact, even as I'm writing these words I'm listening online to her "Canticles of Ecstasy," available on CD at Amazon for less than ten dollars. Her recipe book sells for slightly more, though her cookie recipe is free online. Could Hildegard in her wildest visions have ever imagined this?

As modern as Hildegard may seem with her now-popular music and recipes, she was very clearly a woman at home in the medieval world—more so by far than Héloïse—and she knew how to navigate that world as a woman. How do we evaluate these medieval women in ministry? In many respects they are far removed from contemporary evangelical women, and it is difficult for us to identify with them. Their focus on celibacy as the key to true spirituality was misdirected, as was their intense mysticism that often gave support to erroneous doctrines—all of which may have been fostered by the gender restrictions they endured.

Indeed, some historians have argued that the visionary experiences of these women transported them into priestly roles that the church denied them, authenticating their ministry through messages and revelations given directly by God. As such they took on a role as mediators between God and those who came for spiritual succor.

Visions and Voices

The women discussed in this chapter, particularly Hildegard, were mystics—mystics who, they were convinced, heard the voice of God with clarity. How has God spoken since the era of the apostles? The same way he did in times of old? Did these women hear voices and see visions as did John of Patmos when he penned Revelation, which is now the last book of the Bible?

I turned around to see the voice that was speaking to me. And when I turned I saw seven golden lampstands, and among the lampstands was someone like a son of man, dressed in a robe reaching down to his feet and with a golden sash around his chest. The hair on his head was white like wool, as white as snow, and his eyes were like blazing fire. His feet were like

There were dozens of holy women besides Hildegard who are known to us today through their writings and the roles they played in monasticism. Among them are Julian, Catherine, and Margery. Julian of Norwich, who lived all her adult life secluded in a cell attached to a church, had a significant counseling and writing ministry. Catherine of Siena was a tireless social worker and a traveler who sought to change the course of the Catholic Church. Margery Kempe was a wife and mother, a pilgrim and gadabout, who authored the first autobiography in the English language and left an indelible mark wherever she went.

HILDEGARD OF BINGEN
Renaissance Abbess in Medieval Europe

Hildegard was born in 1098, and her life would span most of the twelfth century—more than eighty years. Despite her reputation as a holy woman for most of a millennium, she was not canonized a saint until May 10, 2012, under the papal reign of Benedict XVI.

bronze glowing in a furnace, and his voice was like the sound of rushing waters. In his right hand he held seven stars, and coming out of his mouth was a sharp, double-edged sword. His face was like the sun shining in all its brilliance.

When I saw him, I fell at his feet as though dead. Then he placed his right hand on me and said: "Do not be afraid. I am the First and the Last. I am the Living One; I was dead, and now look, I am alive for ever and ever! And I hold the keys of death and Hades.

"Write, therefore, what you have seen, what is now and what will take place later."

Revelation 1:12–19

One of the required marks of a saint, properly canonized by the Catholic Church, is to be credited with miracles. On that score, Hildegard's credentials were stellar. For her, miraculous events occurred early in life. She recounted how she had informed her nurse that a calf soon to be born would be white with spots from its head to its feet. Just as she prophesied, the calf turned out to be spotted. She may have related the story to demonstrate that even at a very young age she was able to see things that were entirely hidden from others. Her real visionary life, however, began decades later.

> And it came to pass . . . when I was forty-two years and seven months old, that the heavens were opened and a blinding light of exceptional brilliance flowed through my entire brain. And so it kindled my whole heart and breast like a flame . . . and suddenly I understood the meaning of the expositions of the books.[1]

By this time Hildegard was an abbess, the head of a large convent in what is today Germany. But more than three decades earlier, like so many little rich girls, she was singled out to be a nun. In fact, as the tenth child, she was offered to God as a tithe. Bidding farewell to her family, she left to reside with the anchoress Jutta. Her only other alternative would have been to be betrothed at an early age to an aristocrat and, beginning at

Hildegard, No Proto-feminist

The 12th century anchorite Hildegard of Bingen possessed a clutch of talents, which would make even the most eclectic of media-donnas curdle with envy. Writer, visionary, prophet, composer, artist, herbalist, politician, preacher, property owner, upbraider of emperors and favourite of Popes, she could even exorcise demons and heal the sick. She invented her own language, wrote one of the earliest surviving morality plays, established her own convent, terrorised her detractors. . . . No proto-feminist, she insisted that her influence on the age exposed the lacklustre womanishness of the clergy; only in dire necessity, would God have resorted to her.

Joanna Griffiths, "Nun for All Seasons," *The Observer*, Saturday, March 17, 2001 puberty, hope to survive the pregnancies that would inevitably follow. Here with Jutta, she lived in a small cell attached to a church and spent her days surrounded not only with prayer and meditation but also with liturgy, music, and books.

Though surely missing her family, Hildegard never looked back. This was the very life she longed for. Jutta told her young charge of her visions, and soon Hildegard was receiving her own revelations from God. Mystical experiences were expected, and they served Hildegard well in the years after Jutta's death, when she took charge of what had become a community of nuns.

What Hildegard testified to at age forty-two was very different from what might be considered routine revelations, and it was this claim that most distinguished her from others. Although she was convinced that the blinding light was an opening to God's truth given uniquely to her, she was not without misgivings. There were heresy hunters aplenty, and she was consumed with self-doubt, particularly after she began consulting the opinions of others. A serious illness, however, convinced her that God was commanding her: publish or perish. She had no other choice.

> I started writing this book and received the strength to finish it, somehow, in ten years. These visions weren't fabricated by my own imagination, nor are they anyone else's. I saw these when I was in the heavenly places. They are God's mysteries. These are God's secrets. I wrote them down because a heavenly voice kept saying to me, "See and speak! Hear and write!"[2]

Know the Ways of God (*Scivias*) was completed a decade after the first blinding light. Here the reader sees in vivid detail what Hildegard herself is seeing, whether the spotlight is on the Virgin Mary or the terrors of punishment awaiting sinners after death: "I saw a well deep and broad full of boiling pitch and sulphur, and around it were wasps and scorpions. . . . And I saw a great fire, black, red, and white, and in it horrible fiery vipers, spitting flame; and there the vipers tortured the souls of those who had been slaves of the sin of uncharitableness."[3]

If we imagine Hildegard to be nothing more than a navel-gazing visionary, however, we would be far off the mark. She relocated her convent to the town of Bingen on the Rhine, and there she presided over what could be considered a *ren d'la femme*—a female renaissance—a high point of scholarship and art specifically among women. The breadth of studies was wide-ranging, from literature and letters to art and music, with a heavy dose of natural medicine and even what appears to be elementary psychology.

One does not have to read far in Hildegard, however, to be reminded that she is still very much a twelfth-century woman. Her cures for various ailments border on the ludicrous, no more than superstitious folk remedies. For jaundice, fasten a live bat onto the sick person's back or abdomen and have the person wear it around until the creature dies. To treat a hangover, fetch a container of water, submerge a female—preferably small—dog, and wash the inebriated person's head in the water. Works every time. Or had it not been tested sufficiently in clinical trials?

One of Hildegard's strangest writings relates to women, sex, and how babies are conceived. No bat or dog or even stork is involved in the process. Simply a woman making love to a man—and some unusual bodily responses:

> When a woman is making love with a man, a sense of heat in her brain, which brings with it sensual delight, communicates the taste of that delight during the act and summons forth the emission of the man's seed. And when the seed has fallen into its place, that vehement heat descending from her brain draws the seed to itself and holds it, and soon the woman's sexual organs contract, and all the parts that are ready to open up during the time of menstruation now close, in the same way as a strong man can hold something enclosed in his fist.[4]

Hildegard would never know the love of a man, but she did express a deep bond of love for the young nun Richardis von Stade, who had encouraged her in her writing: "When I wrote the book Scivias, I bore a strong love to a noble nun . . . who suffered with me until I finished this book."[5] When Hildegard was informed that Richardis would be transferred to become an abbess of another convent (a promotion arranged by her archbishop brother), she was heartbroken. More than that, she was enraged. She called on the pope to step in and intervene, but to no avail. Richardis left, and Hildegard wept. It would not be exaggerating to say that she was in love with the young woman. To assume this was a hidden lesbian love, as some have done, however, is not warranted.

Richardis had nursed her beloved abbess during a long sickness. Their relationship was so intimate and intense that certain nuns and others were troubled—perhaps even envious. Hildegard alluded to this in a letter to Richardis: "I loved the nobility of your conduct, your wisdom and your chastity, your soul and the whole of your life, so much that many said: What are you doing?"[6]

There is no doubt about the enormous emotional outlay that Hildegard had invested in Richardis. She fought for the young nun not to relocate and, when she did, placed the blame squarely on her: "Then, however, due to her noble origin, she strove for the honour of a greater name in order to be called the mother of a prestigious church. And she did not strive for this for the sake of God, but for her own secular glory."[7] Though angry, she begged Richardis to return.

But the young woman died soon after at age twenty-eight. The grieving Hildegard would cling to the alleged last words of Richardis. Word came that on her deathbed she had expressed her deep love for Hildegard and her desire to return to the convent. But Hildegard could not let go. She had to have the last word. The faithful Richardis, tempted by fame, met her untimely death: "But the ancient serpent had attempted to deprive her of that blessed honor by assaulting her through her human nobility. Yet the mighty Judge drew this my daughter to Himself, cutting her off from all human glory."[8]

Hildegard would live on for more than a quarter century during which time her fame would spread as her creative genius shone forth in music, poetry, plays, letters, and memoir as well as academic writings. She traveled widely as a sought-after preacher and met with popes and other well-known figures of the era. And she still reigns today as the most celebrated abbess of the Middle Ages.

JULIAN OF NORWICH
English Anchoress

Like Hildegard, Julian captures the religious seeker's imagination even today. A quick check on Amazon reveals dozens of books available under her name, though perhaps not to be outdone by Hildegard, whose cookbook was released in 2010: *From Saint Hildegard's Kitchen: Foods of Health, Foods of Joy* by Jany Fournier-Rosset. From pasta and poultry to jams, jellies, and table grace, the book seeks to re-create medieval monastic meals. If only Julian had left behind recipes! Catherine of Siena also fares well on Amazon, as does Margery Kempe. Even the most established writers today could envy their popularity—and certainly their enduring shelf life.

Julian was an anchoress who like Hildegard in her youth lived in a tiny cell attached to a church. But she would remain clinging like a barnacle to a church in the English town of Norwich for the remainder of her life. She is a nameless mystic, known only for her writings, her name taken from the church to which she was attached: St. Julian. Nor does she write about her life or her loves, and for her there is no travel abroad or encounters with famous people. Her oft-quoted self-description, we know to be patently false: "a simple unlettered creature" who is "lewd, feeble and frail."[9]

Indeed, Julian's personal life is barely more than a blank slate. That has not stopped historians, however, from speculating. Did her family determine she would be an anchoress? Did her family perish in the Black Death, and did she then devote her life to God? Or was she a married woman who lost her husband and children to that terrible epidemic and only then decided to live a life of complete devotion?

Even the most basic questions concerning this fourteenth-century woman have gone unanswered in the seven hundred years since her death (though the exact year, as that of her birth, is unknown). Was she a laywoman rather than a nun? That no monastic order has ever been associated with her perhaps makes the former more probable. Benedictines and others have sought to claim her, but she remains ever elusive. Indeed, so little is known of her that she is not even officially a saint.

Perhaps the most baffling question of all is: Why was there so little curiosity about her personal life? She did not, after all, live in ancient times nor in the medieval Dark Ages. Norwich was the second largest city in the land. And she lived on into the fifteenth century as England was approaching the Renaissance. The life of John Wyclif, some two decades younger than she, is fully fleshed out. But she herself, like that of another well-known English writer, William Shakespeare, remains elusive.

Yet despite her obscurity, then as now, her influence has been enormous. Her contemporaries, including Brigitta of Sweden and most likely Catherine of Siena, were familiar with her writings, and Margery Kempe wrote in her autobiography that she had gone out of her way to consult with her.

As was true with Shakespeare, it was Julian's words, not her personal life, that mattered to contemporaries. She is best known for her *Revelations of Divine Love*, drawn from visions that she experienced during a prolonged illness. It would have been a time when she might have pleaded with God for healing. But she came to understand otherwise:

> Our customary practice of prayer was brought to mind: how . . . we spend so much time on petition. I saw that it is indeed more worthy of God and more truly pleasing to him that through his goodness we should pray with full confidence, and by his grace cling to him with real understanding and unshakeable love, than that we should go on making as many petitions as our souls are capable of.[10]

Most of her writing would be viewed today as spiritual discipline with little that would cause controversy save her feminine images of God. The medieval English text speaks for itself: "God is oure moder," "oure savyouure is oure very moder," "very moder Jhesu," and "oure moder, Christ."[11]

CATHERINE OF SIENA
Saint on the Streets of Siena

On Wednesday, November 24, 2010, Pope Benedict XVI lectured on the fourteenth-century St. Catherine of Siena to a General Audience of the Catholic Church. He told his listeners how she, having been called by St. Dominic in a vision, entered the Third Order of Dominicans when she was just sixteen years old. The pope also reminded them that forty years earlier, in 1970, Pope Paul VI had declared Catherine a doctor of the church. Pope Benedict went on to relate another mystical experience:

> In a vision that was ever present in Catherine's heart and mind Our Lady presented her to Jesus who gave her a splendid ring, saying to her: "I, your Creator and Saviour, espouse you in the faith, that you will keep ever pure

until you celebrate your eternal nuptials with me in Heaven." . . . This ring was visible to her alone.[12]

Benedict's reference to a "splendid ring" that "was visible to her alone" on the surface sounds like an ordinary saint story. What he surely knew but did not elucidate was that Catherine's splendid ring was actually the *holy foreskin* of Jesus. Doctor Catherine, however, did not originate the idea of such an object. Her visionary *Holy Prepuce* was a popular medieval relic that was kept safe and certified authentic by a number of Catholic churches.

From the earliest years of childhood, Catherine knew the horrors of suffering and dying having survived the terrible plague known as the Black Death. She responded with intense religious emotion, and at age seven, as her story goes, she took the vow of virginity. In the years that followed, she spurned social gatherings and settled into a secluded cell of her family home—though perhaps it was a more figurative "cell of the mind." In opposition to her parents' strong objections, and in her desire to sacrifice herself to her holy spouse, she practiced strict asceticism. She not only wore a hair shirt against her skin and around her hips an iron chain, but she also flagellated herself and deprived herself of tasty food and sleep—a rough board her only bed.

Like other medieval holy women, Catherine would emerge from her solitary confinement to take on a public role. Her focus was on those Jesus

Sin So Bad It Repulses Devils

For this [homosexuality] not only causes Me nausea, but is disgusting even to the devils themselves whom these depraved creatures have chosen as their lords. . . . It is disgusting to the devils not because evil displeases them or because they find pleasure in good, but rather because their nature is angelic and flees upon seeing such a repulsive sin being committed. For while certainly it is the devil that first strikes the sinner with the poisoned arrow of concupiscence, nonetheless when a man actually carries out such a sinful act, the devil goes away.

Catherine of Siena, *The Dialogue of Divine Providence*

identified as the least of these—Mother Teresa's poorest of the poor. With the plague still claiming lives and filling people with fear, she did not have far to go—simply outside her door, where the streets of Siena became her mission field. Had she been a fourteenth-century version of Mother Teresa, she might have been upstaged only by St. Francis.

But Catherine was weird—weirder than Francis. She carried her all-consuming asceticism right into the streets with her, and not simply the hair shirt and iron chain. To stoop down and drain and wash a woman's pus-filled sores and apply an herbal balm was not enough. Nor was it enough to carry the pitiful creature home and gently place her on the board bed. No. To demonstrate her utter selflessness, she drank the pus that filled the bowl. God alone, she insisted, gave her—a woman who could barely eat anything without vomiting—the strength to do this. How the suffering woman felt about Catherine's repugnant act is unclear. Many questioned her sanity.

Each day Catherine made a pilgrimage from disease-ridden streets to filthy dungeons where hardened criminals were chained. Here she found holy relics in human form. She symbolically clothed herself in Christ's love for suffering humanity. Of one man she related, "I was there at the place of execution, waiting and praying." When he was brought from his cell, she greeted him and gave him most unusual last rites. She made the sign of the cross and said:

> "Kneel down now, my sweetest brother. To the nuptials! In a moment you will have entered into life eternal." He knelt down gently and I bent over him and held him as he lowered his head, reminding him of the blood of the Lamb. His lips murmured nothing but the names, Jesus and Catherine. I closed my eyes accepting in the Divine Goodness the sacrifice, and as he was speaking I received his head into my hands.[13]

Catherine did turn her attention to larger issues of the day, especially the contentious matter of papal relocation to the French town of Avignon. In fact, she led more than a dozen of her followers to that "Babylon of the West" in an effort to convince the pope to return to Rome. He was unmoved. Her efforts came to naught.

Like that of the other well-known women mystics of the Middle Ages, Catherine's reputation was built in part on her writings, particularly her

Dialogue on Divine Providence, completed two years before her death. Here she recounts the vision of her dialogue with "the eternal Father, indescribably kind and tender," who "turned his eye to this soul and spoke." If the reader is hoping for God to say something extraordinary or perhaps unexpected, she may be disappointed by how bland his words are, at least in comparison to Catherine's own often startling style and demeanor. Here we find a typical example of the messages she heard:

> O dearest daughter, I have determined to show my mercy and loving kindness to the world, and I choose to provide for mankind all that is good. But man, ignorant, turns into a death-giving thing what I gave in order to give him life. Not only ignorant, but cruel: cruel to himself. But still I go on providing. . . . I want you to know: whatever I give to man, I do it out of my great providence.[14]

MARGERY KEMPE
Unconventional Pilgrim

Gregory of Tours, a sixth-century bishop and since canonized a saint, often extolled his ideal for marriage by way of a story. A young couple had just celebrated their nuptials. The groom leads his young bride off to bed. She begins weeping. When he inquires of her sorrow, she responds, "I had determined to preserve my poor body for Christ, untouched by intercourse with man. . . . At this moment when . . . I should have put on the stole of purity, this wedding dress brings me shame." The husband is taken aback but then relents: "If you are determined to abstain from intercourse with me, then I will agree to what you want to do." Gregory's punch line: "Hand in hand they went to sleep." And they lived happily ever after: "For many years after this they lay each night in one bed, but they remained chaste in a way which we can only admire."[15]

Margery Kempe's situation was very different. She "put on the stole of purity" only after having given birth to fourteen children. One day on or around the time of their twentieth anniversary, she proposed to her husband that they live a chaste life, and he agreed. A mystical marriage, she had long before determined, was more suited to her than motherhood. She had given birth to enough children, and now God was calling her to a new life of travel. It was an era of pilgrimages, and she would see herself as God's pilgrim.

Margery's life is easily divided into three nearly equal periods: youth, marriage and family, and pilgrim. In fact, for more than twenty years she would spend much of her time journeying from one shrine to another, always requesting an audience with priests and prelates. Few churchmen had time to listen to her personal revelations, and fellow pilgrims regarded her as a nuisance, if not completely deranged.

Margery was born in Norfolk, England, in 1373, into a prosperous family of wool merchants and statesmen. At twenty she married John Kempe, who himself would become involved in local politics. Soon after the birth of her first child, she suffered a lengthy episode of serious mental illness, which she later described in third person in her autobiography, *The Book of Margery Kempe*:

> For dread she had of damnation . . . this creature went out of her mind and was wonderfully vexed and labored with spirits half year eight weeks and odd days. And in this time she saw, as her thought, devils open their mouths all inflamed . . . sometime ramping at her, sometime threatening her, sometime pulling her and hauling her both night and day . . . with great threatenings and bade her she should forsake her Christendom. . . . And so she did. She slandered her husband, her friends, her own self . . . like as the spirits tempted her. . . . She bit her own hand so violently that it was seen all her life after. And also she [scratched] her skin on her body . . . with her nails.[16]

Her husband had no choice but to restrain her until she came out of her madness by way of a vision of Jesus. In the years that followed, she had babies, ran a brewery, and milled corn, all the while claiming visions and revelations—and weeping. Indeed, her signature spiritual discipline, so to speak, was loud wailing and shedding of copious tears that she was convinced authenticated messages from God. Among her visionary messages was confirmation that she had been actively involved—more than a mere bystander—at both the birth and the crucifixion of Christ.

That Margery's trademark was shedding tears makes all the more amazing her humor and ability to poke fun at her opponents, as her *Book* reveals. Indeed, she might have been a stand-up comedian of her day with

Margery's Sense of Humor

Modern readers of *The Book of Margery Kempe* have considered her narrative the produce of so-called "naïve sincerity" which can be both engaging and frustrating. Yet this reading . . . strikes me as itself naïve, for it overlooks what is one of the fundamental purposes of both her life and her Book: laughter. Or, in her own words, merriment. Whether she is laughing at herself which . . . she does more often than we may be aware, or whether she uses humour to teach wayward archbishops and priests humility, Kempe ultimately relies on the power of laughter to convert.

Karma Lochrie, "Margery Kempe and the Rhetoric of Laughter"

this knee-slapping routine (with my own italicized phrases added): *So the archbishop says to me*: "I hear bad reports about you; I hear it said that you're a thoroughly wicked woman." *And I say to him*: "And I hear it said you're a wicked man, sir. And if you're as wicked as people say, you will never enter heaven unless you mend your ways." *Then he, exploding in rage, says*: "Why you! . . . What do people say about me?" *I say, chuckling under my breath*: "Others can tell you well enough, sir."[17]

Many of Margery's fellow pilgrims, however, failed to catch her humor. To them, she was too often more than just a wacky woman. She was demented, a woman whose shrill cries and claims of God's special calling quickly became tiring. It is tempting today to resurrect her reputation and find her amusing. But at the time, some seven hundred years ago, she was not easy company on a pilgrimage that too often involved arduous travel, dirty, flea-filled inns, and sleepless nights. Tempers ran short even without her in the midst.

CONCLUDING OBSERVATIONS

They are medievals, further along on the evolutionary scale, to be sure, than Cro-Magnons, but too far removed for us to easily comprehend their ways.

How easy it is for us to be consumed with the present, losing sight of history, and relatively recent history at that. It is true that much of medieval Europe was a backwater in comparison to classical Greece and Rome. But these women of the High Middle Ages are ones with whom we can resonate, ones who know the heartbreaks and struggles we ourselves confront.

Yet they lived in an era when, in the name of God, girls resided in little cells. Today we would call social services, reporting the shocking child abuse. We would prescribe drugs for Catherine or confine her to a mental institution. We should not assume, however, that the town folk and extended family members sanctioned such treatment of children or admired someone who drank pus. Margery was shunned in her own day and how much more would we steer clear of her today. We often consider street preachers to be on the edge of insanity in our own age.

Nevertheless, Hildegard, Julian, Catherine, and Margery still speak to us today, reminding us that their spiritual struggles and torn relationships are ours, though often in very different apparel. Hildegard, particularly, demonstrates a love for learning and a lively life of the mind. Margery's story offers a fascinating glimpse of a mother and laywoman who knew so well the hardscrabble life of a medieval village. Unlike the others, she was not devoted to a life of prayer or humanitarian service—yet ever longing for a deeper relationship with God. We do well to invite these women into our lives and living rooms and learn from them.

QUESTIONS TO THINK ABOUT

Do kids grow up too fast today? Faster than Hildegard, Julian, and Catherine? How do you assess their childhood spiritual desires? Have you or anyone you have known had such spiritual longings as a young child?

Was Hildegard overly controlling in her expectations of Richardis? Did she accuse her younger protégée of seeking the very fame and significance that she herself had sought and was continuing to seek? Do you know people today who are blinded in that respect?

Do you agree with Julian that too much time in prayer consists of petition—of making requests for our needs and the needs of others? Do you ever think of God—of Jesus—as a mother, as she did? Is there anything wrong in relating to God in feminine terms?

Have you ever known anyone who in any way resembled Catherine in her effort to demonstrate holiness, or perhaps unworthiness? Would you assume a mental illness for such a person today?

How do you assess Margery's conversion to the life of a pilgrim? Do you assume she may have had mixed motives that involved a true love for God, a strong distaste for another pregnancy, and serious emotional issues?

If you were able to interview one of these women for an in-depth media feature, which one would you choose? Which one do you find most interesting, most authentically spiritual, most colorful?

4

Katherine Schütz Zell
and Protestant Reformers

"I guess, what I will tell you now, won't make you very happy. Most of them say you are a feminist. But I don't think so. What do you think about that accusation? I hope I did not hurt you." These sentences are part of an email message sent from a young man studying at a Bible college in Switzerland. He and his fellow students had read some of my writings, and they were curious about me. Who am I? That is essentially what the suspicious students want to know. No, I wasn't offended at all.

Labeling and name-calling are how we differentiate ourselves from others, particularly those whom we perceive to believe and act differently in ways we don't approve. I've certainly been guilty of that, and it's not all bad. These students labeled me and in doing so sparked conversation. What is a feminist? Is it a bad thing to be a feminist? As a historian, I'm wary about using the word when discussing individuals who lived in earlier generations. Is a feminist one who supports women's suffrage? Today in the West a woman's right to vote and hold office is simply assumed. But in their day, suffragists were considered feminists and liberals.

Today many Christians would label one who supports women's ordination a feminist, but many such *feminists* hark back to the apostle Paul and his affirmation of women in ministry (when there were no such credentials as ordination per se). They would also point to the succeeding generations when women held important roles in the developing church—for example, Marcella and Paula advising and speaking for Jerome on theological matters. Then throughout medieval times women wielded power as abbesses and served in significant roles during the Reformation.

Like the Dear Mary Magdalene

Like many women before and since, Katherine Zell looked to a biblical woman as a role model. She saw herself like "the dear Mary Magdalene, who with no thought of being an apostle, came to tell the disciples that she had encountered the risen Lord."[a] How do biblical figures show women the way to ministry today?

> Early on the first day of the week, while it was still dark, Mary Magdalene went to the tomb and saw that the stone had been removed from the entrance. So she came running to Simon Peter and the other disciple, the one Jesus loved, and said, "They have taken the Lord out of the tomb, and we don't know where they have put him!" . . .
>
> Now Mary stood outside the tomb crying. As she wept, she bent over to look into the tomb and saw two angels in white, seated where Jesus' body had been, one at the head and the other at the foot.
>
> They asked her, "Woman, why are you crying?"
>
> "They have taken my Lord away," she said, "and I don't know where they have put him." At this, she turned around and saw Jesus standing there, but she did not realize that it was Jesus.

But it is during this Reformation era that name-calling and labeling of women really began in earnest. Protestants disdained monasticism, which incidentally had been the primary path to ministry for women. Indeed, we find Reformers and their minions emptying out convents, leaving nuns in precarious positions. *Find them husbands lest worse befall them,* is the cry. Many women, among them nuns, however, welcomed the changes in the air. Martin Luther was condemning the excesses of the church, as others before him had done, reproving ignorant priests and calling for a focus on the Bible. It was a time of radical notions, including the priest-hood of the believer.

> He asked her, "Woman, why are you crying? Who is it you are looking for?"
>
> Thinking he was the gardener, she said, "Sir, if you have carried him away, tell me where you have put him, and I will get him."
>
> Jesus said to her, "Mary."
>
> She turned toward him and cried out in Aramaic, "Rabboni!" (which means "Teacher").
>
> Jesus said, "Do not hold on to me, for I have not yet ascended to the Father. Go instead to my brothers and tell them, 'I am ascending to my Father and your Father, to my God and your God.'"
>
> Mary Magdalene went to the disciples with the news: "I have seen the Lord!" And she told them that he had said these things to her.
>
> John 20:1–2, 11–18

[a] Roland H. Bainton, *Women of the Reformation in Germany and Italy* (Minneapolis: Augsburg, 1971), 55–67.

Women as believers are now part of the priesthood. It almost sounds as rash as the New Testament itself: "You are . . . a royal priesthood . . . that you may declare the praises of him who called you out of darkness into his wonderful light" (1 Pet. 2:9). And some women took such words seriously. They wanted to be a part of this new movement, not as mere bystanders but as outspoken activists. Reformers both needed them and feared them. In fact, every new movement needs all the help it can muster, and thus we typically find women more prominent in such instances. When the religious movement becomes established as a regulated hierarchy, women's roles are typically diminished.

John Wesley's movement that would become known as Methodism is an example. Women preachers were common in his day, but not after the fledgling company of believers became an established church. The situation was not entirely different during the onset of the Protestant Reformation. No longer priests, preachers had wives, some of them as independent and outspoken as Katie Luther and Katherine Zell. Martin Luther welcomed the strong-minded support of Argula von Stauffer, and Calvin similarly relied on both Jeanne d'Albret and Renée of Ferrara. And the Anabaptists simply recruited converts and transformed them into evangelists whether a man or an Elizabeth Dirks.

KATHERINE SCHÜTZ ZELL
Reformer from Strasburg

She was a strong, articulate, and very vocal woman who grew up in a respectable Strasburg family. But as a woman she knew well how to be self-deprecating, often with a touch of humor. Whether she was merely "a splinter from the rib of that blessed man Matthew Zell"[1] or one who had as much right to speak for God as did Balaam's ass, she argued her case. She was a controversial writer and speaker who skillfully supported her positions with scriptural texts.

Perhaps more than any Christian woman before her, Katherine was a defender of women's roles in ministry—and a defender of what she was convinced were true Christian precepts. She spoke out with conviction on the critical importance of Scripture, hymn singing, and religious liberty. But her first published apologetical work was in defense of clerical marriage. In early December 1524, at twenty-six, she married Matthew Zell, twenty years her senior, the most popular preacher in town. The age difference, however, was far less significant than his vow of celibacy.

Not surprisingly, the marriage created an uproar resulting in his excommunication from the Catholic Church. Katherine was sensitive about her own reputation and particularly how laypeople would regard the scandal. So she turned the tables: *Why shouldn't the church support a priest who marries and is faithful to his wife? Everyone knows that priests certainly don't practice celibacy. Is it because,* she boldly demanded, *the bishops pocket the monetary fines they collect from the priests who live with their mistresses? And how many priests are sneaking around seducing women? Their sexual sins are hardly a secret.*

Indeed, Katherine went on to explain that she regarded marriage to a priest as a ministry that "uplifted the moral degradation of the clergy." And from all indications, their union was a model of clerical marriage—a warm and healthy partnership with no apparent effort on Matthew's part to stifle his outspoken wife. When someone started a rumor that he had "thrashed" her (or ought to have thrashed her) for neglecting the house while spending her time speaking her mind, she shot back: "I have never had a maid. . . . And as for thrashing me, my husband and I have never had an unpleasant 15 minutes. We could have no greater honor than to die rejected of men and from two crosses to speak to each other words of comfort."[2]

We can also infer from Katherine's writing that she and Matthew enjoyed laughter and lightheartedness. When he died less than a year shy of their twenty-fifth wedding anniversary, she was bowed down in grief. Sometime later she wrote a note of apology to houseguests: "I wish I could have done better for you but my Matthew has taken all my gaiety with him."[3]

Active involvement in ministry helped Katherine work through her grief. For the remaining fourteen years of her life, she would serve others until her health gave out. She could look back on more than a half century of dedication to God: "Ever since I was ten years old I have been a student and sort of church mother, much given to attending sermons. I have loved and frequented the company of learned men, and I conversed much with them, not about dancing, masquerades, and worldly pleasures but about the kingdom of God."[4]

For their entire childless marriage, Katherine served alongside her husband in the local parish. The first enormous responsibility to fall on her shoulders as a young minister's wife was heading a taskforce to house refugees. The Peasants' War of 1625 had left behind widows and orphans; some three thousand refugees had fled their homes, seeking food and shelter in Strasburg. She tirelessly organized the effort and welcomed many into her own home, which throughout their marriage served as a hospitality house—and not just to the homeless.

We imagine Matthew beaming with pride when they entertained notable guests who were impressed that his wife interacted so intelligently on matters of doctrine that she ranked alongside theologians. Her feelings were

Katie Luther: First Lady of the Reformation

Katrina von Bora, who became the wife of Martin Luther, deserves recognition if for no other reason than that. Luther was a very difficult man to live with. She had been a nun, and as the story is told, escaped the convent with other nuns all on a wagon hiding under a tarp, disguised as barrels of herring. Some returned to their family homes, while others were sent to Wittenberg, where Luther and his fellow Reformers were expected to find husbands for them. After all, they had escaped to follow his teachings. Like Katherine Zell, Katie married at age twenty-six, six months after Katherine and Matthew said their vows. Unlike Katherine, Katie was not actively involved in ministry outside the manse. She did not preach or teach or write tracts and devotionals. But she was consumed with far more than rearing their six children. She maintained a farm (away from the manse in Wittenberg), bred and sold livestock, brewed beer, and administered a med center at their large home. Her husband called her by various pet names, perhaps most appropriately "morning star." Her rising before dawn had been a call to prayer at the convent; now married with children it was a call to work.

mutual: "I honored, cherished and sheltered many great, learned men, with care, work and expense. . . . I listened to their conversations and preaching, I read their books and their letters and they were glad to receive mine."[5]

She may have collaborated with Matthew in his catechism for children, and she was actively involved in ministry to the needy. Following her husband's death, however, she was forced to defend her public speaking and preaching. In fact, so involved had she been alongside her husband that she, amid her grief, felt obligated at his funeral to dispel rumors that she would take over the pulpit as Dr. Katherine: "I am not usurping the office of preacher or apostle. I am like the dear Mary Magdalene, who with no thought of being an apostle, came to tell the disciples that she had encountered the risen Lord."[6]

Whether or not she carried out the work of an apostle, there was very little that Katherine did not do. She was a tenacious defender of the persecuted Anabaptists, daring to defy Reformation leaders who were in some instances guilty of executions and outright brutality. "Why do you rail at Schwenckfeld?" she demanded of a Lutheran clerical leader. "You talk as if you would have him burned like the poor Servetus at Geneva"—an obvious jab at John Calvin. She insisted that Anabaptists were Christians "who accept Christ in all the essentials as we do"; yet they are "pursued as by a hunter with dogs chasing wild boars." What an outrage. "Anyone," she added, "who acknowledges Christ as the true Son of God and the sole Savior of mankind is welcome at my board." Her hospitality was an ongoing aspect of her life. "I have been allowed to keep the parsonage which belongs to the parish. I take any one who comes. It is always full."[7]

In her fight for Anabaptists and so-called radicals, she made a strong case for religious liberty long before the call for toleration in the seventeenth-century Enlightenment, arguing that a government had no right to punish individuals for matters of conscience. As a respected widow and mature Christian, Katherine personally visited those sick and in prison, wrote tracts, edited a hymnal, and preached. As a self-educated biblical scholar and theologian, she defended her right to do so.

You remind me that the Apostle Paul told women to be silent in the church. I would remind you of the word of this same apostle that in Christ there is no longer male nor female and of the prophecy of Joel: "I will pour my spirit upon all flesh and your sons and your daughters will prophesy." I do not pretend to be John the Baptist rebuking the Pharisees. I do not claim to be Nathan upbraiding David. I aspire only to be Balaam's ass, castigating his master.[8]

But there were many who were threatened by Katherine's strong personality and the perception that she was overstepping biblical prescriptions for women. Indeed, to the very end of her life, despite her selfless service, she was hounded by detractors. One such individual was Ludwig Rabus, a younger cleric whom she had known well and who had lived in her home. But when she did not as a matter of course support all his opinions, he turned against her, accusing her of disturbing the peace of the church. "A disturber of the peace am I?" she indignantly shot back. "Yes indeed, of my own peace. . . . I have visited the plague infested and carried out the dead. I have visited those in prison and under sentence of death. Often for three days and three nights I have neither eaten nor slept. . . . Is this disturbing the peace of the church?"[9]

Katherine simply could not be pushed around by someone like Rabus. Nor was she deferential to him whose so-called doctorate didn't impress her one whit. From his perspective, she carried her concepts of religious liberty to an extreme.

The Spiritual Value of Hymns

When I read these hymns I felt that the writer had the whole Bible in his heart. This is not just a hymn book but a lesson book of prayer and praise. When so many filthy songs are on the lips of men and women and even children I think it well that folk should with lusty zeal and clear voice sing the songs of their salvation. God is glad when the craftsman at his bench, the maid at the sink, the farmer at the plough, the dresser at the vines, the mother at the cradle break forth in hymns of prayer, praise and instruction.

Katherine Zell

Perhaps so. She was in her sixties, sick in bed, the hour past midnight when she heard a knock at the door. The grieving man's wife had died, and he wanted her to officiate at a surreptitious graveside service before dawn. The woman was considered a radical—a Reformation heretic. Katherine agreed. When town leaders learned, they were determined to reprimand her. The flap ended in a draw. She died before the documents were drawn up.

ARGULA VON STAUFFER GRUMBACH
"A Singular Instrument of Christ"

She was born into Bavarian nobility in 1492 (when Columbus "sailed the ocean blue"). Wealthy and well educated and for a time a lady-in-waiting to the queen, Argula led a life that was anything but tranquil. Political turmoil, religious reform, and leftover pockets of the plague served to make central Europe a dangerous place to live. While she was yet in her teens, her parents both died of that scourge, and some years later her uncle, a high court official (who had become her guardian), was embroiled in a royal scandal and executed for his alleged crimes. Amid her rage at the awful injustice, she found nowhere to turn but to God.

Raised in a religious family, Argula had from childhood found solace in Scripture. When she was ten years old, her father had given her a gift of a beautifully illustrated Koberger Bible, a treasure that she repeatedly read and memorized. Such activity, however, was considered highly objectionable by Catholic clerics, who feared reading the Bible would lead to dissent. Their fears were actualized in Argula.

Indeed, her admiration of Martin Luther was based largely on his emphasis on the Bible and his demand that church tradition be validated by Scripture. To Argula his teachings were a breath of fresh air. But her freedom to interact with religious ideas was thwarted by her husband, Friedrich von Grumbach, whom she had married in 1516, the year her uncle was executed. The following year Luther nailed his Ninety-Five Theses to the church door in Wittenberg, and nothing would ever be the same again.

Although her husband was not particularly interested in the Bible or religious ideas, he was caught up in the conflict politically. And from his vantage point it was advantageous to support the Catholic side of the controversy. The mother of four children, Argula became so taken up in the religious excitement of the day that she was accused by some of neglecting her household. In 1523, with the publication of Luther's tracts and his translation of the New Testament, she took a bold stand and was soon in the thick of it.

Arsacius Seehofer, an eighteen-year-old university-educated teacher, had been arrested and exiled for his refusal to recant his Lutheran beliefs. Such an incident would have easily gone unnoticed but for Argula's involvement. She wrote a letter, citing more than eighty Scripture references, that stands to this day as a monument to the Protestant Reformation. Her salutation, with perhaps more than a hint of disdain, belies her fury: "To the honorable, worthy, highborn, erudite, noble, stalwart Rector and all the Faculty of the University of Ingolstadt."[10] So much for niceties.

The opening lines of the letter lay out her position: "When I heard what you had done to Arsacius Seehofer under terror of imprisonment and the stake, my heart trembled and my bones quaked. What have Luther and Melanchthon taught save the Word of God? You have condemned them. You have not refuted them."

She then went on to accuse them of "pull[ing] God, the prophets and the apostles out of heaven with papal decretals drawn from Aristotle, who was not a Christian at all." She likewise demanded to know: "Where do you read in the Bible that Christ, the apostles, and the prophets imprisoned, banished, burned, or murdered anyone?" Such a terrible crime will soon be "known to all the world."[11] And soon it was—when her letter was printed as a pamphlet and widely distributed.

What kind of a woman would stir a ruckus like this? Her accusers were many. She was a "daughter of Eve," worse than that, "a shameless whore." But she also had supporters in high places. One German reformer praised her for knowing more of the Bible than all the "red hats" (cardinals and canon lawyers) combined. She might have relished being at the center of the debate but for the criticism of those who had most to lose—her family.

Despite the personal cost, however, she refused to be intimidated. In fact, she dared the members of the Diet of Nürnberg to a debate, and they took the bait. Unfortunately for her, she was not taken seriously. In her assessment, "the princes [took] the Word of God no more seriously

Jeanne d'Albret: Christmas Day Conversion

The daughter of Marguerite of Navarre, Jeanne was profoundly influenced by her mother, who studied the works of Reformers. Unlike her mother, however, who remained a lifelong Catholic, this queen of Navarre went a step further. On Christmas Day in 1560, having been strongly encouraged to do so, she publicly professed her conversion. By doing so, she was essentially stating that she was following Scripture as Calvin set forth. As such she became a strong supporter of the French Huguenots, though not without risk. In fact, her Catholic husband threatened to divorce her and locked her up. Her aid to the Huguenots was bad enough; worse was her influence over their young son. When accused of heresy, she responded, "I am not planting a new religion but restoring an old one." As queen she decreed that the crucifix and other religious ornaments represented idolatry. She died in 1572, the very year Protestants were defeated during the infamous St. Bartholomew's Day Massacre.

than a cow does a game of chess."[12] Many others, however, were taking the Word of God seriously and were playing the game of chess with great skill. Among them, Martin Luther, whom she had met in person in 1530.

Sidling up to this audacious monk—and university professor—was very risky, and she paid a heavy price. "I understand that my husband will be deposed from his office. I can't help it. God will feed my children as he feeds the birds and will clothe them as the lilies of the field."[13]

Luther's own words in a letter to a friend confirm her precarious situation:

> The Duke of Bavaria rages above measure, killing, crushing and persecuting the gospel with all his might. That most noble woman, Argula von Stauffer, is there making a valiant fight with great spirit, boldness of speech and knowledge of Christ. . . . Her husband, who treats her tyrannically, has been deposed from his prefecture. . . . She alone, among these monsters, carries on with firm faith, though, she admits not without inner trembling. She is a singular instrument of Christ.[14]

"A singular instrument of Christ." Although she would carry on in her reform efforts for several more years, those words offer a fitting epitaph for her life's work.

RENÉE OF FERRARA
Reformer and Friend of John Calvin

> Had I had a beard I would have been the king of France.
> I have been defrauded by that confounded
> Salic law [which denied women succession to the throne].[15]

Though minus a beard, Renée lacked nothing of boldness or brilliance. She was anything but a princess of fairy tales and little-girl dress-up parties. Nor was she the first French woman of royal birth to make a name for herself in Reformation Europe. Marguerite of Navarre and Jeanne d'Albret had also espoused Protestant principles from inside palaces. And like Renée they had taken great risks.

Though Renée did not articulate fine points of doctrine, as had Marguerite, she stands alone in her spirited interaction with her mentor, John Calvin, and her refusal to kowtow to his demands. Born in 1510, she was a year younger than Calvin, who regarded her as a royal trophy. And no wonder. Her father was King Louis XII of France, her mother Anne the Duchess of Brittany, the richest woman in all of Europe. With no brothers (or half-brothers), Renée would have succeeded her father, but for the Salic law. Instead, a nephew inherited the throne, and she became a political pawn in her father's foreign alliances.

Matchmaking deals were in the works when she was but a child, and at seventeen she was married off to Ercole, son of Italy's infamous Lucrezia Borgia. Her new home at the court in Ferrara was at the very center of the Italian Renaissance. She had everything that a princess could want—a lavish palace, priceless art, manicured gardens, dazzling gowns, precious jewels, culinary delicacies, and a handsome husband. Renée's plain features, according to one wag of the day, "were more than compensated by her superior intellect."[16] What Ercole most desired of her was an heir, and on that score she succeeded, bearing five children, including two sons, all in the space of seven years.

Marital bliss, however, was not aided by the fact that she was strong willed and did not play the part of a submissive wife, egged on in her independent ways by Calvin. Indeed, her religious sympathies would become a serious bone of contention. The Reformed movement had made significant inroads in France, and news of bloody persecution—perhaps conveyed by her friend and cousin Marguerite of Navarre—was alarming.

Renée could not turn down the call for help. When French "heretics" secretly sought refuge in Ferrara, she welcomed them without her husband's knowledge. Among the fleeing heretics was Charles d'Espeville, aka John Calvin, who arrived in the spring of 1536 and stayed for a month. His influence on matters of theology was enormous, but she submitted to Calvin no more readily than she did to her husband.

From Calvin's correspondence, however, it is clear that a friendship had developed. "If I address you, madam," he wrote, "it is not from rashness or presumption, but pure and true affection to make you prevail in the Lord." He was no doubt dazzled by her wealth and perceived influence. "When I consider the pre-eminence in which He has placed you," he wrote her, "I think that, as a person of princely rank, you can advance the kingdom of Jesus Christ." He went on to praise her spiritual maturity: "I observe in you such fear of God, and such a real desire to obey Him, that I should consider myself a castaway if I neglected the opportunity of being useful to you."[17]

Renée, however, was caught between a rock and a hard place, and she carried on publicly as though she were a devoted Catholic. Calvin was more than a little upset: "I have heard that your domestics have been scandalized by the word of a certain preacher who says that one may go both to Mass and to the Lord's Supper," he wrote, alluding to her as well. "I cannot suffer a wolf in sheep's clothing. I esteem the word of this preacher no more than the song of a jackdaw. . . . The Mass is an execrable sacrilege and an intolerable blasphemy."[18]

Renée was caught in the middle. When word of her apostasy was reported to King Henry II, a staunch Catholic who had succeeded her father, he pleaded with his beloved "only aunt" to be "restored to the bosom of [their] holy mother church, cleansed and purified from those cursed dogmas and reprobate errors." In order to help her in her restoration process, he informed her that the Inquisitor Ori would be coming to give her spiritual guidance. If she were to resist his kindly teaching, the king added, the inquisitor would bring her "to reason by severity."[19]

When Ercole learned how devious his wife had been in sneaking the Reformed heresy into his very palace, he forcibly placed her under house arrest and threatened to place their daughters, Lucrezia and Leonora, in a convent. Her maternal instincts firing on all cylinders, Renée sent for a priest to hear her confession and administer communion. The solution worked. She was set free to care for her young girls.

Fleeing in disguise and with an alias, John Calvin himself had not hesitated to escape persecution in Paris, but now he scolded her. "I fear you have left the straight road to please the world," he wrote her. "And indeed the devil has so entirely triumphed that we have been constrained to groan, and bow our heads in sorrow."[20] He told her to humble herself before God and come back to the faith, offering no counsel as to what she should do about her daughters. Although she did not attend mass in the years that followed, she did not enjoy the freedom of publicly professing her Reformed faith.

When Renée was approaching her fiftieth birthday, her husband died, and her oldest son, a staunch Catholic, succeeded his father as Duke of Ferrara. She had lived in Ferrara for more than three decades. The time was right. She returned to her beloved homeland to stay. She left behind her ministry to the poor and needy, many of whom wept at her departure. Back home she had more religious freedom, and her estate became a refuge for Reformed Christians fleeing persecution.

As she had in the past, she maintained her correspondence with Calvin, often on testy terms. When her daughter's Catholic husband was assassinated, she was not ashamed of her sorrow, and she was furious that Calvin had consigned him to hell. She was also troubled that she was not permitted to be part of church decision making. One of Calvin's former students, who had been assigned to keep Renée on the straight and narrow, discovered that she was no pushover. "Renée wants to attend the meetings of the synod," he wrote to Calvin. "But if Paul thought that women should be silent in the church, how much more should they not participate in the making of decisions. How will the Papists and the Anabaptists scoff to see us run by women!"[21]

Renée wanted her voice heard and resented the fact that the Salic law had denied her the crown and that a set of arbitrary rules would silence her at a synod—especially when so much was at stake. She decried the religious persecution of any stripe, and that included the terrible atrocities conducted against Catholics by Reformed vigilantes in France. To "Monsieur Calvin," she wrote: "I am distressed that you do not know how the half in this realm behave. They even exhort simple women to kill and strangle. This is not the rule of Christ. I say this out of the great affection which I hold for the Reformed religion."[22]

To the very end Renée fought for religious toleration, but it would be a lost cause. In 1572, she would learn of the carnage carried out against Protestants—a slaughter of thousands that would forever be remembered as the St. Bartholomew's Day Massacre. She lived on for two more very sad years and was then laid to rest in France, even, as many feared, was the Reformed faith.

ELIZABETH DIRKS
Teacher, Preacher, Deaconess, Martyr

The year was 1549. The setting was a house in the Netherlands, the town of Leeuwarden. The young refugee had been hiding there in plain sight. Roman Catholic authorities tracked her down, thinking she was the wife of the well-known "heretic" and Anabaptist leader Menno Simons. She was not, but her story of conviction and courage would be indelibly marked in blood in the annals of martyrdom for ages to come. There was little on which Catholics and Protestants agreed in this era of religious rancor, except for the belief that Anabaptists ought to be put to death.

That Catholic authorities would have a particular interest in Elizabeth Dirks was not surprising since she had spent much of her life in a convent. And the questions they asked her clearly indicated that she had abandoned her convent education. They demanded to know what she believed about the sacraments of the mass and baptism—and whether she had been rebaptized.

Her responses reflected standard Anabaptist teachings. Mass no longer meant anything to her, and neither the Lord's Supper nor baptism was a sacrament. Regarding a second baptism, she responded: "No, my lords, I have not been re-baptized. I have been baptized once upon my faith; for it is written that baptism belongs to believers."[23]

Born into Frisian nobility, Elizabeth was shipped off to a convent at a young age where some time later she learned of the persecution and martyrdom of Anabaptists through the social media of the day. Printing in the sixteenth century was comparable to the internet today. Whether through pamphlets or word of mouth, forbidden religious messages found their way beyond the barriers of brick walls. What most stunned young Elizabeth was that people were willing to die for their faith. She had known all about the practice of killing for the cause of the church, but to refuse to fight back and die for one's beliefs was an amazing concept.

In addition to *heretical* tracts, Bibles had made their way into convents, and Elizabeth, under lax supervision, had secretly studied a copy of a Latin Bible. That Anabaptist beliefs were supported with Scripture verses impressed her, as had the claim that much of Catholic belief and practice was not supported by Scripture, or worse, was contradicted by Scripture. Monasticism itself, she soon realized, was not practiced in New Testament times. Deep in the heart of convent life, a new world was opening up to her. Perhaps not surprisingly, she was unable to keep her discoveries to herself. When word of her deviant ideas leaked out, she was placed in quarantine—convent arrest. Soon after, through her own ingenuity and the help of others, she escaped, disguising herself as a milkmaid.

In Leeuwarden, Elizabeth refused to live a life underground. Instead, though obviously not wearing a nun's habit, she went about town functioning as an evangelist, teacher, and preacher. Had she quietly practiced her faith behind closed doors, she likely would have avoided inquisitors' questions. But she dared to speak her mind right under their noses. When she was hauled in for questioning, she might have nuanced her answers. Instead she quoted long passages from the Latin Bible that, at least to her way of thinking, proved that Catholics themselves were the real heretics.

Even then, had she been willing to simply name some Anabaptists as her teachers, she might have avoided torture. But she refused to implicate anyone but herself. So the screw torture was inflicted—so tight that her fingernails spurted blood. Screws were also applied to her shins and elsewhere.

She cried out for mercy but refused to divulge names. So severe was the torture that she fell unconscious. Such a death, her tormentors realized, was too easy and would defeat their purpose. They revived her, fastened heavy weights to her body, tied her inside a bag, and deposited her alive and fully conscious into the icy waters of the Potmarge on March 27, 1549.

CONCLUDING OBSERVATIONS

Drowning Anabaptists, who believed in adult immersion, has since been dubbed the cruelest joke of the Reformation: *If they insist on rebaptism, we'll gladly comply!* The story of Elizabeth is difficult to read. Her prolonged torture and cruel death were not carried out by a totalitarian regime or by terrorists. Rather by professing Christians. And Catholics were certainly not alone in their pursuit of peaceful Anabaptists. The Swiss and German Reformers also took part in executing other Christians, as did church leaders in the British Isles and the Puritan divines in America.

John Calvin, Ulrich Zwingli, and papal emissaries have sometimes been excused because they did not have the benefit of the Enlightenment—the philosophical movement that swept Europe in the eighteenth century and demanded, among other things, religious toleration. But Katherine Zell was hardly a product of the Enlightenment. She was outraged that people were being executed for their so-called heresies. She cited "the poor Servetus" in particular, who was burned at the stake in Geneva, when Calvin had the power to prevent it. Too many history books have unfortunately left this wise woman out of their pages, though she stands forever as a monument to religious toleration amid the hysterical voices of the Reformation.

Renée censured John Calvin on matters of religious toleration. Again, he could have stepped in and called on his followers to stop their vicious attacks on Catholics. But he did not. Nor did he offer understanding and true pastoral counseling to Renée when she was threatened with the loss of her little girls. As mothers and daughters we can only cringe at his callousness.

Though all four of these women demonstrated incredible fortitude in the face of danger, the most determined and outspoken of them all was Argula. Though she had everything to lose, it is a credit to her convictions and chutzpah that she dared to stand up to theological thugs. She stood tall before the Diet of Nürnberg and cited one scripture after another to support her beliefs. She was fearless, "though not without inner trembling." Luther's words still ring out today: "She alone, among these monsters, carries on with firm faith . . . a singular instrument of Christ."[24]

QUESTIONS TO THINK ABOUT

Do you agree with Katherine's defense-of-marriage argument—that marrying a priest is a ministry? Is there any justification in the Roman Catholic Church's forbidding priests to marry?

How should we respond to individuals like Katherine who have lost their gaiety and find little pleasure in life after the loss of a loved one? Have you ever sought to help bring someone out of deep depression?

Have you ever known a mother like Argula, who seemed to put ministry above domestic concerns? Should Luther's praise of her have been more tempered? Did Calvin expect too much of Renée by way of ministry and fail to understand her concerns as a mother?

Are women more likely than men to be less concerned about fine points of doctrine and more concerned about ecumenical harmony? In what ways did these four women speak out or show empathy for those who were being persecuted? Do you admire or fear people who seek to bring unity among Christians?

Would you, like Elizabeth, be willing to die for your faith in Christ? Would you be willing to die for particular beliefs associated with your faith? Would you have advised Elizabeth to agree to be a good Catholic in order to avoid execution?

Which of these women do you think would be the most effective minister—or minister's wife—in your congregation?

5

Teresa of Ávila
and Sectarian "Heretics"

I recently finished reading Cathleen Medwick's excellent book, *Teresa of Ávila: The Progress of a Soul*. At about the same time, my husband, who reads to me every night, began a book we had chosen for our own private book-club selection: Abraham Verghese's highly rated novel *Cutting for Stone*. The story is set primarily in an Ethiopian mission hospital. The narrator is a non-Christian Indian surgeon who tells his life story. What a coincidence, then, that Teresa of Ávila, albeit dead, is such an important character in the book. And Verghese even raves about Medwick's biography in his acknowledgments at the end of the book.

Cutting for Stone was criticized by one reviewer for its mystical artificiality: "The first hundred pages or so make the book look almost like a Rushdie-esque magic realist novel, complete with mystically communicating twins, an apparent virgin birth, divine intervention, and other anti-realist devices."[1] But so too with Medwick's scholarly biography, which lays out in a systematic way Teresa's incredible accomplishments while at the same time relating her mysticism and miracles in an objective and almost rational manner.

I found the biography fascinating, though I realized again that Teresa's spirituality is something I do not easily relate to. God entered her world in strange ways that are foreign to my way of thinking. But if Teresa could experience incredible raptures, who's to say that her spiritual memoir itself would not inspire great—and small—wonders? *Cutting for Stone* is exactly what I needed to better understand her and her profound legacy. What a coincidence—or *God thing*—that one book would follow so seamlessly after the other.

Like Teresa, Anne Hutchinson is a longtime acquaintance of mine, one who has also been favored with a great scholarly biography. *Divine Rebel* by Selma Williams was first published in 1981, and several more books on her life have appeared since then. She too was persecuted for her religious beliefs, as was Margaret Fell Fox, known as the Mother of the Quakers. American evangelist Clarissa Danforth traveled and preached freely though critics claimed she was infringing on what was rightfully a man's turf. But like the others she was convinced she had a profound calling from God.

Besides being intrepid evangelists, Teresa, Margaret, Anne, and Clarissa were all involved in what are typically considered sectarian movements. Teresa fought the Roman Catholic establishment as much as Margaret fought the seventeenth-century religious establishment in the British Isles. Anne, like Teresa and Margaret, was regarded as a heretic, in her case and in the case of Mary Dyer, by Puritan divines. Only Danforth had ministerial credentials, albeit from the sect known as Free Will Baptists.

St. Teresa in the News

If higher powers are helping to lift Spain out of its economic crisis, one political party wants to know exactly who they are and what they're doing [by asking] a series of questions to the governing People's party after the interior minister . . . said recently he was certain that Saint Teresa was "making important intercessions" for Spain "during these tough times."

In a letter to the government [an opposition party leader] asked for clarification about what help the government was getting from one of Spain's most popular holy figures. "In what ways does the minister of the interior think Saint Teresa of Avila is interceding on behalf of Spain?"

Ashifa Kassam, "Spanish Government Questioned," *The Guardian*, January 30, 2014

TERESA OF ÁVILA
Strong-Willed Catholic Reformer

Keeping track of Catholic religious orders, as I have discovered, is a mind-boggling project even for seasoned Catholic monastics themselves. Many of these movements were repeatedly reformed and in the process were renamed or had a qualifier added to their original name. Such is the case with the Carmelites, both calced and discalced.

In the thirteenth century St. Albert of Jerusalem organized hermits who had already taken up their abode in caves and huts on Mount Carmel for

Jesus and the Discalced Carmelites

Christians before and since Teresa have at times sought to literally follow the commands Jesus gave to his followers. Teresa focused on footwear, insisting that her followers travel shoeless, thus the label Discalced Carmelites.

> After this the Lord appointed seventy-two others and sent them two by two ahead of him to every town and place where he was about to go. He told them, "The harvest is plentiful, but the workers are few. Ask the Lord of the harvest, therefore, to send out workers into his harvest field. Go! I am sending you out like lambs among wolves. Do not take a purse or bag or sandals; and do not greet anyone on the road.
>
> "When you enter a house, first say, 'Peace to this house.' If someone who promotes peace is there, your peace will rest on them; if not, it will return to you. Stay there, eating and drinking whatever they give you, for the worker deserves his wages. Do not move around from house to house.
>
> "When you enter a town and are welcomed, eat what is offered to you."
>
> Luke 10:1–8

the purpose of poverty, prayer, and penance. Albert wrote a rule for them and set the stage for a monastic order. The significance of their location on Mount Carmel was that here the great prophet Elijah prevailed over the prophets of Baal. This blazing miracle would conclude with the slaughter of all the false prophets—an unusual setting perhaps for peaceful hermits to congregate. Mount Horeb, where God came to Elijah in a still small voice, might appear to be a more appropriate locale. But when we consider the Carmelites of Teresa's day, the site of the killing fields is fitting.

To imagine St. Teresa as a beloved reformer or a placid nun receiving revelations from God is to miss the upheaval surrounding her ministry. She was anything but a contemplative in a hermit's cave. Her reforms were hated by a majority of the Carmelites, and she was considered a heretic by many outside her discalced order. Violence often accompanied reform in the sixteenth century, as was true in the autumn of 1571. Having departed La Encarnación (her convent just outside the city walls of Ávila) to establish more convents, she returned to defend her turf after learning of fierce opposition. With armed bodyguards and supporters, her procession was announced before her arrival. Onlookers gathered for a good view of the impending melee.

Angry nuns had locked themselves behind bolted doors while the two sides scuffled outside. Then Teresa's armed band forced its way in, jostling and kicking the screaming, irate enemy nuns. They fought back, punching, scratching, and hurling obscenities. Indeed, the commotion was so loud it could be heard some distance away inside the city walls. At the end of the day Teresa's reform-minded henchmen claimed victory. The nuns in the convent were defeated, even as were the false prophets of Baal on Mount Carmel, though in this situation they were forced to live under the rule of Teresa, whom they hated—perhaps a punishment worse than death.

This altercation occurred barely a decade before Teresa's death at sixty-seven. She is known primarily for her founding, with John of the Cross, the Discalced (or barefoot) Carmelites. The reform was largely an effort to bring the movement back to its very strict initial practices. That Teresa would one day become a beloved saint would not have appeared to be an obvious eventuality to most contemporary observers. But the unshakable loyalty of her followers, combined with her published spiritual memoir and a boatload of alleged miracles, led to her canonization forty years after her death—and a miraculous death at that. Her corpse, smelling as fragrant as roses a month later, did not naturally decompose.

For those who might be skeptical about a sweet-smelling corpse and, prior to death, a miraculous capability of levitating, there ought to be no doubt about Teresa's punishing lifestyle of privation and almost nonstop arduous travel and work. And entirely by choice. She grew up in affluence, a daughter of wealth and privilege. She would easily fit in with today's upwardly mobile American family—a typical teenager with trashy novels, a love for dancing, chess, and horseback riding, her iPhone only a ringtone away. She later reflected on her dreamy fascination with the romance of chivalry: "So excessively was I absorbed in it that I believe, unless I had a new book, I was never happy. . . . I began to deck myself out and to try to attract others by my appearance, taking great trouble with my hands and hair, using perfumes and all the vanities I could get."[2]

But then came the hard times, the death of her mother and her own extended illness. She had previously taken religion for granted. Sixteenth-century Spain was saturated with spirituality. With her reading of St. Jerome's *Letters*, however, her life changed. She learned that Marcella and Paula had worked alongside him. And what was barring her from becoming a woman of God even as they were? So at age twenty she stole away from home to join a Carmelite monastery. There she saw laxity all around her, and she was no better than the rest, that is until she determined to devote herself entirely to God. She would forfeit all but the barest necessities with self-imposed solitary confinement and strenuous asceticism, lashing herself "until the walls of her cell dripped with gore."[3]

For most of the next two decades, Teresa's life in the convent was relatively routine—if near-fatal physical ailments and severe doubt and terrifying temptations could be considered in any way routine. But then in 1554, as she was approaching forty, her life made a radical turn. In a flood of tears, she was converted. Something suddenly happened in a momentary flash that endless hours of prayer and meditation and self-flagellation could not accomplish. But with the conversion came horrendous battles with the powers of darkness, as well as heart-pounding raptures.

These intense times of spiritual warfare, revelations, and raptures served to fuel the engines of Teresa's reform. A visionary tour of hell revealed to her how Satan was snatching souls—souls who had been deceived by the "Lutherans" (actually French Calvinists). They were souls worth any sacrifice to redeem and bring back to the true church. The Protestant Reformers were to her as dangerous as were the false prophets of Baal. God stood with Elijah on Mount Carmel, and he was standing with her and her Carmelite reformers in the face of heresy.

Teresa's most memorable mystical experience was an erotic ecstasy that she recorded in her *Life*. Here she revealed graphic details of "an angel . . . in human form . . . [who had in his hands] a large golden spear. . . . I felt as if he plunged this into my heart several times, so that it penetrated all the way to my entrails. When he drew it out, he . . . left me totally inflamed with a great love for God. The pain was so severe it made me moan several times. The sweetness of this intense pain is so extreme, there is no wanting

St. Teresa: Navigating a Fine Line between Saint and Heretic

Although Teresa had been the object of examination by the Inquisition and a controversial figure during her lifetime, she was canonized only decades after her death, the first Spanish woman to receive that honor. Following canonization, she came to be viewed as a swooning, ecstatic mystic, a miraculous healer, and a humble proponent of absolute orthodoxy and absolute obedience.

However, in recent years this stereotype has been challenged. She has become the focus of intense religious and historical criticism by scholars . . . who have attempted to establish that Teresa of Avila was actually an independent, free-thinking, strong woman. . . . Because of her charismatic personality and her ability to reform the church while acting within the political constraints of the clerical and patriarchal hierarchy, Teresa was able to keep from crossing the fine line between "saint" and "heretic."

"Teresa of Avila," http://www.csbsju.edu/Documents/libraries/teresaofAvila.pdf

Portrait of a Nun on a Divine Mission

[She was] a determined, middle-aged nun on a divine mission. . . . Teresa, the woman who left her convent to roam about the countryside wheeling and dealing like a man, putting ideas into the heads of nuns who were better off ignorant, wreaking havoc in the lives of prelates and municipal officers, invading cities in the dead of night. The papal nuncio Felipe Sega scorned her as . . . "an unstable, restless, disobedient, and contumacious female."

Cathleen Medwick, *Teresa of Avila: The Progress of a Soul*

it to end."[4] Such love would impel her to carry out a ministry in the face of intense opposition. In the next two decades she established more than a dozen new houses, and she would be named among the great leaders of the Catholic Counter-Reformation.

Yet Teresa's actual success as a founder of convents was questionable. Many of these so-called Carmelite houses were small and regularly in a state of turmoil. Powerful opposition from secular Carmelites and high-ranking clerics was marshaled against her. She was repeatedly accused of heresy and charged with leaving "her cloisters against the orders of her superiors contrary to the decrees of the Council of Trent." Proud and disobedient, she was out of control: "She is ambitious and teaches theology as if she were a doctor of the church in spite of St. Paul's prohibition."[5]

Despite the attacks, Teresa managed to curry the favor of certain high-placed individuals. Though questioned by papal inquisitors, she repeatedly managed to avoid prison. The pope ruled in her favor largely because of her effort to rid Spain of the "mischief and ravages those Lutherans had wrought in France." Were she to have "a thousand lives," she vowed she "would give them all to save a single one of the many [such] souls which were going to perdition."[6]

Teresa's writing has stood the test of time, especially her *Life*. So also her volume on spiritual discipline, *The Interior Castle*, which guides the seeker through seven stages toward complete union with God. She has long been a revered Catholic saint, and more than that. In 1970 Pope

Paul VI gave her (as well as Catherine of Siena) the title doctor of the church.

ANNE HUTCHINSON
New England "Heretic"

The town of Boston was barely ten years old when Anne Hutchinson arrived with her large family. She quickly became a popular teacher, was then banished from town, and died in 1643, less than a decade after she had arrived. In 1660, Mary Dyer, a Quaker preacher, was hanged in that same town. Then in the early 1690s, the Bay Colony presented a full-length feature show in Salem, now remembered as the infamous witch trials of 1692. Dozens of individuals, primarily women, were accused, imprisoned, and condemned, no less than twenty of whom were executed. Hangings were the hottest shows in town.

Imagine such awful spectacles. Here were Puritans who had been severely persecuted in England now turning these same vicious tactics against those whom they deemed heretics. In recent decades New England Puritans have been heralded for their noble legacy, but we dare not forget their damnable religious bigotry. Fortunately, Anne's contemporary Roger Williams, also banished from Boston, articulated a position of religious liberty that would serve to turn the tide toward religious toleration and significantly influence later constitutional rights.

Growing up in England, Anne was a deeply religious girl whose favorite haunt was the well-stocked library of her father, an Anglican vicar who died when she was nineteen. Two years later, she married William Hutchinson and soon thereafter became acquainted with the preaching of the young John Cotton, already an influential English Puritan. In his message she found the theology that would frame the remainder of her life: God's overpowering grace and the Holy Spirit's mystical union with a believer—an "elect saint," in Puritan terminology. So profoundly inspired by his teaching was she that a dozen years later, in the 1630s when Cotton emigrated from England to the Bay Colony, Anne was bound and determined to follow. Only pregnancy with her fourteenth child delayed the voyage.

When the large family arrived in Boston, they were warmly welcomed. Anne quickly became a much-sought-after midwife, working closely with other women to keep the mothers and their infants alive during the most perilous days just before and after the birth. She also started what would today be called a ladies' Bible study. Her minister described her work during those early years:

> Shee did much good in our Town, in womans meeting at Childbirth-Travells, wherein shee was not onley skillful and helpfull, but readily fell into good discourse with the women about their spiritual estates . . . By which means many of the women (and their husbands) were . . . brought to enquire more seriously after the Lord Jesus Christ.[7]

Indeed, Anne was an engaging teacher—too engaging for her own good. The women enjoyed lively interaction, and they shared their thoughts with their husbands, who started attending her weekly meetings as well. In fact, she became a sensation. So many people attended that she had to schedule extra meetings. But the criticism quickly piled on. She was just like Eve, some said. Indeed, the neighborhood women were proving that. They were "as by an Eve catch[ing] their husbands also."[8] In fact, so many women and men did she catch that they were collectively called Hutchinsonians.

Essentially what she had done was to draw from John Cotton's theology of grace, while adding her own emphasis on personal guidance from the Holy Spirit, testifying of her own revelations coming directly from God. Such divine messages were regarded as dangerous. "If they be allowed in one thing [they] must be admitted a rule in all things," Governor Winthrop warned, "for they being above reason and Scripture, they are not subject to control."[9] That she denied the doctrine of original sin only added fuel to the fire. The storm surrounding her quickly spread as the accused and the accusers multiplied, and the controversy took on a life of its own.

Yet her unique story stands out. She was rebuked not only as an Eve but also as a Jezebel who, like that wicked Old Testament queen, had spread "abominable" doctrine and carried out her agenda as a "thing not tolerable nor comely in the sight of God, nor fitting for [her] sex."[10] Brought before the Bay Colony's General Court and charged with insubordination, she insisted that her only authority was the Great Jehovah. The verdict

Inscription on Statue in front of the Boston State House, Dedicated 1922

IN MEMORY OF
ANNE MARBURY HUTCHINSON
BAPTIZED AT ALFORD
LINCOLNSHIRE ENGLAND
20 JULY 1595 [sic]
KILLED BY THE INDIANS
AT EAST CHESTER NEW YORK 1643
COURAGEOUS EXPONENT
OF CIVIL LIBERTY
AND RELIGIOUS TOLERATION

was banishment, but she was permitted to stay in her home until spring. When she again appeared in court, this time begging that her sentence be reversed, there was no backing down. Even her mentor and onetime friend John Cotton spoke of her detestable "errors and pride of spirit" that had brought great harm "to many a poore soule."

But John Cotton desired to give her another chance. For a week he and another minister counseled her until she recanted her errors. But when brought back into court, her enemies brought new evidence and quickly ended the trial with an unambiguous sentence read by Rev. John Wilson: "I doe cast you out and . . . deliver you up to Sathan . . . and account you from this time forth to be a Hethen and a Publican. . . . I command you in the name of Ch[rist] Je[sus] and of this Church as a Leper to withdraw your selfe out of the Congregation."[11]

Although her husband had gone on ahead to Rhode Island to prepare a home, Anne's life quickly went from bad to worse. She was pregnant again, and the trauma resulted in a miscarriage. Word got back to Boston, and her misfortune quickly became a story of God's righteous judgment. This, the rumor mill hissed, was no mere miscarriage. Rather, "20 monstrous births," none of them "of human shape." Even John Cotton joined in these cruel accusations: She had delivered "twenty-seven . . . lumps of man's seed, without any alteration or mixture of anything from the woman, and thereupon gathered that it might signify her error in denying inherent righteousness."[12]

What a travesty! Where was his sense of decency? What about his calling to pastoral care? He should have been ashamed of himself.

Sometime later when word reached Boston that Anne and some of the children had been slain by Native Americans on Long Island, the Puritan divines haughtily insisted that they now had solid evidence God was on their side. "I never heard that the Indians in those parts did ever before this, commit the like outrage," wrote the Reverend Thomas Weld, "and therefore God's hand is the more apparently seene herein, to pick out this wofull woman, to make her . . . an unheard of heavie example of their cruelty above al others."[13]

MARGARET FELL FOX
Mother of the Quakers

She was a rich, highborn lady who married George Fox, a smelly itinerant preacher trudging about from town to town in the English countryside with a message that drew mockery and derision. Not only that, imprisonment. His attempts to shout down ministers who were waxing eloquent in their Sunday morning sermons did not sit well with local law enforcement. He was a tormented man, many people claimed, but outwardly he was brash and self-possessed. An early Quaker song, "The Ballad of George Fox," depicts him boldly "walking in the glory of the light . . . in [his] old leather breeches and [his] shaggy, shaggy locks."[14] By his own account he slept under haystacks and hedges and foraged for food.

What did Margaret Fell see in this man? Even if she recognized him as a true prophet of God, what possessed her to marry him? I pondered that question a decade ago wandering the grounds of her lovely Swarthmore mansion, and I still mull over it today. On that cloudless September morning, the grass still wet and sparkling from an overnight rain, I tried to put myself in her shoes. I've certainly made my share of rash decisions, but to marry a frenzied fanatic so devoid of social graces is something I cannot comprehend. If her biological clock had been running down and there were no other eligible bachelors, I might give her some slack. But she was in her midfifties, a widowed mother of nine children.

George Fox, more than ten years younger than she, however, had received a message from God: "I had seen from the Lord, a considerable time before, that I should take Margaret Fell to be my wife; and when I first mentioned it to her, she felt the answer of life from God thereunto."[15] What happened next is left to our imaginations, but we cannot assume that their relationship revolved around romance. To his credit, he did not rush matters, and he consulted with her children and with other Quakers.

Margaret had married her first husband, Thomas Fell, when she was seventeen, he some sixteen years her senior. A barrister and country gentleman and later a member of Parliament, he trusted his young wife with the management of the Swarthmore estate during his frequent travels. It was while he was away in 1652 that George Fox paid a visit. Soon she, her children, and most of the household servants were "convinced and converted unto God." When Thomas returned home, nosy neighbors met him and warned him of the fate of his household. He no doubt entered his house with some serious trepidation. But his confidence in Margaret was so great that later the same evening he agreed to listen to the message of George Fox himself.

Although Thomas Fell did not become a Quaker himself, he never presumed to restrain Margaret in her active involvement with George Fox and his ragtag following. In fact, she freely donated large sums of money and opened Swarthmore Hall not only as a meetinghouse but also as the nerve center of the new movement. So significant was her support and leadership in these early years and throughout her life that it is difficult to imagine the movement ever getting off the ground without her involvement.

When Thomas Fell died in 1658, six years after her conversion to Quakerism, Margaret was devastated. She had lost not only her beloved husband but also the movement's most reliable defender. The matter of religious toleration in seventeenth-century England was dicey at best, and Quakers were a natural target for harassment. Now with Fell's death and the restoration of King Charles II to the throne, the threat of street violence and state-sponsored persecution spiked. It is hardly a surprise, then, when the arm of the law reached into the very inner sanctum of Swarthmore.

George Fox was hauled off to languish for months in a foul dungeon in Lancaster Castle.

Margaret managed to secure his release, but then she was locked up. Her crime? Failing to honor the king with an oath of allegiance—though hardly rubbing it in his face:

> I love, own, and honor the King and desire his peace and welfare [and desire to] live a peaceable, a quiet and a godly life under his government, according to the Scriptures. . . . And as for the oath itself, Christ Jesus, the King of Kings, hath commanded me not to swear at all, neither by heaven, nor by earth, nor by any other Oath.[16]

Although the judge handed down a life sentence, she ended up serving less than five years, during which time she wrote her now most widely quoted booklet, *Women's Speaking Justified, Proved and Allowed of by the Scriptures*. . . . The Bible, she argued, raised no roadblocks to women serving God in the pulpit or on the evangelistic circuit. Rather the roadblocks came from "the bottomless pit, and the spirit of darkness that hath spoken for these many hundred years together in this night of apostasy." The Scriptures, she argued, presented perfect equality—in marriage as well. The word of God to Abraham: "In all that Sarah hath said to thee, hearken to her voice."[17]

It was two years after the pamphlet was published that Margaret, more than a decade a widow, had married George Fox, a union that afforded her an opportunity to put her egalitarian proposal into practice. But if equality was a mark of the marriage, togetherness was not. Again she was hauled away to prison, this time for holding unauthorized religious meetings. She was released in less than a year, barely in time to see her new husband off on his sea voyage to America. After he returned, he was imprisoned again. And so went their marriage until his death at age sixty-seven.

It is no surprise that the company of Quakers remained scattered, disorganized, and ravaged with infighting. When Fox was not imprisoned, he was traveling, as was the case with many of his followers. Margaret, more than he, kept the movement from falling apart entirely. As early as 1660, she published her declaration on pacifism, which clearly stated what her husband a decade earlier had put forward. In the years that followed she continued to write and to clarify the beliefs of the growing movement.

Throughout her twenty-one-year marriage with George Fox, there were questions about their lengthy separations. Marriage had not put a damper on his itinerant ministry. Was this a real union or a marriage in name only? Prior to his death, with his health declining, he was living in London and had not seen Margaret for some six months. She was sensitive about any such censure:

> My concern for God and His holy and eternal truth was then in the north, where God had placed and set me; and likewise for the ordering and governing of my children and family; so that we were willing both of us to live apart some years upon God's account and His truth's service, and to deny ourselves of that comfort which we might have had in being together. . . . If any took occasion, or judged hard of us, because of that, the Lord will judge them; for we were innocent.[18]

Margaret carried on in the ministry until her death at eighty-eight. Three years earlier she had made the arduous journey to London for the purpose of delivering a letter to the new king, William of Orange, refusing to return home "until [she had] cleared [herself] unto this government." The letter includes a brief summary of more than four decades of persecution and imprisonment for no other crime than following their "consciences towards God." Truly, for no crime they had "suffered very much, as it is well-known to the nation of England, even to the death of several hundreds by imprisonment and other hardships." All of that, "and yet," she stated, "we were never found in transgression of any just or righteous law, but only upon account of our consciences towards God."[19]

She ended her letter with praise for this king who had promoted religious toleration: "Now God has placed you over us, in this government, which has been very moderate and merciful to us, and we live very comfortably. . . . I pray God for your preservation, who am His servant, and your faithful subject."[20]

It is interesting to note that the year after Margaret Fell's death in 1702, John Wesley, often considered the child of his parents' reconciliation, was born. Samuel Wesley (his father) had allegedly walked out on his wife, Susanna, because of a bitter political clash over King William's legitimacy as an English monarch. That story is told in a later chapter, but it is cited here only to point out that Susanna strongly opposed this same king to whom Margaret Fell expressed such gratitude.

Although Susanna was a strong woman involved in ministry herself, it would be left to her son John to commission women preachers. In doing so he was accused of being—God forbid—a Quaker. Indeed, it was often assumed, thanks to Margaret Fell, that any woman preacher must be a Quaker. Perhaps she would have smiled at that thought. John Wesley did not. But if the seventeenth century belonged to her, the eighteenth belonged to him. Both continued in their respective ministries until they died in their eighty-eighth year.

CLARISSA DANFORTH
New England Evangelist

Can a woman preach and teach and conduct revival meetings? This was an issue in the early nineteenth century when Clarissa Danforth began her ministry in New England. Well why not? Why should anyone deny women the pulpit? "If an Ass could reprove the prophet Balaam, and a barn-yard fowl could reprove Peter, may not a woman rebuke sin?"[21] So went the reasoning of Dr. Clark, one of Clarissa's supporters.

Whether the same rationale was used to support people of color in the pulpit was not immediately apparent, but the records show that she had on more than one occasion shared the pulpit with a black man. Like Clarissa, Charles Bowles was an ordained Free Will Baptist minister, and in January 1817, they were both billed at the same venue. For some the appearance of "a colored man and a woman" was "a novel spectacle" that they might never witness again in a lifetime.

It is tempting to include Clarissa in a book on American religious history simply because of gender. But it is important to note that her ministry as an early American revivalist is significant apart from her sex. In another series of meetings the following year in New Hampshire, she is credited with the conversion of more than two hundred individuals. It was reported that scarcely a person in this sparsely populated region was left unconverted. And we should not imagine that collecting converts was an easy job in early nineteenth-century New England—certainly no easier than it

Mary Dyer: Condemned New England Quaker

Mary was a Quaker convert, a onetime upstanding Puritan who had been led astray by Anne Hutchinson. In fact, when Anne was excommunicated from the Boston church, Mary got up from her seat and walked out with her. Years later after Anne had died, Mary returned to England, where she joined the Society of Friends in 1652, the very year that Margaret Fell also joined the movement. Some years later, Mary returned to the Massachusetts Bay Colony, publicly testifying of her newfound faith despite laws forbidding Quakers to enter the colony. For her disobedience, she was sentenced to be hanged in 1659 along with two male Quakers. But the Puritan divines got cold feet: "As the Hangman was ready to turn her off, they cryed out to stop." Rather than do a little dance on the scaffolding, she told the crowd that she wanted to die like "her Brethren" unless the colony annulled its "wicked Law." They sent her packing, but she returned the following spring and was hanged May 31, 1660. One of her Puritan enemies, General Atherton, offered justification: "Mary Dyer did hang as a flag for others to take example by."[a]

[a] G. T. Paine, ed., *A Call from Death to Life*.

had been for Jonathan Edwards some two generations earlier. In fact, she might be favorably compared with him as a revivalist and thus might be well known to us today, except that unlike him she left behind no writings or a reputation as a theologian and philosopher.

Though Clarissa's ministry reached people from a wide variety of denominations, her own loyalties did not waver. Wherever she went, she organized Free Will Baptist churches, several, in fact, in Rhode Island alone during her preaching tour of 1819–20. Here she was credited with some three thousand converts. Such success was considered a "glorious work" of God, not a result of her remarkable speaking ability and engaging personality. Among her converts was Nancy Towle, a young woman who would herself become an iterant evangelist in the 1820s, preaching in New England and beyond, traveling to a dozen states as well as Canada and the British Isles.

Revivals: A Work of God, Women, and African Americans

There's a camp meeting in New Hampshire in 1817, where Clarissa Danforth, who is a very popular female preacher, shared the pulpit with Charles Bowles, who was a black Freewill Baptist preacher. When I think about that event and what it was like for people in the audience—in New Hampshire, of all places, a white audience—to see a white woman and a black man standing together in the pulpit and preaching, this is a really remarkable moment . . . [for] many people . . . a sign that God was doing something extraordinary in the world. These people think that the revivals are a work of God, and all the normal rules of life have been suspended.

Catherine Brekus, PBS Interview, June 23, 2009

CONCLUDING OBSERVATIONS

So that woeful woman Anne is banished from New England, and some two centuries later in the 1820s Clarissa, a Free Will Baptist, is winning souls by the thousands among the great-great-grandchildren of those who banished Anne. Now some two centuries after Clarissa's heyday of pulpit pounding, most Baptist women who wish to preach are again prohibited. The argument calling forth Balaam's ass and the barnyard fowl did not settle the matter.

For a woman to carry the torch as a preacher or an evangelist required a clear call from God and more than a little chutzpah. Such was the case with Teresa, whose influence is still powerfully felt. I wonder, though, how I would assess her today if she were a sister nun or a neighbor? Would I report her to social workers and insist that she be treated with appropriate meds? I remind myself that this much beloved and honored St. Teresa would be fighting against me as surely as she fought demons. The Protestant Reformation was to her a terrible blight, the worst calamity to ever befall her beloved Catholic Church.

And what about Anne Hutchinson? Would I have stood in solidarity with her against her accusers, those hypocritical Puritan leaders who deemed her a heretic? I surely admire her confidence and skills as a midwife and her willingness to pass her expertise along. And like me, she questions tradition and authoritarian church control. She naturally assumes women's intelligence is equal to that of any man. But does she carry her freedom too far? After all, her teaching of the inner light essentially claimed that her own direct access to God trumped the rules laid down by the church.

Margaret Fell, "mother" of the Quakers, made a decision to marry a movement—and George Fox to a lesser extent. I cannot comprehend what might have been going through her mind, other than her confidence in his having actually heard the voice of God. The decision in the end afforded her a platform—as well as harsh persecution—that transformed her into a church mother far beyond the borders of the Society of Friends.

QUESTIONS TO THINK ABOUT

Do you understand the popularity of St. Teresa and her writing today? Do mystical and miraculous experiences in everyday life resonate with you? Do you think that Christians today easily gravitate to spiritual experiences while ignoring the sacrifice and asceticism of such holy women as Teresa?

Does it seem strange that historically (and even today) women such as Anne Hutchinson were referred to as an Eve or a Jezebel, while similar slurs were not made against wayward men, calling them an Adam or an Ahab?

Had you been living in Boston in the early 1640s, how would you have reacted to the treatment of Anne? Would you have stood by her right to express her own opinion even if you did not agree with her? Would you have strongly spoken against her banishment and the smearing of her reputation after she had been so brutally killed?

What do you most admire about Judge Thomas Fell and his relationship with his wife Margaret? How do you view her decision to become the wife of George Fox and their seemingly distant marriage?

Why do you think Clarissa was permitted to be a preacher and evangelist in the sectarian Free Will Baptists at the same time the more liberal established churches were almost universally banning women in the pulpit? Is there any justification today in allowing women to preach in small mission churches, while banning them from the pulpit in large churches?

Have you ever considered abandoning the good life, as Teresa and Margaret did, to live on the edge, barely knowing where your next meal is coming from? Which of these four women would you be most inclined to join with in a ministry partnership?

6

Susanna Wesley and Eighteenth-Century Evangelists

What is poverty? Is it a line on a graph below which large numbers of people fall? I look back at my own childhood and imagine that many people today would say I lived in poverty. My earliest memories are of lantern lights, an outhouse, hand-me-down clothes, and a one-room school. But I kept warm on winter days huddling over the heat register fueled by the wood furnace, and I always had plenty to eat. Our family of seven was many things, but we insisted that we were not poor. We always had something to give to those we considered poorer than we were. Such was the case in the Wesley home, particularly under the influence of Susanna.

The Wesleys were small farmers as were we, though Samuel, Susanna's husband, was also an Anglican minister. I can almost picture myself among all the children in that poorly heated, dilapidated house, having to go to the barn and tend the cows on bitterly cold mornings. I have visited the Wesley home in Epworth. It is a rather substantial dwelling, rebuilt after the original thatched-roof house was destroyed by fire when John (the fifteenth child of Susanna) was six years old.

Though I understand privation, it is difficult to envision the poverty into which John Wesley was born. It is very different from my own childhood situation. We worked hard and saved every penny and avoided debt like the plague. Not so Samuel Wesley. Never good with money, he was sent to debtor's prison more than once, leaving Susanna to suffer alone with the children. On one occasion when she was asked about privation, she responded: "I will freely own to your grace that, strictly speaking, I never did want for bread. But then I had so much care to get it before it was eat, and to pay for it after [that] . . . it has made it very unpleasant to me. And I think to have bread on such terms is the next degree of wretchedness to having none at all."[1] Though she admitted that such a hand-to-mouth existence had "made it very unpleasant to [her]," Samuel insisted, "[It] does not in the least sink my wife's spirits. She bears it with courage which becomes her."[2]

For young John, poverty was a way of life that he almost escaped through a servitorship at Oxford. With an education he was convinced he would never live that way again. But an incident there would change the course of his life:

> He had just finished paying for some pictures for his room when one of the chambermaids came to his door. It was a cold winter day, and he noticed that she had nothing to protect her except a thin linen gown. He reached into his pocket to give her some money to buy a coat but found he had too little left. Immediately the thought struck him that the Lord was not pleased with the way he had spent his money. He asked himself, Will thy Master say, "Well done, good and faithful steward"? Thou hast adorned thy walls with the money which might have screened this poor creature from the cold! O justice! O mercy!—Are not these pictures the blood of this poor maid?[3]

Wesley's movement from the beginning focused on humanitarian outreach. The Holy Club, scoffed at by other Oxford students, not only emphasized prayer, accountability, fasting, and Bible study, but also pushed its paltry membership into the outside world of destitution and misery. The young men ministered to orphans and prisoners and distributed food to the hungry. They accomplished their goals very methodically, and thus they were tagged Methodists.

In subsequent years, many women joined the movement as preachers and humanitarian workers. Among them were Mary Fletcher and Sarah Crosby. Selina Hastings, the Countess of Huntingdon, a wealthy supporter, made generous gifts, though favoring the work of George Whitefield over that of Wesley. A High Church Anglican and never a Methodist herself, Susanna Wesley is rightly regarded as the mother of the movement.

SUSANNA WESLEY
Anglican Mother of the Methodists

It is too simplistic to present Susanna Wesley as the ultimate mother—a nineteen-kid-quiver-full, homeschooling, disciplinarian supermom and writer of rules—who stands up to her authoritarian husband and to King William III, a monarch who she insisted usurped the throne of England.

Submitting One to Another

Marriage problems should not be viewed as relating exclusively to modern households where career opportunities for the wife compete with those of the husband. In this chapter we see several situations involving marriage dysfunction. The apostle Paul was fully aware of such problems when he wrote his Letter to the Ephesians, where he introduces a passage on marriage with the words: "Submit to one another." It was this passage with its demands on him as husband that gave John Fletcher pause at the time of his marriage to Mary.

Submit to one another out of reverence for Christ.

Wives, submit yourselves to your own husbands as you do to the Lord. For the husband is the head of the wife as Christ is the head of the church, his body, of which he is the Savior. Now as the church submits to Christ, so also wives should submit to their husbands in everything.

The story contains more than an element of truth, but it bears examination that is rarely offered as it is repeated again and again online and in books. Those who know the story will find this two-sentence online response amusing: "She didn't like the king, so her husband didn't think they should keep sleeping together? After 19 kids, I'm thinking . . . okay!"

But is the account even true? The story of Susanna's failure to say amen to her husband's prayer for the king (which I have unwittingly repeated in my own earlier writings) deserves further examination. Indeed, it is tempting to turn the Wesley marriage into an extended stalemate of strong wills interspersed by enough sexual intimacy to account for nineteen babies.

Susanna, however, seems to be just as authoritarian—if not more so— than her husband. And King William of Orange, as a result of the Glorious Revolution, was on the English throne a dozen years before she supposedly refused to say amen to her husband's prayer. Would her husband not have known that she held tenaciously to the concept of the divine right of kings (seeing William as a usurper) before that evening prayer? It is highly unlikely since she had made a habit of not joining in public days of prayer during

Husbands, love your wives, just as Christ loved the church and gave himself up for her to make her holy, cleansing her by the washing with water through the word, and to present her to himself as a radiant church, without stain or wrinkle or any other blemish, but holy and blameless. In this same way, husbands ought to love their wives as their own bodies. He who loves his wife loves himself. After all, no one ever hated their own body, but they feed and care for their body, just as Christ does the church—for we are members of his body. "For this reason a man will leave his father and mother and be united to his wife, and the two will become one flesh." This is a profound mystery—but I am talking about Christ and the church. However, each one of you also must love his wife as he loves himself, and the wife must respect her husband.

Ephesians 5:21–33

the near decade-long span of King William's War: "Since I am not satis-
fied of the lawfulness of the war, I cannot beg a blessing on our arms. . . .
In the meantime, I think it my duty, since I cannot join in public worship,
to spend the time others take in that, in humbling my soul before God for
my own and the nation's sins."[4]

Born in London, the twenty-fifth—and last—child of Dr. Samuel An-
nesley, a noted Puritan preacher, Susanna grew up surrounded by older
siblings and books. Times were tough, however, for nonconformist preachers, especially when the government levied heavy fines or confiscated their
belongings. But in 1669, the year Susanna was born, her father was presiding over a congregation of some eight hundred in East London. With his
encouragement, she was an independent thinker, in fact, so much so that
at age thirteen she decided to align herself with the Church of England.

When she was twenty, Susanna married Samuel Wesley, twenty-eight.
There is no reason to assume that he did not love and respect his strong-
willed young wife, whom he affectionately called Sukey. Many years later
he wrote to his son Samuel, admonishing him to "reverence and love your
mother." He went on to make his point very clear: "Though I should be
jealous of any other rival in your breast, yet I will not be of her. The more
duty you pay her, and the more frequently and kindly you write to her, the
more you will please your affectionate father."[5]

The most oft-repeated account about the aforementioned relationship
between his parents was passed along by John himself. He had been told
as a young boy that he was the child of his parents' reconciliation. As the
story goes, one evening more than a year before his birth, his father, during evening devotions, prayed for King William III. Susanna refused to say
amen. Samuel said: "Sukey, if that be the case, you and I must part; for if
we have two kings we must have two beds."[6] So he walked out on her—and
the church, of which he was rector—returning only after Queen Anne, a
Stuart whom Susanna could support, had ascended the throne. So with
both supporting the same monarch, they could now sleep in the same bed.
Nine months later John was born.

It's a good story, but there are many reasons why it does not ring true
of Samuel and Sukey. Indeed, it is not difficult to imagine that Sukey spoke
her mind on political issues on many occasions. She possessed far more

chutzpah than one single meek failure to say amen. She was a demanding mother who homeschooled her children with a combination of severity and sympathy. One observer described her children as "a cluster of bright, vehement, argumentative boys and girls."[7]

Susanna maintained strict standards of child discipline that have been praised far more often than emulated. "No one can, without renouncing the world, in the most literal sense, observe my method," she later wrote. "There are few, if any, that would entirely devote above twenty years of the prime of life in hopes to save the souls of their children, which they think may be saved without so much ado; for that was my principal intention, however unskillfully and unsuccessfully managed."[8] In a letter to her husband, she noted how she made a schedule so as to give each child private instruction and counsel: "I take such a proportion of time as I can spare every night to discourse with each child apart. On Monday, I talk with Molly; on Tuesday, with Hetty; Wednesday, with Nancy; Thursday, with Jacky; Friday, with Patty; Saturday, with Charles; and with Emily and Suky together on Sunday."[9] But despite her efforts, her method had mixed results at best. One after another, her children struggled with serious problems in their relationships and suffered failed marriages.

John would later speak of his mother as a "preacher of righteousness," identifying her thus alongside "her father, and grandfather, her husband, and her three sons." In explaining this high tribute, he quoted letters from her to his father during one of his father's prolonged absences. Here Susanna is defending her preaching, which began very innocently while she was teaching her own children on the Sabbath. The letter, dated "February 6, 1711 [or] 12" (when John would have been eight years old) is quoted in John Wesley's journal:

> This was the beginning of my present practice. Other people's coming and joining with us was merely accidental. [One] lad told his parents: they first desired to be admitted; then others that heard of it begged leave also: so our company increased to about thirty, and it seldom exceeded forty last winter. . . . With those few neighbors that then came to me, I discoursed more freely and affectionately. I chose the best and most awakening sermons we have. And I spent somewhat more time with them in such exercises, without being careful about the success of my undertaking. Since this, our company

increased every night; for I dare deny none that ask admittance. . . . Last Sunday I believe we had above two hundred. And yet many went away for want of room to stand.[10]

This is, for my money, one of the most fascinating letters in the whole of the eighteenth century, and what's more, it is a direct challenge to her insecure husband. The letter leaves no doubt that it had been prompted by a missive from Samuel, apparently upset by her sudden popularity. His harsh preaching had never endeared him to the congregations, and, as her letter suggests, he was threatened by the feelings of admiration the people had for her:

> I cannot conceive, why any should reflect upon you because your wife endeavors to draw people to church and to restrain them from profaning the Lord's day by reading to them, and other persuasions. For my part, I value no censure upon this account. I have long since shaken hands with the world. And I heartily wish I had never given them more reason to speak against me. . . . As to its looking [peculiar], I grant it does. And so does almost anything that is serious, or that may any way advance the glory of God or the salvation of souls.[11]

Samuel insisted that she stop speaking to the newly formed home congregation. He offered a "proposal of letting some other person read." She reminded him in no uncertain terms why his idea would not work—that he had failed to "consider what a people these are." They were essentially illiterate, and no one had a voice that carried except for her: "I do not think one man among them could read a sermon, without spelling a good part of it. Nor has any of our family a voice strong enough to be heard by such a number of people."[12]

So there! Stifle yourself, Samuel. Let me do the work of the Lord. But Susanna had her own struggles about what she was doing. She was a woman after all.

> But there is one thing about which I am much dissatisfied; that is, their being present at family prayers. I do not speak of any concern I am under, barely because so many are present; for those who have the honor of speaking to the Great and Holy God need not be ashamed to speak before the whole

world; but because of my sex. I doubt if it is proper for me to present the prayers of the people to God. Last Sunday I would fain have dismissed them before prayers; but they begged so earnestly to stay, I durst not deny them.[13]

Susanna, well versed in theological and biblical studies as well as literature and languages, had no inclination to make a statement for women's rights or to demonstrate her own capabilities over her husband's. She regarded herself first and foremost as a wife and mother.

That John looked back on her ministry and identified her as a preacher of righteousness is most interesting, particularly in light of his assessment of her when she died at age seventy-two. He and his hymn-writing brother Charles, both still in their thirties, agreed that she should be honored with a poem for her tombstone. The epitaph, though a bit of a jingle, begins with typical sentimentality, but then goes on to speak of her "legal night of seventy years"—as though devoid of the light of the gospel until two years before she died. What an incredible insult to this devout Christian woman.

> In sure and steadfast hope to rise,
> And claim her mansion in the skies,
> A Christian here her flesh laid down,
> The cross exchanging for a crown.
>
> True daughter of affliction, she,
> Inured to pain and misery,
> Mourn'd a long night of griefs and fears,
> A legal night of seventy years.
>
> The Father then revealed his Son;
> Him in the broken bread made known;
> She knew and felt her sins forgiven,
> And found the earnest of her heaven.
>
> Meet for the fellowship above,
> She heard the call, "Arise, my love!"
> "I come!" her dying looks replied,
> And, lamb-like as her Lord, she died.

Samuel Wesley's early biographer, Luke Tyerman, responded to such nonsense with strong words:

> This is a monstrous perversion of facts, and can only be accounted for on the ground that John and Charles Wesley were so enamored of their blessed and newly discovered doctrines, that as yet they felt it difficult to think any one to be scripturally converted except those who . . . had experienced an instantaneous change of heart, under circumstances similar to their own. . . . Having read her letters and her other literary productions, we are satisfied that, if there ever was a sincere and earnest Christian, she was one.[14]

SELINA HASTINGS, COUNTESS OF HUNTINGDON
"Methodist Archbishop"

She was a "Methodist Archbishop," so identified by George Whitefield, though she ranked herself a notch lower, and then only in jest when she wrote: "Dear Mr. Jones must indulge this bishop with his presence."[15] She was a wealthy woman who saw herself as a key player in "this present Reformation" of the Church of England.

Lady Selina was born into wealth and nobility, and her marriage at age twenty-one to Theophilus Hastings brought her the title Countess of Huntingdon. Like John Wesley, her life would span most of the eighteenth century (1707–91). Her childhood was marred by her feelings of abandonment by Lady Mary, her mother, who, unbeknownst to the young Selina, had contracted syphilis. Ever loyal to her beloved father, she did not know that his infidelity was the cause of her mother's terrible affliction. As an adult, Selina herself would endure serious physical ailments as well as the early deaths of four of her seven children. She also slogged through decades of disputes with siblings over her father's estate.

In 1739, in the midst of her troubles, she joined John Wesley's new movement. In fact, only a year earlier he had testified that he felt his "heart strangely warmed" while attending a meeting at Aldersgate Street. After her husband died some seven years later, Selina embarked on full-time ministry in an effort to convert well-heeled aristocrats. By that time her taste for lively preaching had drawn her more closely to Whitefield. Indeed, she invited guests to her home, to hear not a gifted musician but rather a fiery evangelist.

Soon Selina was funding chapels, sixty-four altogether, as well as Trevecca House, a preacher training school. She served as an unofficial bishop, supplying chapels with young men whose preaching carried a decided Calvinistic slant. In fact, she became deeply embroiled in the much-publicized doctrinal dustup between Wesley and Whitefield, clearly siding with the latter, while at the same time seeking harmony.

Like Wesley's ministers, those who served under Selina were circuit preachers. She mapped out their territories and often accompanied them on their tours of England and Wales. Speaking of her own call to preach, she wrote: "With respect to myself this has been the matter between the Lord and my own heart. . . . He has favoured me with many more voices for Him, and where mine could not have reached; yet always this constant reserve before Him that His call . . . should carry me to the ends of the earth for Him."[16]

Ever loyal to the Church of England, Selina walked a tightrope, especially after 1779, when the church began requiring that all chapels be registered as "dissenting places of worship." As such, wealthy aristocrats stayed away in droves. Labeled a dissenter, Selina was heartbroken: "I am to be cast out of the Church now only for what I have been doing this forty years—speaking and living for Jesus."[17] Yet she carried on in ministry until her death in 1791 despite tight regulation and frequent bouts of illness.

Selina's physical frailties and loss of young children, as well as her struggles with siblings and her ecclesiastical and doctrinal disputes, were surely enough to turn her into an autocratic and cranky old lady as she was sometimes accused of being. But she was also beset with inner conflict. John Wesley's teaching on entire sanctification did not countenance the sin of pride, the very trademark of British high society. To Charles Wesley, her confidante and counselor, she wrote that his brother John believed him to be too lenient with her on spiritual matters: "He wants me to be more a poor sinner . . . and indeed when I think of myself at all I feel it as a sore burden too heavy for me to bear."[18]

In an effort to cast out her pride, she frequently employed various forms of self-deprecation: "I often think of myself a very Herod in a gorgeous robe of profession, such a poor, wretched, creature do I seem to myself." To eradicate pride, she repeatedly referred to herself in demeaning terms:

"unworthy worm," "poor, vile and foolish creature," "vile worm," "worthless worm," "poor worm," "poor, vile, blind fool," "poor, worthless, simple worm,"[19] and the list goes on.

As obsessed as she was with the sin of pride, Selina appeared to be entirely oblivious to the sin of slaveholding. Perhaps her blind admiration for Whitefield played a part. A one-time critic of slavery, he had sought to support his orphanage work in colonial Georgia with a slave plantation. On his death, Selina inherited the oversight of both the orphanage and the plantation. In an effort to keep them both afloat, she increased the number of slaves from fifty to well over one hundred—that, despite the strong antislavery stance of the Wesleys and many of her circuit preachers.

How she could justify her actions is difficult to comprehend. Unlike antebellum planters, who had often been born into the system, she became a slaveholder as a mature woman who could have found other means of fund-raising for the orphanage. Did the utter incongruity of her actions ever occur to her? Perhaps not. Lady Selina Hastings was a complicated woman who utilized her social status and wealth to carry out God's work as she saw fit. That she was unable to see the evil of slavery scuffs the shine on any sort of saintliness we might want to bestow on her.

SARAH RYAN
Social Activist and Enemy of John Wesley's Wife

If we wish to look back at a time when marriages were rock solid and separation was rare among Christians, the early Wesleyan movement would not be the place to start. Although John Wesley's parents had endured conflict and frequent separations in their marriage, they were married until death did them part. Not so with John's sisters, Susanna, Hetty, and Martha. And John's own marriage to Molly also fell apart. Such was the case as well with some of his most prominent followers. Sarah Crosby, who would later become a trusted preacher, married in 1750 and became a Methodist class leader in 1752. The marriage was troubled from the start, ending in 1757, when her husband left her for the final time. Of this marriage she had written:

A short time after this I married, and can truly say, my ultimate end in so doing was to live more to the glory of God. . . . Before this I desired to suffer, but now I began to do so in reality; and because I can hardly bear to reflect on some of my trials, much less relate them, I shall pass over what I now went through in silence: it is sufficient, God knoweth it all. The Lord had before allured me, now he began to lead me into the wilderness.[20]

It was her colleague and friend Sarah Ryan, however, whose marriage problems and relationship with Wesley created scandal in the movement. Sarah Ryan was converted through the preaching of George Whitefield and then was actively involved in the Foundry, an abandoned building that became the center for John Wesley's Methodist movement. Soon after this, at nineteen, Sarah married a man who she learned was not only destitute but also married to another woman. When he abandoned Sarah, she married a sailor who left her to live in America. Her third marriage was to an Italian who likewise abandoned her.

That she was married three times was considered bad enough, but that she had married twice without ever having been divorced was no less than scandalous—though apparently not regarded as such by Wesley. In fact, she later related how he had influenced her in her second marriage:

And now I received a letter from my husband, reminding me of an agreement between us, that I should follow him to New-England . . . and I really imagined, that it was the will of God, that I should go to him. But after some time, I thought I will ask Mr. Wesley's advice, which I accordingly did. After we had conversed a little, he said, "Can he maintain you there[?]" I answered, "Yes: but can I go, and save my soul?" He replied "What do you think of it, Sally?" Instantly light broke in, and I said, "No, Sir, I cannot." I went home, and soon after wrote, and told him, "At the peril of my soul I dare not come."[21]

After her third husband had abandoned her, Wesley appointed Sarah, then in her early thirties, housekeeper at the Kingswood School in Bristol, a managerial position that required strong leadership skills and spiritual maturity. Wesley's wife, Molly, was furious when she learned of it. According to Mary Fletcher, Molly blasted Sarah during a conference at the school when dozens of preachers were seated around a large table. Sarah was in charge of the meal service. Molly entered and said in a loud voice: "See that whore who is serving you! She hath three husbands now alive!" And she did not end there as Mary went on to relate: "With all the depreciating things she could say, as she was going on, Sister Ryan set down in a chair which stood near her, with her eyes shut."[22]

Molly had reason to be upset, and not simply because her husband had given a "whore" an important position at the Bristol school. Wesley, like at least three other men before him, had apparently become more than a little enamored of Sarah. His marriage was already on the rocks, and she had captured his heart, as he confided in a letter to her:

> The conversing with you, either by speaking or writing, is an unspeakable blessing to me. I cannot think of you without thinking of God. Others often lead me to Him; but it is, as it were, going round about: you bring me straight into His presence. Therefore, whoever warns me against trusting you, I cannot refrain, as I am clearly convinced He calls me to it.[23]

In the jargon of entire sanctification, this was no less than a love letter. Molly, who rifled through his coat pocket and read the letter before he sent it, recognized that in a heartbeat. She was livid. "Last Friday, after many severe words, my wife left me, vowing she would see me no more," Wesley wrote to Sarah in January 1758. "In the evening, while I was preaching at the chapel, she came into the chamber where I had left my clothes, searched my pockets, and found the letter. . . . I afterwards found her in such a temper as I have not seen her in for several years. She has continued in the same ever since."[24]

Wesley was smitten by Sarah, perhaps panting as he wrote: "I am eager to receive your next letter with excitement as always." At one point, she had apparently apologized for being too familiar with him. He wrote back: "I not only excuse but love your simplicity; and whatever freedom you use it will be welcome." He couched his words in spiritual tones, but she would have understood the double meaning: "You have refreshed my bowels in the Lord: I feel your words, and praised God on your behalf. . . . Surely God will never suffer me to be ashamed of my confidence in you. I have been censured for it by some of your nearest friends; but I cannot repent of it."[25]

Many in Wesley's movement blamed Sarah for the dissolution of his marriage. Each spouse blamed the other, and Molly spread the word that her husband had traveled alone with Sarah. But despite the accusations and scandal, Molly came back time and again until 1774. She died in 1781, a fact that Wesley grudgingly acknowledged: "I came to London, and was informed that my wife died on Monday. This evening she was buried, though I was not informed of it till a day or two after."[26]

Despite the rumors surrounding her, Sarah continued on in her position at the Kingswood School for some years after Molly's outburst. In that capacity she also served as a class leader, meeting with dozens of people each week. She also traveled widely, meeting with Methodist societies. In 1762, she moved to London to work with Sarah Crosby and Mary Fletcher in establishing the Leytonstone orphanage, later relocated in Yorkshire to accommodate Sarah's failing health. She died six years later at forty-three.

In 1782, a year after his wife had died, Wesley published some of his correspondence to and from Sarah, stating that her letters "breathe deep, strong sense and piety. I know few like them in the English tongue."[27] Sarah had also been praised by Mary Fletcher, fifteen years younger than she, who described her as her "mother in Christ" and wrote: "Our hearts were united as David and Jonathan's."[28]

MARY BOSANQUET FLETCHER
Megabarn Preacher

For nearly sixty years she served as one of the most capable associates of John Wesley. Born into wealth, Mary turned away from the affluent lifestyle of her family and left home at eighteen to set out on her own. It was nothing short of scandalous. That she identified herself as a Methodist only added to the disgrace her family felt. But she had John Wesley—and God—on her side, and she never looked back. With money from her grandmother's estate and the help of Sarah Ryan, she established an orphanage as well as a Methodist society in Leytonstone, where they found themselves most unwelcome.

Methodists were persecuted, and Mary and Sarah, like John Wesley himself, were assailed with obscenities and pelted with dirt. Mary carried on after Sarah's death. But as time passed and her inheritance dwindled, she began dreaming of the unmarried John Fletcher, a brilliant Anglican vicar and strong supporter of Wesley. She did not know that Fletcher had written to Charles Wesley, asking his advice about a marriage proposal to her, though confiding his fears that she might not make a good wife. Fifteen years went by as each contemplated the other. Finally Mary wrote to Wesley about him, and shortly thereafter Fletcher wrote to her. After several months of correspondence and private meetings, they were married. Mary was forty-two, he, ten years her senior.

After their brief wedding ceremony, they spent time in hymn singing and discussion with friends. Fletcher read the familiar words from the apostle Paul: "Husbands, love your wives as Christ loved the Church." His spontaneous comments would serve Mary well: "My God, what a task! Help me, my friends, by your prayers to fulfil it. As Christ loved the Church! He laid aside his glory for her!" He continued with Paul's words: "Wives, submit yourselves unto your own husbands," and Mary added, "as unto the Lord." Again, his words were reassuring: "Well, my dear, only in the Lord. And if ever I wish you to do any thing otherwise, resist me with all your might."[29]

Encouraged by her husband, Mary continued preaching at Methodist meetings as she had done before. Yet she was very conscious of criticism, not wishing to offend anyone opposed to women preachers, especially one who delivered what was thought to be an actual sermon (as she had done). "For some years I was often led to speak from a text," she explained. "Of late I feel greater approbation in what we call *expounding*, taking a part or whole of a chapter and speaking on it."[30] Thus she was only offering spontaneous commentary on the reading of the Scripture, rather than reading a prepared sermon. She likewise stood on the steps in front of the pulpit rather than behind it.

John and Mary's was a strong marriage, but it lasted only "three years, nine months, and two days." Fletcher was a sickly man who had been near death on several occasions. Mary was heartbroken. "It seems to me," she later wrote to a friend, "I both *love and miss him* every day *more* and *more*. . . . Never did I know three years of such suffering."[31]

Although Wesley wanted her to relocate in London (150 miles southeast), where he believed her ministry would be more fruitful, she continued her work at Madeley, at the invitation of the new vicar. Here she strengthened the bond of unity between the Methodists and the Anglicans that her husband had labored to maintain. She was a popular preacher and was able to draw crowds in the thousands, though not in the Anglican church building itself. Her primary venue was the nearby "tythe barn," where she preached on Sunday afternoon and evening and weekday evenings as well. Though convinced that God had empowered her in ministry, she understood her opposition:

> I know the power of God which I have felt when standing on the horseblock in the street at Huddersfield; but at the same time I am conscious how ridiculous I must appear in the eyes of many for so doing. Therefore, if some persons consider me as an impudent woman, and represent me as such, I cannot blame them.[32]

Mary continued preaching, sometimes three or four times a week, until her death at seventy-six. She had lived thirty years as a widow, and the searing sorrow that had so consumed her in the years immediately after her husband's death had all but vanished. She testified of her mystical communion with him. "My house is a sweet rest," she wrote in later years. "I have peace within. . . . I have communion with my friends above."[33]

Concluding Observations

What an incredibly fascinating group of women surrounded John Wesley. One measly chapter does not begin to capture their story. Susanna's life and legacy have particularly captivated me. On a recent holiday in England, I spent a sunny September afternoon meandering through her house and gardens in Epworth. As a onetime minister's wife and mother myself, I resonate with her, though as children go, she trumps me 19:1. I can't imagine how she alone, when her husband was away, managed to conduct an organized household and even do a little preaching on the side.

But if we imagine that Susanna Wesley would fit in with our book club or Bible study, we might be sadly mistaken. She was a High Church Anglican, a very strict disciplinarian, and a drinker (though vowing never to "drink above two Glasses of any strong Liquor at one time") who was convinced a resident ghost was living upstairs. She talked back to her authoritarian husband, and her engaging sermons drew people to church when he was absent.

John Wesley worked closely with *Bishop* Selina and affirmed women preachers, the most noted of whom was Mary Fletcher. Sometimes drawing thousands, she would be the first of such intrepid Methodist women, with dozens more highly acclaimed women in the nineteenth century and later. Wesley's life spans most of the eighteenth century as does the life of the famed literary critic and philosopher Dr. Samuel Johnson, who remarked: "A woman's preaching is like a dog's walking on its hind legs. It is not done well; but you are surprised to find it done at all."[34] The prejudice embodied in this remark has persisted over time, thus impeding a serious assessment of the female preaching tradition and its role in shaping social and literary discourse.

Today as I write, online media seems almost obsessed with matters relating to insurance coverage for birth control and the definition of marriage. But when we travel three centuries back in time to the early decades of the eighteenth century, we might wonder how Susanna would have responded to easily accessible birth control. And what do we make of the definition of marriage? Did Samuel simply walk out over a trivial difference of opinion? If not, how did John come up with such a tale? And what of his own marriage, and his apparent emotional affair with Sarah Ryan, who never bothered to obtain a divorce before remarrying? Sarah Crosby likewise had an estranged marriage, as did Susanna's daughters. Only Mary's marriage to John Fletcher, though short, stands as a model for today.

QUESTIONS TO THINK ABOUT

Which of Susanna's qualities and attributes do you most admire? If you had a magical opportunity to welcome her into your home for a few days, how would you entertain her? Besides the Bible, what books would you make available? What favorite haunts would you visit, and what friends would you invite along?

What do you make of Lady Selina's verbal self-abnegation? How might you counsel her—or would you suggest a therapist more qualified than yourself? What do you imagine she was thinking in her involvement as a slaveholder, despite strong criticism? Are you ever inconsistent in what you perceive as sinful—perhaps emphasizing minor misconduct while ignoring major transgression?

Imagine yourself a friend of both Sarah Ryan and Molly Fletcher. How would you have separately counseled them? Have you ever had to stand between two women involved with the same man?

How do you assess Mary's long interest in John and her subsequent marriage? Would you have wanted to interfere and get them together many years sooner? Do you have any experiences that help you to resonate with her years of deep grief? Have you ever had a mystical sense of communicating with deceased loved ones?

How would you relate to Mary Fletcher as a preacher? Do you know of any women preachers today who can draw large crowds as she did?

Which one of the lives of these four women would you most want to unravel if you had the resources to research and write a full-length biography?

7

Narcissa Prentiss Whitman and American Protestant Missionaries

I'll never forget that sunny August morning, walking alone through the grounds of the Whitman Mission in Walla Walla, Washington. Tall clumps of rye grass still grow on this site that the natives called Waiilatpu, "place of the rye grass." There I sensed a melancholy that still lingered from that Sunday, June 23, 1839, when little Alice Clarissa, only child of Narcissa and Marcus, drowned in the nearby stream—the Walla Walla River. I could not comprehend the indescribable anguish this mother must have endured. But when such searing sadness settles into a place, it is sometimes felt for centuries. Here on that clear and cloudless morning the tears of sorrow still seemed to saturate the soil and nurse the swaying reeds of grass.

I have related Narcissa's story in other books I've written, sometimes zeroing in on the discord at the Waiilatpu mission. As the mistress of the house, she often had to contend with other missionary families and run-of-the-mill settlers who assumed she somehow owed them free lodging for weeks on end. One flare-up, according to a guest, "came on so sharp that I was compelled to leave. . . . It is enough to make one sick to see what is the state of things in the mission."[1] When criticism is leveled at Narcissa, I become defensive. I put myself in her situation, and I can only imagine how easy it would be for a carefree individual to become cranky and resentful.

On the arduous covered-wagon journey to the *foreign* land of Oregon, Narcissa was upbeat, often reveling in the glories of nature—the wildlife, the trees and flowers and spectacular sunsets and snowcapped mountains. She was, by her own account, truly happy. Her marriage appeared to be solid, unlike that of Mary Walker, another Oregon missionary who, in her diary, repeatedly lamented the insecurities she felt about her marriage. How many times she wondered to herself if her husband really loved her, and how many times she longed for stimulating conversation. Elkanah, her husband, enjoyed lively interaction with men, but not with her.

The decision to marry, for many missionaries, was often a hurried affair based solely on mutual missionary callings. That the couple would have fallen in love or would have been compatible emotionally or intellectually was not necessarily a high priority.

Present Yourselves a Living Sacrifice

The women featured in this chapter would have been very familiar with Paul's words of admonition to his followers, in this case those living in Rome. I memorized the passage in the King James Version as these women would have also known and memorized it.

> I beseech you therefore, brethren, by the mercies of God, that ye present your bodies a living sacrifice, holy, acceptable unto God, which is your reasonable service.
>
> And be not conformed to this world: but be ye transformed by the renewing of your mind, that ye may prove what is that good, and acceptable, and perfect, will of God.
>
> Romans 12:1–2

For Narcissa Prentiss in her midtwenties, the call of God came through a story she had heard of the Nez Percé, who had pleaded that someone bring them the "Book of Life." She would have packed her bags and set out for the Oregon Territory on her own, but single women were required to find husbands first. When Marcus Whitman, thirty-three and still single, heard of her predicament, he arranged a meeting, and, without the benefit of romance, they were married the following year.

The contributions of married women to missions were enormous, despite the fact that many, like America's first celebrated woman missionary, Ann Judson, would die young in childbirth. For Narcissa Prentiss Whitman, mission work would be sandwiched between tragedy—the drowning of her little girl and her own grisly death in the midst of a wholesale massacre. A generation later, by the time Lottie Moon, Adele Fielde, Maude Cary, Malla Moe, and Mabel Francis were pursuing overseas ministry, mission agencies were accepting single women. Grateful for such opportunities, they nevertheless battled loneliness and the sting of second-class status.

NARCISSA PRENTISS WHITMAN
Mission Matron and Martyr

Growing up in Prattsburgh, New York, in 1808, Narcissa was one of nine children born to Judge Stephen Prentiss and his wife, Clarissa, devout Presbyterians. In 1824, having been schooled at the local Franklin Academy, sixteen-year-old Narcissa sensed God's call during a religious revival and committed herself to foreign missionary service. The Nez Percé of the Oregon Territory, she had learned from an oft-repeated story, were pleading with someone to bring the "Book of Life." More than a decade would pass, however, before she could answer that call. As those years passed, she feared she would have to resign herself to being an old-maid schoolteacher.

Indeed, she might have remained single, teaching school for the remainder of her life, but for a visit from Marcus Whitman, who was about to set out for Oregon on an exploratory expedition in the spring of 1835. If mission work in the West proved feasible for him, accompanied by a wife, he proposed that he return to marry her and they then set out for Oregon together. He returned, and they were married in February 1836.

The cross-continent trip to Oregon, from western New York, was arduous. The weather was either too hot or too cold; the natives hostile; and the mountain trails so steep that cattle and wagons had to be left behind. Yet during most of the trip, Narcissa enjoyed good health and great optimism as is indicated in her letters and journal from March 15 to September 1, 1836. Her greatest anguish came from poor mail service—not receiving letters from home, particularly from her parents and four younger sisters:

> We left Pittsburgh this morning at ten o'clock and are sailing at the rate of thirteen miles an hour. It is delightful passing so rapidly down the waters of the beautiful river. . . . Can scarcely resist the temptation to stand out to view the shores of this majestic [Mississippi] river. Varied scenes present themselves as we pass up beautiful landscapes. . . . We are now in port. Husband has been to the office, expecting to find letters from dear, dear friends at home, but find none. Why have they not written? . . . But I am not sad. My health is good. My mind completely occupied with present duty and passing events. . . . I have one of the kindest husbands, and the very best every way. . . . Twilight had nearly gone when we entered the waters of the great Missouri, but the moon shone in her brightness. It was a beautiful evening. . . . I wish I could describe to you how we live so that you can realize it. Our manner of living is far preferable to any in the States. I never was so contented and happy before neither have I enjoyed such health for years. . . . I do not know as I was ever so much affected with any scenery in my life. . . . You can better imagine our feelings this morning than we can describe them. I could not realize that the end of our long journey was so near. We arose as soon as it was light, took a cup of coffee, ate of the duck we had given us last night and dressed for Walla Walla. We started while it was yet early, for all were in haste to reach the desired haven.[2]

Along the way, Narcissa had become pregnant, and on March 14, 1837, on her twenty-ninth birthday, baby Alice Clarissa was born. She was the darling of her parents, and her death as a toddler, at just over two years and three months, was devastating to them. On June 25, 1839, Narcissa wrote to her sister:

> You make some important inquiries concerning my treatment of my precious child, Alice Clarissa, now laying by me a lifeless lump of clay. Yes, of

her I loved and watched so tenderly, I am bereaved. My Jesus in love to her and us has taken her to himself. Last Sabbath, blooming in health, cheerful, and happy in herself and in the society of her much loved parents, yet in one moment she disappeared, went to the river with two cups to get some water for the table, fell in and was drowned. . . . Husband and I were both engaged in reading. She had just a few minutes before been reading to her father; had got down out of his lap, and as my impression, was amusing herself by the door in the yard. . . . But she had gone; yes, and because my Saviour would have it so. He saw it necessary to afflict us, and has taken her away. Now we see how much we loved her, and you know the blessed Saviour will not have His children bestow an undue attachment upon creature objects without reminding us of His own superior claim upon affections.[3]

The following year, on May 2, 1840, Narcissa wrote of issues they were having with the nearby Native Americans. As was true of all the Oregon missionaries, merchants, and traders, she saw whites as superior and could not comprehend why the native peoples were not more appreciative of their ministry and why they would resent the landgrab:

A tide of immigration appears to be moving this way rapidly. What a few years will bring forth we know not. . . . [The natives] said we must pay them for their land we lived on. They are an exceedingly proud, haughty and insolent people, and keep us constantly upon the stretch after patience and forbearance.[4]

The tension between missionaries and native peoples only increased in the following years. Marcus provided medical assistance, but the natives suspected that he was trying to poison them. Though many of them continued to attend meetings, Narcissa felt uneasy in their presence. A series of letters in 1842, especially those to her single sister, Jane, expressed her loneliness, sickness, and terror of being alone when Marcus was traveling.

Jane, I wish you were here to sleep with me, I am such a timid creature about sleeping alone that sometimes I suffer considerably, especially since my health has been not very good. . . . Dear Jane, I am sick tonight and in much pain—have been scarcely able to crawl about all day. . . . I have this day entered upon my thirty-fifth year, and had my dear Alice C. been alive she would have been five years old, for this was her birthday as well as mine. Precious trust! She was taken away from the evil to come. I would not have it otherwise now. . . . I got dreadfully frightened last night. About midnight I was awakened by some one trying to open my bedroom door. . . . Soon the latch was raised and the door opened a little. I sprang from the bed in a moment and closed the door again. . . . Thanks be to our Heavenly Father. He mercifully "delivered me from the hand of a savage man."[5]

Settlers pouring into the Oregon Territory took advantage of the Whitmans, whose mission station had essentially turned into a trading post and inn. Or was it the other way around? Were the Whitmans taking advantage of travelers by charging exorbitant prices, as some claimed? Their fertile land and bountiful harvests were the envy of new immigrants. Among those who came to the mission in 1844 were seven orphans, whom Narcissa took into her home—in addition to the four children she had already taken in.

I have now a family of eleven children. . . . I get along very well with them; they have been to school most of the time; we have had an excellent teacher, a young man from New York. . . . I wish you could see me now in the midst of such a group of little ones; there are two girls of nine years, one of seven, a girl and a boy of six, another girl of five, another of three and the baby, she is now ten months.[6]

By the summer of 1847, immigrants were passing through nonstop, all but Jane. Despite the increasing tension with the natives, Narcissa was somehow convinced that things would be much better for her if only her sister would join her.

For the last two weeks immigrants have been passing, probably 80 or 100 wagons have already passed and 1,000 are said to be on the road. . . . Two men are at this place on their way to the States. One of them, Mr. Glenday, intends to return to this country next spring with his family. I have importuned him, and made an arrangement to have you accompany them to Waiilatpu. Now Jane, will you do it? I know you will not refuse to come. . . . Believe me, dear Jane, and come without fail, when you have so good an opportunity.[7]

Only six weeks after her last letter begging Jane to come, Narcissa was dead. The grim statement detailing the slaughter was not dated until several months later in a letter from a fellow missionary, Henry Spaulding. His opening lines relating to his own deliverance by the hand of God must have seemed hollow and almost crass to Narcissa's grieving family:

> Through the wonderful interposition of God in delivering me from the hand of the murderer, it has become my painful duty to apprise you of the death of your beloved daughter, Narcissa, and her worthy and appreciated husband, your honored son-in-law, Dr. Whitman. . . . They were inhumanly butchered by their own, up to the last moment, beloved Indians, for whom their warm Christian hearts had prayed for eleven years. . . . The massacre took place on the fatal 29th of November last, commencing at half past one. Fourteen persons were murdered first and last. Nine men the first day. . . . Sister Whitman in anguish, now bending over her dying husband and now over the sick; now comforting the flying, screaming children, was passing by the window, when she received the first shot in her right breast, and fell to the floor. . . . Your dear Narcissa, faint with the loss of blood, was carried on a settee to the door. . . . She groaned, she lingered. The settee was rudely upset.[8]

What had begun with so much promise ended with the most shocking missionary massacre in the history of Christianity. The killers were motivated not by a hatred of the gospel message but by fear—fear fused with rage against those who were taking their land and threatening their way of life.

ADELE MARION FIELDE
"Mother of Our Bible Women"

It was a clear May morning in 1865 as the ship entered the Hong Kong harbor after a perilous sea voyage from America. The journal entries tell the story: After having weathered a series of storms and a typhoon "that mauled and drove our ship for days . . . jungle fever seized all on board save the captain," leaving ten of the crew dead. The writer herself, while in a coma, "was thought to have died." But now having arrived she hoped the worst was behind her. "I was barely able to stand, and Miss Sands, who had partially recovered arrayed me in white."[9]

Adele was arrayed in white because it was to be her wedding day. Her fiancé, Cyrus Chilcott, a newly appointed Baptist missionary, would be rowed out to the ship, and the captain, as he had promised, would perform the ceremony. They waited only to learn that Cyrus was not among those who had been ferried from the shore. Instead, the small delegation boarded the ship for the grim purpose of informing her that the intended groom had died of typhoid fever a few months earlier.

Born into a working-class Baptist family in East Rodman, New York, Adele was a curious child who was quick to question matters of creed and doctrine. As a teenager she determined she would hang her hat with the Universalists, who, to her liking, consigned no one to hell. After studying at a state college, she became a schoolteacher, earning enough to live on half her salary while sending the remainder to her aging parents. At twenty-five she was a "confirmed old maid," until she met Cyrus, her best friend's brother. She fell in love, became engaged, and agreed to become a Baptist and sail to Hong Kong to serve as a missionary wife in Thailand.

With his death, her dreams had been dashed. The ship's captain pleaded with her to wait in Hong Kong and return with his vessel to America. Hardly capable of rational thinking, she turned him down, deciding instead to continue on to Thailand to at least kneel at his grave and feel his presence in the house he had prepared for her, as she wrote in a letter in the *Baptist Missionary Magazine*:

> I have journeyed seven weary months over tempestuous seas and in strange lands to meet my beloved and I found his grave with the grass upon it seven months old. I have come to my house; it is left unto me desolate. While I stood holding out my hand for a cup of happiness, one of fearful bitterness was pressed violently to my lips. I looked joyful to Providence and it turned upon me a face of inexpressible darkness. And because I believe in God I have been able to endure it.[10]

Through sheer determination, she vowed to carry out the mission work Cyrus had been commissioned to do. That was not, however, what the mission director had in mind. There was no place for a single woman—particularly one who wanted to do the work of a man. But considering her sorrow, she was permitted to stay on. There, amid her deep grief, she learned Chinese and began ministering to Chinese people in Bangkok. A brilliant linguist, she communicated effectively with the people, all the while struggling to fit into the tight strictures of the Baptist mission. When she discovered that her salary was only half that of a single male colleague, she demanded equity. The conflict stretched out for two years before her salary was doubled to match his, with one year of retroactive pay.

But now the tables were turned on her. True, she was very effective in her mission outreach, but she did not fit into the mission community. She was accused of socializing with unbelieving merchants and diplomats during her free time, joining in card playing and dancing. When she was warned that such activities put her ministry in "extreme peril," she agreed to give up card playing. To renounce dancing, however, was simply too much to ask. For months she was in limbo as letters were exchanged and controversy raged. Then it was over. After serving six years in Thailand, she was ordered to return home. So upset was she that she fashioned a pipe and "smoked six thimblefuls" of hashish.[11]

Thinking her missionary service was behind her, Adele set sail for America on a ship that made a stopover in a South China port. There she was befriended by resident missionaries who recognized her capabilities and dedication to evangelism. With their appeal to the home office, she was permitted, after a stay in America, to return and work with them. During the next two decades, she would focus her attention on training Bible women. Others before her had worked alongside such native assistants, but she took the concept to another level by establishing schools, writing and publishing materials, assigning and supervising circuit ministries, and working herself out of a job by training the women to teach new recruits and carry out the work themselves.

During a furlough in America in 1883, Adele discovered that she had become somewhat of a celebrity. Besides writing materials for Bible women, she had written stories about these women for magazine publications, later compiled in a book, *Pagoda Shadows*. Speaking invitations piled up, but she spent most of her two-year furlough studying at the Academy of Natural Sciences in Philadelphia. She was recognized as a scholar, and before she returned to China, she turned down an invitation to serve as president of Vassar College.

Upon returning to China, Adele spent the next four years stabilizing her work before retiring to America in 1889. In the space of twenty years, she had trained some five hundred Bible women, several of whom were competently teaching others. She had faced many problems along the way, but her work would serve as a model for other Western missionaries and Chinese women.

In the remaining quarter century of her life, she devoted herself to nonmissionary activities, summed up in the subtitle of a recent biography: *Feminist, Social Activist, Scientist.* These three roles were closely tied together, her work as an entomologist, for example, serving to inform public understanding of the spread of disease by fleas. Her social activism included her efforts to establish hospitals, and she viewed her demand for women's rights in terms of betterment of humankind.

During this period of her life, she maintained very little association with Baptist missions. In fact, some might view her as a brilliant young woman who fell in love with a missionary only to become sidetracked in China missions for two decades until she escaped to follow her true calling as a scientist and a proponent of social causes. When she died in 1916, the Baptist Foreign Mission Society did not even publish her obituary. Ten years later, however, the society eulogized her as the "mother of our Bible women and also the mother of our Bible schools."[12]

CHARLOTTE (LOTTIE) DIGGS MOON
Southern Belle, Equal Rights Advocate

"What women want who come to China is free opportunity to do the largest possible work. . . . What women have a right to demand is perfect equality." Even for today those are fighting words in Southern Baptist circles, where male headship reigns. But these words were hurled at a male superior in the nineteenth century by Lottie Moon, the most celebrated missionary of that denomination. To her mission board back home, she wrote: "Simple justice demands that women should have equal rights with men in mission meetings and in the conduct of their work."[13]

A southern belle born in 1840, Lottie grew up on a thirteen-hundred-acre Virginia slave plantation some twenty miles from Monticello, the home of Thomas Jefferson. With the outbreak of the Civil War, as the boys went off to fight, she was forced to stay home and help her widowed mother with the work. After the war she became a teacher, but the work was tedious. What else could she do but marry and have babies and become a proper matron? She longed to travel, to move beyond the struggles and confines of the post-war South. But she was stuck as a teacher in a tiny school in Cartersville, Georgia. Then in 1872, her younger sister Edmonia, still in her teens, sailed for China to serve as a missionary. The next year, Lottie followed. It might have become an illustrious partnership but for Edmonia's "good for nothing" behavior and her knack for being "very burdensome" to other missionaries.[14] Despite Edmonia's bent for doing "queer and unreasonable things," when she left after four years, Lottie became lonely and depressed.

Another individual who contributed to her loneliness and depression was Crawford Toy, a Confederate army chaplain. He had "come a-wooing" soon after the war, and now he was wooing again. He was contemplating mission work in Japan and was convinced she would be a perfect partner. There was just one problem. He had been influenced not only by German higher criticism of Scripture but also by Darwinian evolution. On that count alone, Lottie broke up with him. He would become a professor at Harvard, while she, as she later reflected, was left to "plod along in the same old way."[15]

In China, the exciting life that she had imagined was nowhere to be found. She was assigned to teach in a girls' school, where she encountered only

Patron Saint of Southern Baptist Missions

No one—missionary, pastor, or denominational leader—is as powerful a symbol in Southern Baptist circles as Lottie Moon. Her name is a mission shibboleth. Her life epitomizes foreign missions.

Alan Neely, "Saints Who Sometimes Were"

"dull" and "unstudious" minds. She had her heart set on evangelism—to "go out among the millions." In exasperation, she asked: "Can we wonder at the mortal weariness and disgust, the sense of wasted powers and the conviction that her life is a failure, that comes over a woman when, instead of the ever broadening activities she had planned, she finds herself tied down to the petty work of teaching a few girls."[16]

Finally at age forty-four, after twelve years in China, Lottie struck out on her own as an evangelist. She relocated in Pingtu, where she quickly discovered what life was like when she was no longer protected by the walls of a little school surrounded by other missionaries. She was now the local "devil woman," taunted as she made her way through the narrow streets. But slowly the taunts turned to curiosity. Men demanded to learn, even as women had, about the strange stories she had in her book. Within a few years her first converts were baptized. The little church, soon with a Chinese pastor, grew to more than one thousand, becoming the fastest growing Baptist work in China. To loved ones back home, she wrote: "Surely there can be no deeper joy than that of saving souls."[17]

During these years Lottie continued her village evangelism, taking long breaks in Tengchow, where her accommodations were more suitable. Here she wrote letters and articles that would transform her into a household name in Baptist circles throughout the South. Despite her cynicism and frequent rebukes, her popularity soared. "It is odd," she scolded in an article, "that a million Baptists of the South can furnish only three men for all China. Odd that with five hundred preachers in the state of Virginia, we must rely on a Presbyterian to fill a Baptist pulpit [here]. I wonder how these things look in heaven. They certainly look very queer in China."[18]

In her writings, she often appealed for "vigorous healthy women" to join her in China and for funds to support them. She called for a special Christmas offering to be collected by women, the first of which in 1888 brought in enough money to support three young women. Lottie was elated: "What I hope to see is a band of ardent, enthusiastic, and experienced Christian women occupying a line of stations extending from Pingtu on the north and from Chinkiang on the south, making a succession of stations uniting the two."[19]

In the years that followed, Christmas offerings increased, and more women joined her in China. If we imagine Lottie as an imposing figure, talking down superiors and raising money among women as no one had ever done before, we do well to remember that her full height in sturdy shoes was considerably less than five feet—and, according to one source, barely more than four feet in height. The fact that she was not a tall, big-boned, blonde woman wearing a size-10 shoe no doubt served her well in an Asian culture where foot binding was still the custom.

But times were changing in China. The Boxer Uprising of 1900, followed by famines and outbreaks of the plague, created widespread turmoil and political upheaval. People all around her were starving. Lottie pleaded for relief offerings and resented the fact that Christians back home were so tight with their money. She depleted her own bank account, going without

Malla Moe: Forceful Evangelist

A Norwegian immigrant to Chicago, Malla Moe graduated from an eleven-day evangelist course in Chicago and was commissioned in 1892 to serve as a missionary in Swaziland with the Evangelical Alliance Mission. Within six years she was established at her mission site, Bethel, where she remained until her death more than a half century later. There she welcomed dozens of converts for weekly services, and in subsequent years she trained and commissioned pastors and evangelists. In 1927 after "the mission had seriously considered not allowing her to rejoin them because of her dominating behavior," she began traveling in her covered house wagon, evangelizing new regions and serving as a bishop over her African preachers at various church sites. One of the most colorful stories about her is drawn from a letter from a coworker. Malla had encountered a Swazi man and "told him she was going to pray till he got saved." The next day when they met again, he ran the other way with her hot on the trail. "She shouted to him to come back and grabbing him by the arm pulled him down into the grass and prayed mightily to God to save him from Satan and hell. It was more than he could stand. He wept and prayed and got saved."[a]

[a] Letter from Grace Sanders, February 10, 1940.

sustenance herself. She became depressed, even more so with the news in 1909 that her sister Edmonia had committed suicide by putting a gun to her head. They had faithfully corresponded, and Lottie was a world away, shrouded in grief.

That Lottie, amid severe depression, committed suicide herself is probably not entirely accurate. But she did starve herself to death. By the time that others realized how severe her condition was, it was too late. She died on Christmas Eve 1912 on a ship at port in Kobe, Japan. It would be impossible to exaggerate how much this news would influence the future of the "Lottie Moon Christmas Offering." She was a symbol of self-sacrifice—one who *presented her body a living sacrifice*. Through fund-raising and recruitment, she exercised a profound influence on Southern Baptist missions.

MAUDE CARY
"Old-Maid Missionary" to Muslims

In 1901, when Lottie Moon was entering her final dismal decade in China, Maude Cary, with four other missionaries, was sailing to Morocco, under the banner of the Gospel Missionary Union. She might also have been filled with dreary thoughts of the future. It was no secret that work among Muslims came with few rewards—no hope of a thousand converts such as Lottie had in Pingtu. Nor could she ever muster the support of women in a large denomination.

Born on a Kansas farm in 1878, Maude, at age eighteen, enrolled at a Bible institute to prepare for a career in overseas missions. She was smart and independent, necessary qualities for success, but not ones well suited to her gender. Language training thus proved problematic, particularly considering her competitive nature. When she outscored the other students—perhaps with a bit of smugness—she was accused of being proud and aggressive. This would be only the beginning of her problems, however. Her first full review came at a field conference, during which time discussion was opened for the missionaries to critique one another. Having imagined things were going well, she heard otherwise. Indeed, she was bluntly told that she was forgetful and selfish, given to frivolous talk and unbecoming laughter. When the president of the mission arrived some weeks later, he advised her to return home. Utterly humiliated, she promised to mend her ways and was permitted to stay.

In the years that followed she studied Arabic and conducted village evangelism with no visible results. In her spare time she spent countless hours in an effort to learn the difficult Berber tongue. Why would she voluntarily put so much effort into learning a language not spoken among those to whom she was ministering? Is it possible her interest related to the fact that the unmarried George Reed was working among that tribal group? They had corresponded, and she no doubt hoped that learning Berber might be enough to spark his interest in her. Her ploy worked, and during the 1907 field conference he made overtures serious enough for her to consider his intentions equal to a marriage proposal.

By the following year, however, his ardor—if he ever had any—had cooled. To commemorate her thirtieth birthday she determined that she would *seek meekness*, because George let it be known that humility is what he wanted most in a wife. For the next six years until 1914, she saw little of George and was unsure of his intentions. Then without communicating to her, he made the decision to leave Morocco and begin mission work in the Sudan. Her dreams were dashed. She would spend her life as an "old-maid missionary."

After serving in Morocco for more than two decades, she took a furlough and returned to America, now transformed by the Roaring Twenties. How odd she must have appeared, wearing the same hat and dress she had worn on her outbound voyage in 1901. Back in Kansas, she found her parents so frail that neither would survive to see her off again. Indeed, she questioned whether she should even go back to the field. What had she accomplished during that first lengthy term of service? Nothing at all if faithful converts were a measure of success. Knocking her head against the brick wall of Islam was a hopeless cause. But what were her choices? She had no immediate family, and at forty-seven, what other options were there? She returned to Morocco.

Once again submersed in Moroccan culture and mission outreach, Maude began to witness very slow and steady progress. Here and there were converts who did not back down in the face of persecution. But at the same time the mission force was dwindling until she and another single

Mabel Francis: Decorated Missionary to Japan

In 1962, the Japanese emperor honored Mabel with the nation's highest civilian award, membership in the exclusive Fifth Order of the Sacred Treasure for her sacrifice for "the welfare of the Japanese people in their distress and confusion at the time of their defeat."[a] A missionary to Japan since 1909, Mabel had refused to evacuate after the bombing of Pearl Harbor. She was placed under house arrest, but after the war ended, she carried on with her ministry. Growing up in New Hampshire, Mabel began teaching school at age fifteen and then traveled as a schoolhouse evangelist until she was commissioned by the Christian and Missionary Alliance to serve in Japan. There, she was joined by her brother and later her widowed sister Anne, who was in charge of teaching while Mabel and her brother engaged in evangelism and planted twenty churches before he returned to America. Mabel served in Japan for fifty-six years and was known widely as the American lady on a bicycle who was always smiling.

[a] Robert L. Niklaus, *All for Jesus.*

woman were the only missionaries left in the field. Two young women arrived, and then, with the onset of World War II, the doors were shut. There the women waited out the war, though hardly idle. By splitting up, they were able to continue the work at three outposts, Maude and the other seasoned missionary each working alone, while the two new recruits worked together.

When the war ended, more missionaries arrived, finding ministry opportunities already in place for them. Now the most seasoned of the missionaries, Maude worked with new recruits, and at age seventy-one was assigned to open a new mission station in El Hajeb. When the mission established a Bible institute in 1951, it enrolled three students its first year, two from El Hajeb. The following January she returned to America for health reasons and, it was presumed, for retirement. But later that year, now seventy-four, she returned and carried on in the work for another three years, setting the stage for widespread evangelism, with some thirty thousand Muslims enrolled in correspondence courses.

121

In 1967, twelve years after her departure, however, all missionaries were forced to leave Morocco. That same year, Maude Cary died. Apart from mission colleagues, very few others noticed. One of the missionaries forced to leave the Moroccan field was Evelyn Stenbock. She had arrived twelve years earlier in 1955, when Maude was departing. She had heard the accounts of Maude's perseverance against all odds and made the decision to write the story down in a short biography, *Miss Terri: The Story of Maude Cary*. Without Evelyn's work we would have never known of Maude, who represents thousands of missionary women whose stories would remain forever buried.

CONCLUDING OBSERVATIONS

One of the benefits of being a writer is the gratefulness that often comes my way from people who have been inspired or challenged by one of my books. I trust that Evelyn Stenbock also enjoyed such expressions for her writings, more than a dozen of which are still available on Amazon. Although I profited from her biography of Maude Cary, I was disappointed that no excerpts from letters or diary entries were quoted—especially those between Maude and George. Were there none available? Without such sources, it is difficult to determine George's investment in what Maude took to be a marriage proposal. Nevertheless, anyone who is interested in Maude owes a debt to Evelyn, who died at age eighty in 2009. In fact, I have now learned that she grew up on a farm in northern Wisconsin, less than seventy miles from the farm on which I was raised. She was a teenager the year I was born—so close and yet so far away, our only connection a book.

It is difficult to read that book without an incredible sense of wonder at Maude's sacrifice. Today the term is often used where it is not warranted. The accounts of missionaries of prior generations, however, offer much-needed perspective on the call to sacrifice, to take up their cross to follow Jesus. It is true, however, that part of the appeal to mission work was the opportunity for adventure, though women were far less susceptible to the adrenaline rush that propelled men into unwarranted risk.

We shudder to read of Narcissa's all-consuming terror when her door is nearly knocked down in the dead of night. She struggled with loneliness and depression, as did Adele, Lottie, and Maude. Families were worlds away, and letters and packages from home were few and far between. Mail service was unreliable, and when letters actually did arrive from home, the news often came in the form of sorrow and death, sometimes six months or a year old.

In many remote places in the world today, missionaries are only a text or email or Skype away from family back home. But as recently as the late 1980s, I found myself in a situation desperately trying (and failing) to reach Grand Rapids by phone from Kijabe, Kenya. Little more than a decade after that, Rift Valley Academy, an easy walk up the mountain, was boasting high-speed internet.

QUESTIONS TO THINK ABOUT

A 2014 check on Amazon shows no recent biography on the life and times of Narcissa Whitman (or her husband, Marcus). Do you think an up-to-date biography is perhaps overdue? Does her life interest you enough to want to know more about her?

How would you assess Adele Fielde as a Christian, as a missionary, and as a turn-of-the-twentieth-century modern American woman? Can you envision her life if she had never met and fallen in love with her fiancé? Has a chance meeting with someone ever made a life-changing difference for you?

Do you think Lottie Moon was too outspoken with her mission superiors? How would you compare and contrast these two China missionaries, Adele and Lottie? Which one would you most welcome into your home for a one-week visit?

If you were a woman's mission board counselor or therapist and Maude Cary sought your advice, what are some suggestions and guidelines you might offer her in the realm of relationships?

Can you identify an author like Evelyn Stenbock who has influenced you by expending time and energy to bring to life an otherwise obscure woman of faith? Does her example inspire you to write and publish such a story?

Which of these women sacrificed the most for the least apparent results? Which one do you admire the most?

8

Jarena Lee and African American Evangelists

For twenty-eight years I lived in an integrated neighborhood, more blacks than whites. My son's education from kindergarten through high school was the same. Whites were a minority. There my son found friends as I did. In fact, I often visited with my friend and neighbor Claretha, and it was to her arms I would go when my son was in trouble. I've likewise worked alongside a black woman as my business partner (and we were guests on a radio talk show featuring the topic "business in black and white"). I dedicated a book to friends, husband and wife, both black. My son and granddaughter have both dated across color lines. I have taught courses with segments on racism.

With that backdrop, I opened one of my lectures on racism with controversial remarks. After distributing handouts and briefly introducing the topic, I paused and made a statement that caught my students off guard. They were mature seminary students, all white males, many with families. My remark was anything but startling. In fact, it should have been regarded as the most obvious statement I could have made regarding race. I repeated my words twice, as I slowly and solemnly looked at each of them: "There is racism here in this classroom. There is racism in this room." Another pause. (I had prepared for these introductory remarks.) Then I said: "I know there is racism right here in this room" (pause) "because I am here."

I'm not sure what they had expected me to say during those fleeting moments. Was I going to reveal an incident that related to one of them? Was I going to remind them of a comment someone had made in class the previous week? Whatever was going through their minds, my confession forced them to think seriously about racism.

I recently read an online article by Tyler Glodjo on white privilege. After laying out a lengthy factual premise, Glodjo writes:

> But this article is not ultimately about racialization, nor is it about white privilege. These are simply concepts that are necessary in order for us to begin engaging a much deeper conversation on race within the body of Christ in our nation. So with all of the aforementioned said, I begin with a confession: I am a racist.[1]

Many of us (who are white) go through life without the slightest awareness of white privilege. Those confronted with the term typically deny that it relates to them. Likewise, they would be horrified at the thought of being racist. It is very easy for white people today—ones who strongly affirm equality and integration—to deny their own racism and white privilege.

One of the most searing personal examples of racism was told to me by my neighbor Jack. He was an easygoing trucker, and typically our chats were lighthearted. Not that day. The setting of his story was Mississippi in the early 1960s. He was on a double date, the car parked along a river on a moonlit night. It was an area typically consigned to black teenagers. Headlights flashed behind them. In a matter of moments a white sheriff and his deputy were ordering them out of the car at gunpoint. Their girlfriends, crying out and sobbing, were brutally raped.

Though the story was decades old, Jack couldn't tell me without choking. The utter awfulness of it. And the guilt after all those years. The guilt for having done nothing to save the girls. He couldn't have. The sheriffs had guns. He shook his head and twice repeated almost under his breath: "They called me *boy*."

I've often wondered about the girls. How did they fare in the years and decades that followed? And I wonder about Jarena Lee, Harriet Tubman,

Amanda Berry Smith, Mary McLeod Bethune, and Eliza Davis George. Did they too suffer such terrible violence, often excused on the basis of their perceived double inferiority—black and female? They encountered racism and blatant discrimination in ministry. Yet in each instance they overcame all odds and effectively fulfilled the call to serve.

JARENA LEE
First AME Woman Preacher

During the early nineteenth century, when the preaching of Mary Fletcher was still ringing in the ears of English Methodists, Jarena Lee heard God calling: "Preach the gospel. I will put words in your mouth." She consulted with Richard Allen, the bishop of the African Methodist Episcopal Church (AME), only to be told that the Methodist Church made no provision for women preachers. Had he known or heeded the precedent of John Wesley himself, Allen might have welcomed her as a circuit preacher during a time when the AME was barely getting off the ground itself. But his bias or ignorance got the best of him, and Jarena backed down—though not for long.

Jarena was born in Cape May, New Jersey, in 1783, the last year of the long and drawn-out Revolutionary War. Unlike the vast majority of African Americans at the time, she was born free. That freedom suddenly seemed to end, however, when she was sent away to be a servant at the tender age of seven. In her autobiography she mentions very little of these years except for a few occasions when she was prodded along in her spiritual quest. In one instance she lied to her mistress: "At this awful point, in my early history, the Spirit of God moved in power through my conscience, and told me I was a wretched sinner." In the years that followed, the weight of sin, prompted by Presbyterian preaching, distressed her to the point that she contemplated suicide: "There was a brook about a quarter of a mile from the house, in which there was a deep hole, where the water whirled about among the rocks; to this place, it was suggested, I must go and drown myself."[2] This is a haunting confession. What sin was awful enough to tempt her to take her own life? Might she have been raped and perceived herself to be in some way culpable? One can only wonder.

Your Sons and Daughters Shall Prophesy

Peter's message at Pentecost was a message of hope for all those who were listening. Thousands were baptized. The message had particular significance to women and bondservants and slaves. The Spirit would be poured out on them even as it would be poured out on freeborn men. Such good news was shocking, and many took it to heart, including African American women.

> Then Peter stood up with the Eleven, raised his voice and addressed the crowd: "Fellow Jews and all of you who live in Jerusalem, let me explain this to you; listen carefully to what I say. These people are not drunk, as you suppose. It's only nine in the morning! No, this is what was spoken by the prophet Joel:
>
> "'In the last days, God says,
>   I will pour out my Spirit on all people.
> Your sons and daughters will prophesy,
>   your young men will see visions,
>   your old men will dream dreams.
> Even on my servants, both men and women,
>   I will pour out my Spirit in those days,
>   and they will prophesy.'"
>
> Acts 2:14–18

It was not until she was in her early twenties that under the preaching of Richard Allen she was converted. There, amid a crowd of hundreds and with no apparent hesitation or embarrassment, she jumped to her feet and declared that God had pardoned her sins. But as she later testified, the devil began harassing her the moment she took her stand.

So oppressed was she that for four years she was "under the awful apprehension" that she "could never be happy in this life." Again she was tempted to take her own life, this time by hanging. As she escaped this temptation, she saw herself held only "by a spider's web" over "the awful gulf of hell," hearing "the howling of the damned" and seeing "the smoke of the bottomless pit."[3] Her image may very well have been drawn from the late Jonathan Edwards's still-popular, oft-repeated sermon "Sinners in the Hands of an Angry God"—sinners dangling over hell, held only by the thread of a spider's web.

After a lengthy time of further temptation by Satan, Jarena found assurance of salvation, only to be informed by a minister that she must experience sanctification. Again she endured a lengthy period of torment until finally she heard a voice telling her, "Thou art sanctified!" Several years after that, she heard God's call to preach the gospel and was then told by Allen that there was no place for women preachers among those in the AME. She mulled over his words:

> O how careful ought we to be, lest through our by-laws of church government and discipline, we bring into disrepute even the word of life. For as unseemly as it may appear now-a-days for a woman to preach, it should be remembered that nothing is impossible with God. And why should it be thought impossible, heterodox, or improper for a woman to preach? seeing the Saviour died for the woman as well as for the man.[4]

Jarena was convinced that God had called her to preach. Why else, she asked, would her ministry be accompanied by the testimonies of so many conversions?

In 1811, at the age of twenty-nine, Jarena married a pastor of a Methodist society. Six years later she was a widow with a toddler and an infant. Still the call to preach weighed heavily on her. Eight years had elapsed since Bishop Allen had denied her request to preach. Then on a particular Sunday she was in his congregation. He announced his text from the book of Jonah. "But as he proceeded to explain, he seemed to have lost the spirit." At that moment, Jarena sprang to her feet and took over:

> I told them I was like Jonah; for it had been then nearly eight years since the Lord had called me to preach his gospel to the fallen sons and daughters of Adam's race, but that I had lingered like him, and delayed to go at the bidding of the Lord, and warn those who are as deeply guilty as were the people of Nineveh.[5]

She sat down, fearing that she might be expelled from the assembly. Amazingly, Allen was not offended by her interrupting his sermon. In fact, he took her spontaneous exhortation as a sign from God. He admitted that he had denied her the opportunity to preach eight years earlier but now believed she had indeed received a genuine calling from God.

With his public pronouncement, she became the first woman preacher in the AME. In the years that followed, she traveled thousands of miles throughout New Jersey, New York, Pennsylvania, Ohio, and beyond, often leaving her little ones with others. In 1832, she began a preaching tour in Canada, and in a little more than a year had traveled nearly three thousand miles, preaching two or three times each week. She even ventured into the South, preaching to slaves during the perilous decades before the Civil War.

Along the way, Jarena returned to Cape May to visit her elderly mother, whom she had not seen in eleven years. Here she had several opportunities to preach:

> Goshen School-house, to both white and colored . . . some were Baptists and some Methodist. . . . Four miles from there I preached in the Court House to a congregation of different denominations, and the house was crowded. . . . On the following Sabbath I spoke in a School-house to a white Methodist congregation.[6]

In the early 1840s, when she was approaching sixty, Jarena again visited her aged mother, who was eighty-two and not in good health. Nor was Jarena. Nevertheless she eagerly accepted opportunities to preach, with walking often her only means of travel. Her autobiography ends shortly thereafter, and her life seems to fade away, with no record of her death.

AMANDA SMITH
Evangelist, Preacher, Missionary, Worldwide Traveler

One of the most revered nineteenth-century missionaries to India, James Thoburn, an American, served for many years as the Methodist bishop. In 1876, back in Ohio, he first observed the "colored lady dressed in a very plain garb . . . expounding a Bible lesson to a small audience." He was not impressed, but he inquired who she was. "I was told that the speaker

Harriet Tubman: Railroad Conductor

She was dubbed *Moses* for her tireless efforts to set her people free, and she became the most noted "conductor" on the Underground Railroad. In 1849 she had run away from slave captivity in Eastern Maryland. Once safe, she could not comprehend that she was even the same person, and freedom felt like heaven. She went on to lead many others to freedom, and for that effort a large reward for her capture was widely circulated. But she kept making forays into the South, her fearlessness fueled by her faith in God. In fact, she believed God was directly leading her. Reflecting on her, abolitionist Thomas Garrett wrote: "I never met any person of any color who had more confidence in the voice of God." She served the Union cause during the Civil War and in the years that followed was involved in a variety of humanitarian endeavors. She died in 1913, when she was in her eighties, having lived for more than sixty years as a free woman.

was Mrs. Amanda Smith, and that she was a woman of remarkable gifts, who had been greatly blessed in various parts of the country." Three years later, after he had returned to India, he learned that she would be visiting. They were scheduled to minister together on many occasions, and she later returned to India a second time. Of her time there, he wrote: "During the seventeen years that I have lived in Calcutta, I have known many famous strangers to visit the city, some of whom attracted large audiences, but I have never known anyone who could draw and hold so large an audience as Mrs. Smith."[7]

Amanda's autobiography is a classic, and the subtitle sums up her life: *The Story of the Lord's Dealings with Mrs. Amanda Smith the Colored Evangelist; Containing an Account of Her Life Work of Faith, and Her Travels in America, England, Ireland, Scotland, India, and Africa, as an Independent Missionary*.

Unlike Jarena Lee, she was not born free. Her parents were slaves on small farms adjacent to each other. Her father, after his master died, essentially took over the farm, traveling some twenty miles to Baltimore twice each week to sell produce. His mistress, according to Amanda, "was very kind, and was proud of him for his faithfulness, so she gave him a chance to buy himself." His situation certainly was not the norm, but it does illustrate what one man was able to accomplish with his owner's goodwill:

> She allowed him so much for his work and a chance to earn what extra he could for himself. So he used to make brooms and husk mats and take them to market with the produce. This work he would do nights after his day's work was done for his mistress. He was a great lime burner. Then in harvest time, after working for his mistress all day, he would walk three and four miles, and work in the harvest field till one and two o'clock in the morning, then go home and lie down and sleep for an hour or two, then up and at it again. He had an important and definite object before him, and was willing to sacrifice sleep and rest in order to accomplish it. It was not his own liberty alone, but the freedom of his wife and five children. For this he toiled day and night. He was a strong man, with an excellent constitution, and God wonderfully helped him in his struggle. After he had finished paying for himself, the next was to buy my mother and us children.[8]

With their freedom, the family remained in the neighborhood and farmed, though there were harrowing times when it was feared that her father—and all of them, for that matter—might be kidnapped and taken out of state and back into slavery. Otherwise, family life was routine:

> My father and mother both could read. But I never remember hearing them tell how they were taught. Father was the better reader of the two. Always on Sunday morning after breakfast he would call us children around and read the Bible to us. I never knew him to sit down to a meal, no matter how scant, but what he would ask God's blessing before eating. Mother was very thoughtful and scrupulously economical. She could get up the best dinner out of almost nothing of anybody I ever saw in my life. She often cheered my father's heart when he came home at night and said: "Well, mother, how have you got on today?"[9]

Barely in her teens, Amanda began working as a live-in maid, with opportunities for further education and religious instruction. Soon thereafter she experienced a religious awakening, but the fervor was quickly dissipated.

Then she came upon a book that featured "an argument between an infidel and a Christian minister." As she read page after page, the minister was winning the debate. But then "by and by the minister began to lose, and the infidel gained." She continued reading and was soon convinced: "His questions and argument were so pretty and put in such a way that before I knew it I was captured; and by the time I had got through the book I had the whole of the infidel's article stamped on my memory and spirit, and the Christian's argument was lost."[10]

Sometime later, the opportunity came for Amanda to test her faith as an infidel. She was taking a walk with her aunt, who commented: "How wonderfully God has created everything, the sky, and the great waters." Amanda might have agreed, but that was not her style. She "let out with [her] biggest gun" and startled her aunt with, "How do you know there is a God?" and then answered her own question "with just such an air as a poor, blind, ignorant infidel is capable of putting on." Her aunt gave her an arrow-piercing look and stamped her foot as she gave the ultimatum: "Don't you ever speak to me again. Anybody that had as good a Christian mother as you had, and was raised as you have been, to speak so to me. I don't want to talk to you."[11]

With that, "God broke the snare." Had her aunt come back with proofs for God, Amanda, clever as she was, might have bested her. "If she had argued with me," she later wrote, "I don't believe I should ever have got out of that snare of the devil."[12]

During her teen years, Amanda frequently returned home to live with her parents and siblings, eventually twelve of them. Poor as they were, life was good except for the constant fear that the powerful arm of slavery and savagery might reach into their home and strangle them and their little ones. Nevertheless, the family was willing to risk all for black people in bondage, as Amanda movingly recorded:

Our house was one of the main stations of the Under Ground Railroad. My father took the "Baltimore Weekly Sun" newspaper; that always had advertisements of runaway slaves. After giving the cut of the poor fugitive, with a little bundle on his back, going with his face northward, the advertisement would read something like this: Three thousand dollars reward! Ran away from Anerandell County, Maryland, such a date, so many feet high, scar on the right side of the forehead or some other part of the body,—belonging

Black Pride

> One day a lady asked me if I did not think all colored people wanted to
> be white. I told her that I did not think so—I did not. I never wished I
> was white but once, that I could remember, and that was years ago. . . .
> No, we who are the royal black are very well satisfied with His gift to us
> in this substantial color. I, for one, praise Him for what He has given me,
> although at times it is very inconvenient. For example: When on my way
> to California last January, a year ago, if I had been white I could have
> stopped at a hotel, but being black, though a lone woman, I was obliged
> to stay all night in the waiting room at Austin, Texas.
>
> Amanda Berry Smith, Autobiography

to Mr. A. or B. So sometimes the excitement was so high we had to be very
discreet in order not to attract suspicion. . . . I have known him to lead in
the harvest field from fifteen to twenty men. . . . After working all day in
the harvest field, he would come home at night, sleep about two hours, then
start at midnight and walk fifteen or twenty miles and carry a poor slave to
a place of security; sometimes a mother and child, sometimes a man and
wife, other times a man or more, then get home just before day. Perhaps he
could sleep an hour then go to work, and so many times baffled suspicion.[13]

Her father was suspected of harboring slaves and was on more than one
occasion seriously roughed up and almost killed, but Amanda was convinced that God was watching over him.

Still in her teens at the height of Underground Railroad activity, Amanda
herself did not actively participate in this dangerous work. Amanda's early
adult years were characterized most by domestic difficulties. At seventeen,
she married a minister who turned out to be a wretched alcoholic. When
the Civil War broke out, he joined the Confederate army, and she never
heard from him again. Soon she was courted by another minister, whom
she married with the hope of establishing a Christian home. Her hopes
were quickly dashed, though the marriage would hang on for many years,
often with lengthy separations. Her husband died in 1869, leaving her
impoverished with a sickly baby soon to be buried as well.

That same year she began preaching in neighboring towns, supporting herself by washing dirty clothes for white folks. After receiving five dollars on one occasion, she determined that God had called her to preach full-time. Nevertheless, she struggled with the same kinds of questions and doubts that almost derailed her when she was very young: "Some time after the Lord had sanctified my soul [in 1868], I became greatly exercised about the Trinity. I could not seem to understand just how there could exist three distinct persons, and yet one. I thought every day and prayed for light, but didn't seem to get help. I read the Bible, but no help came." Later, she testified, "God made me understand it so I have had no question since."[14]

In the years that followed, Amanda would become perhaps the most celebrated woman preacher in America. Her work began primarily in Methodist camp meetings and continued in England and Scotland. She received an invitation to go to India in 1878, where she would spend time with Bishop James Thoburn. On the way she went to Paris, Florence, Rome, Naples, and Egypt. Impressive travel for one who was so recently a penniless washerwoman. On her return trip she visited West Africa, including Sierra Leone, Liberia, and Calabar (in present-day Nigeria), where she would spend nearly eight years. From there she returned to England at the invitation of Hannah Whitall Smith, after which she sailed back to New York in 1890.

Two years later she moved to Illinois, where she established an orphanage for destitute black children. She retired from that work in 1912 and died three years later at age seventy-eight. Three years after her death the orphanage burned to the ground and was never rebuilt.

MARY MCLEOD BETHUNE
Educator and Counselor to Presidents

As a little girl, perhaps seven years old, she was one day playing at the home of a white neighbor girl. She reached for a book, and the neighbor girl grabbed it away, handing her instead a picture book. It was at that moment that the sensitive Mary McLeod vowed that she would one day learn to read. Visiting with a white neighbor girl, however, was hardly part of Mary's daily routine. At the tender age of five, she was often out in the fields working with her parents and siblings.

She was born in Mayesville, South Carolina, in 1875, the fifteenth child in a poor family of sharecroppers, her parents having been slaves. Mary prayed for a miracle, and when she was ten the miracle arrived in the form of a newly established local school for black children and a young teacher, Emma Wilson, all sponsored by a Presbyterian mission society. "The whole world opened to me when I learned to read."[15] After three years of exceptional progress, Mary was sent to a boarding school in North Carolina, and after graduating she continued her education at Moody Bible Institute in preparation for service as a missionary in Africa.

She later spoke well of her experience at the school and of the occasions when D. L. Moody had shown his concern for her well-being. Her great disappointment came, however, when she learned that the Presbyterian mission had no place for an African American missionary. The enforced segregation of travel and living arrangements, she was told, would create too many problems. Instead, she was asked to serve as a teacher in an all-black mission school in Georgia.

Soon thereafter in 1898, Mary married Albertus Bethune and moved to Florida, with a baby on the way. During the early years she and her husband were separated much of the time, and in 1907, he left altogether. Before their final separation, Mary had opened a day school for African American girls that would grow to more than two hundred students. It began with five girls and her son Albert, in a small rented house next to the Daytona dump. Soon neighbors and church members got on board, and before the school year ended she had thirty students.

In subsequent years Mary brought in additional teachers and devoted her own time to administration and fund-raising, pleading for support from rich and poor alike. Her hard work brought rewards, including a gift of more than sixty thousand dollars from John D. Rockefeller.

In 1931, under Methodist sponsorship, the school merged with a boys' school to become Bethune-Cookman Collegiate Institute. In addition to educational work, Mary served with the Red Cross, established a hospital, organized a public housing project, and became the first president of the National Council of Negro Women. Presidents Coolidge, Hoover,

Roosevelt, and Truman all called upon her participation in White House conferences. In fact, with Eleanor Roosevelt as a go-between, she had the president's ear on several occasions.

> In 1953, she served as an American delegate to Liberia for the country's presidential inauguration. At last, she was convinced, she had in some way fulfilled her missionary calling: "Ever since my student days at Moody Bible Institute in Chicago, in the 'Nineties,' when I so much wanted to find happiness as a missionary to Africa, I had seen myself doing just this— counseling and praying with the native people in the far-away land of my ancestors—and here I was. It was wonderful." She died two years later, age seventy-nine.[16]

Her active involvement in civic and charitable organizations gave her wide recognition and awards, but it was her educational work, particularly in the early decades, that most distinguished her. She was a dominant force, head held high, always carrying an unnecessary cane that added to her flair. To the children she was known as "Mama Bethune," but not one to be trifled with. Early morning Bible study was followed by home economics, math, and science. Strict hours of study were enforced. Of her, one of President Roosevelt's advisors said: "She had the most marvelous gift of effecting feminine helplessness in order to attain her aims with masculine ruthlessness."[17] Africa's loss was truly America's gain.

In her social activism Mary calls to mind Sojourner Truth, who died in 1883 (when Mary was seven) after a long life of struggle for equal rights for blacks and for women. Like Mary, Sojourner consulted with a president, Ulysses Grant, at the White House. She is remembered for, among other things, her riveting speeches, particularly "Ain't I a Woman?," delivered in 1851 at the Women's Rights Convention in Akron, Ohio.

ELIZA DAVIS GEORGE
African American Missionary to Liberia

There are many incredible tales told of the work of "Mother George" in Liberia, West Africa. One particular story was about a harrowing journey, when she walked some two hundred miles, wading and swimming rivers with her two adopted African boys. She had run out of money and was making the trek to claim a two-hundred-dollar gift from America that had been incorrectly sent to Monrovia instead of the town near her mission outpost. On arrival, worn out and hungry, she learned that the money had been returned—or perhaps confiscated.

Eliza Davis lived a long and fruitful life that spanned a century, from 1879 to 1979. Born into a large impoverished family of former slaves turned sharecroppers, she was an eager learner who through sheer tenacity enrolled at Central Texas College, determined to excel despite prevailing race prejudice. Like Mary McLeod, her goal was to follow God's call to Africa. Initially turned down as a missionary candidate by the Texas Baptist Convention, she boldly appealed the decision. So impressive was her testimony that the board agreed to appoint her a missionary to Liberia.

It was not until 1914, when Eliza was well past thirty, that she arrived at her post to work with another single woman. In the years that followed she conducted successful evangelistic outreach and established an industrial academy for boys. That she was ill-equipped for supervising such a school may have been a factor in the decision of the Texas Baptists to discontinue her support, though the immediate issue was a split between the Texas and the National Baptists. Eliza was now on her own, alone in Africa with no financial support. Her options were very limited, that is until prince charming came calling with a marriage proposal.

Actually, Thompson George was in her eyes anything but a charming suitor. A native of British Guyana, he was employed by a Portuguese company. She had spurned his advances before, but now she was in no position to do so. She agreed to the marriage, though surely not for love. In fact, she was repulsed by his expectation of sexual intimacies. He did, however, join her in the work, and despite his issues with alcohol and later, adultery, they continued to work together for a number of years.

By the time he died in 1939, she had sought and received support from the National Baptist Convention, which had recognized her gift for evangelism and for planting churches. Only a few years later, however, she was recalled to America due to health reasons—or so the board claimed. She was to turn her work over to others. She refused, and her missionary service was terminated in 1945. Again, she felt abandoned. But by this time, certain individuals had become aware of her work and began supporting her through what became known as Eliza Davis George Clubs.

In a little more than a dozen years, there were nearly thirty churches in the Eliza George Baptist Association, supported by more than one hundred churches in her homeland. Whether most of the funds were properly spent or whether, through her generosity and lack of oversight, they slipped too easily through her fingers is uncertain. By the time she left Africa, however, her work was well established and being run by native believers. She continued to raise funds for the work until she was ninety-nine.

Several years before she died, Joseph Jeter, a black evangelist and mission founder from Philadelphia, encountered her on the job in Liberia. His commentary speaks to her dedication and perseverance: "I met Mother George at the Evangelical Negro Industrial Mission deep in the bush at the age of 91. Her ministry was vast. She was almost blind. She walked with a walking stick. She had a large tropical cancer on her leg, and she was still pressing the claims of Christ."[18]

CONCLUDING OBSERVATIONS

Jarena Lee was born in Cape May, New Jersey, and returned decades later to preach. I lived just up the road from that town in the late 1970s, working in the field of social services. My assigned territory included the tiny village of Whitesboro, then almost entirely African American. Many years later I returned to the area to preach at a church missions conference. The Sunday night service at the all-white church included the congregation of a nearby sister church, all black. I recall that evening as truly memorable. Nothing routine about it. Here, with audience participation, I delivered a rousing sermon. I stuck to my text, all the while being spurred on by the black congregation's response. What might have taken on the tone of a lecture turned into an inspirational oration, affecting me as much as anyone there. Now as I reflect on Jarena and the obstacles she faced, I can only hope that she found a welcome in Cape May as warm as I did.

The odds were stacked against Jarena, as they were against Amanda, Mary, and Eliza. But a profound sense of calling spurred them on. Born into slavery, Amanda would travel the world challenging listeners not so much with her own story of rescue from slavery but with the gospel story of salvation from sin and degradation, passed down by her mother and grandmother.

Although Mary was not born into slavery, sharecropping was often little better. Education, however, was the path to freedom. And when the door was closed for mission work in Africa, she made education her primary ministry. There are photos posted online of her entering the White House and visiting with Eleanor Roosevelt and other dignitaries, but the most telling of them all is a photo of her standing on a dirt road, long black skirt, white Victorian long-sleeved blouse, Bible in hand, her head crowned with a stylish hat. Behind her are dozens of children lined up in single file, the first five in white dresses with similar stylish hats, and behind them dozens more clad in white blouses, dark skirts, hats—every one of them wearing shoes. More than that, every one of them acquiring an education.

Eliza also found a path out of poverty through education. She might have become an educator herself, but the call to Africa took precedence. But a black American woman, with no cross-cultural training, is not necessarily an obvious fit in Africa. Complicating matters were her lack of administrative skills and a marriage fraught with moral issues and misunderstandings. But like Jarena, Amanda, and Mary, she was highly motivated. Determination and a call from God transformed them all into the very prophesying daughters of whom the apostle Peter spoke.

QUESTIONS TO THINK ABOUT

Have you ever known anyone personally who was targeted by Satan as Jarena believed she was? Do you believe in a personal devil? Have you ever felt as though you were being attacked by the devil or an evil presence?

Have you ever struggled with atheism as did Amanda? Would you recommend in your situation or other similar instances the forceful response of her aunt? Have you ever interacted with anyone who professed atheism?

How should we assess Mary's incredible career, which might not have occurred were it not for the malice of segregation and racism that prevented her from going to Africa? Have you ever experienced good coming from evil in your own life?

Is it ever okay to marry someone for reasons other than love, as Eliza did? Have you ever known of such a marriage that fell apart—or one that eventually developed into a loving relationship? Why is marriage often so difficult to maintain even when both parties have fallen in love with each other?

Have you ever discussed the sin of racism with others—with others across racial lines? Do you believe most people who enjoy white privilege are unaware of personal or institutionalized racism?

If you were assigned to serve as a partner in ministry to one of these four women, which one would you choose? Which one would be the most difficult to work with?

9

Elizabeth "Betsy" Fry and Women of the Social Gospel

July 1990. I was on holiday, having just finished teaching two three-week intensive courses at Moffat Bible College in Kijabe, Kenya. My son and I, along with our good friends Bud and Joan, were on an overnight train to the lovely coastal tourist town of Mombasa to spend a long weekend in delightful thatched-roof cottages on the Indian Ocean. We dined at seaside buffets and bartered for carvings and masks. We sunbathed on the white sand and snorkeled among the reefs.

I look back at those brief, warm, sunny days with fond memories, though always qualified with a sense of shame. There is a picture that is firmly lodged deep in my memory. After our night on the train en route to Mombasa, we enjoyed an elegant breakfast in the dining car. Then we leisurely strolled along the railed open walkway of the train, taking in the morning sun. We passed fields of women hoeing corn and villages of tiny thatched houses, a few lazy dogs lounging in the dirt yards. Young boys calling out with arms outstretched ran near the tracks hoping for tourist coins.

And then as the train clanged along the tracks, we passed another thatched settlement. Here four small girls scantily dressed stood in a row close enough for me to see their pigtails and dark round eyes. I'll never forget them. We waved. They looked back with a vacant stare. At that moment I felt ashamed of myself. I perceived sadness more than anger on their faces, each one of them. Were they aware that we rich tourists were on our way to a seaside resort in their own country that they could never afford to visit? Were they resentful of my wealth? And who was I that I dared to wave my rich *white-gloved hand* at them—these impoverished little girls? By world standards, I truly am rich.

Today controversy swirls when Pope Francis speaks of the injustice of massive income inequality—a serious problem in America itself. But when we contemplate worldwide poverty, the situation is much worse, particularly where there is no safety net for those in desperate circumstances.

With the picture of those little Kenyan girls in mind, my husband and I decided to get serious about poverty and to significantly increase our giving to a charity that subsidizes school fees for such children. It's one small way that I can respond to the sense of shame that still haunts me. Yes, shame. Misplaced, some would say. Go to a therapist and be done with it. But maybe that visual panorama—a passenger train, a dining car with white tablecloths, formal waiters, a rich American lady waving at sad-faced

I Was in Prison and You Came to Visit Me

Elizabeth, Phoebe, Catherine, and Carry committed themselves to what some define as the "social gospel." Indeed, some would insist that their work is of lesser importance than defending the doctrines and truth of the Bible. But it is critical to point out that their ministries were doing just that in following the very commands of Jesus. Far more than that they were simply doing the work the Bible commanded.

Then the King will say to those on his right, "Come, you who are blessed by my Father; take your inheritance, the kingdom prepared for you since the creation of the world. For I was hungry and you gave me something to eat, I was thirsty and you gave me something to drink, I was a stranger and you little girls—is not forgotten for a reason. Hopefully our funding subsidizes schooling for just such girls.

In the West today it is often assumed that government services support the poor. Sure there is dire poverty in Africa and Asia but not in the developed world. No one would have ever made that false assumption, however, in the nineteenth century. Cities such as New York and London were cesspools of poverty. If you were to climb the rickety steps of a multistory tenement, you would find a dark narrow hallway with one-room, rat-infested family dwellings, sometimes ten or a dozen crammed together with no indoor plumbing. Fathers often hooked on cheap gin, mothers working fourteen-hour days in the mills, children picking up rags or picking pockets. Then, a raging winter fire leaving behind no more than a pile of ashes.

Fortunately there were some rich ladies (and many others) who took up the cause of the poor. Elizabeth Fry was a tireless worker for women and children imprisoned in London. Phoebe Palmer founded the Five Points Mission in New York City. Catherine Booth cofounded the Salvation Army; Evangeline, her daughter, also served the needy as did Carry Nation, Frances Willard, and Florence Nightingale. As a group they illustrate the diversity among hundreds of women who served in similar capacities.

> invited me in, I needed clothes and you clothed me, I was sick and you looked after me, I was in prison and you came to visit me."
>
> Then the righteous will answer him, "Lord, when did we see you hungry and feed you, or thirsty and give you something to drink? When did we see you a stranger and invite you in, or needing clothes and clothe you? When did we see you sick or in prison and go to visit you?"
>
> The King will reply, "Truly I tell you, whatever you did for one of the least of these brothers and sisters of mine, you did for me."
>
> Matthew 25:34–40

ELIZABETH "BETSY" FRY
Prison Reformer

Unlike her predecessor Margaret Fell, who risked wealth and social status to convert to the low-class *cult* of Quakers, Elizabeth "Betsy" Gurney Fry was born into Quaker wealth more than a century and a half later. Members of this once-despised movement had quickly moved into the merchant class and beyond. Betsy's father, John Gurney, was a partner in the Gurney Bank; her mother, Catherine Barclay, grew up in the family of the Barclay banking giants. Two wealthy fashionable Quaker families. How times had changed. And it is no surprise that Elizabeth married banker Joseph Fry.

For Margaret Fell and Elizabeth Fry, prison was a common denominator. Margaret was a religious outlaw repeatedly sentenced to languish in foul dungeons, while Elizabeth freely entered these stinking hellholes to serve the inmates and fight for reform. Although Quakers over the generations

Florence Nightingale: Lady with a Lamp

That she was beautiful, as photographs attest, did not hurt her reputation. Wounded soldiers called out and kissed her shadow as she passed by in the night. Queen Victoria sent her words of praise and later became her friend. She was England's most celebrated nineteenth-century heroine. She was born into privilege, and it was simply assumed that she would marry well and carry on the family pedigree. But in 1837 at age seventeen, though not spiritually inclined, she sensed the voice of God calling her to service. But what could a woman do? In England, only Catholic women served God in full-time capacities. Despite her parents' objections, she later traveled to Germany and trained as a nurse at a Lutheran deaconess training school. Through family connections, she had known the British secretary of war, and when the Crimean War broke out, he appointed her to head the nursing corps for the English hospitals in Turkey. That position launched her into a vocation that profoundly changed life back home as well. She set up nursing schools and published literature and is considered by many to be the founder of modern nursing. Hers was a lifetime of service that began with the voice of God.

had made incredible progress, the prisons had not. What an awful shame on the English people. This was an age of lavish wealth. But those on the lower rungs of society suffered as much as they had during the English civil wars—during the days of Margaret Fell Fox.

Life even among the wealthy—then as now—did not escape tragedy. When Elizabeth was only twelve years old, her mother died, a great sorrow that suddenly turned her into a mother of younger siblings. Responsibility, to be sure, but certainly not without riches. There were household servants and liberal allowances for all the fancy clothes and accessories Betsy and her sisters could want. And how fun it was to either skip Sunday meeting altogether or to strut with their finery in front of plain-dressed Quakers.

It was during one such meeting that the eighteen-year-old Elizabeth, clad in a colorful dress and "wearing purple boots with scarlet laces," heard a message by a visiting preacher from America. His words pricked her heart. Her life would never be the same. But not so fast. How could she give up all that was rightfully hers? Back home from the meeting she was of two minds. How awful it would be to turn into a "plain" Quaker. She loved her clothes and her visits to London, the opera and theater.

In the months that followed she struggled. She shunned the idea of being different from her father and siblings, and she knew that plain dress would embarrass them. But her own conscience and the sense of God's calling proved strong. She determined to devote her life to serving those whom Jesus identified as the least of these: the sick, the poor, and prisoners. And she would begin immediately. Her first outreach effort took her no further than the laundry room of the family estate. She invited poor children to listen to Bible stories at her Sunday school—more than that, she taught them to read and write. Her sisters lightheartedly called the ragtag assembly Betsy's imps.

Elizabeth would never renounce her call to minister to the less fortunate, but that sense of duty would be interrupted by her marriage and the eleven children she bore. Then during the Christmas season of 1816, only months after her tenth child was born, she began the prison work for which she is remembered today. Some years earlier she had visited Newgate Prison and observed the appalling conditions. Now she was determined to do something about the situation. Her first order of business, at the recommendation of the women prisoners themselves, was to set up a school for children who were incarcerated with their mothers. Her next order of business was to form the Newgate Association and corral other women to join her in the work and, perhaps equally important, to testify before a committee in the House of Commons.

In the years that followed she instituted sewing, cooking, and literacy classes at the prison and launched other societies to serve the needy outside prisons. As hectic as her schedule was, she would later establish a nursing school that predated the work of Florence Nightingale by several years. Through this training program she supplied nurses for Nightingale's work of mercy in the bloody Crimean War.

During these years of service, Elizabeth held forth as the matron of her large household. Her husband's family, wealthy merchants who imported coffee, tea, and spice, had moved into banking. As affluent as they were, they held tight to their Quaker speech of *thee* and *thou* and their plain dress. Elizabeth, in their eyes, was not plain enough. Her husband agreed, suggesting that her personality was too high-class—*too much of the courtier*. Try as she might, it was not easy to entirely abandon the sense of style that had previously been so much a part of her life.

Besides criticism from husband and in-laws, Elizabeth struggled with the exhaustion of childbirth and constant household demands. Her diary expressed what she could not say outwardly. She was becoming "a careworn and oppressed mother." Later she lamented: "I fear that my life is slipping away to little purpose."[1] Yet she soldiered on, working among the most downtrodden of society. In her spare time she wrote a book on the necessity of better treatment of female prisoners, published in 1827.

Then in 1828, the unthinkable occurred. Her husband's bank went under and with it, not only the assets of her immediate family but also the investments of many others, particularly people they knew well among the Quakers. He was removed from membership—"disowned"—by the Quaker meetinghouse, and she was accused of using investors' money for her charities. From available records, it appears as though Fry was guilty of mismanagement, if not fraud. That Elizabeth had raided the family coffers for her work was widely known. That investors' money was comingled with family funds is entirely possible.

For Elizabeth the shame of the scandal was only part of the awful anguish. The family was forced to leave Plashet House, a grand mansion facing a large fishpond on a beautifully landscaped estate with manicured lawns. Who knew? That she had slept on the floor in prisons with coarse women inmates, it turns out, was only a small portion of her story. She had lived a life of luxury with costly furniture and rugs and artwork and tableware. Now her possessions were being hauled away by creditors. Memories were all that was left to fill the empty rooms with high ceilings—rooms that were soon to be furnished and filled by others. A cloud of darkness and depression descended upon her. In her diary, she wrote that it was like living through a funeral.

But Elizabeth had lost far more than her good reputation and material possessions. With no money, how could she carry on with her charitable work? Many impoverished people depended on her for bare sustenance and for sustaining the village schools. Now everything was lost. In subsequent years she only slowly came to terms with her new life. Indeed, by 1835, she viewed herself in the prime of life. Her Friday Newgate readings were once again popular prison events, drawing large crowds, and she was seeing real changes among the prisoners.

As is often true, there was competition from others—"reformers" sought to counter Elizabeth's work with strong bureaucratic oversight that left no place for the "meddlesome" women's societies. But before she died in 1845, she had been heralded as a true British treasure. She was widely recognized for her selfless service to prison inmates and the underprivileged in all realms of society. Among her admirers were Queen Victoria, who supported her ministry, and the king of Prussia, Frederick William IV, who, while on state business in 1842, visited Newgate Prison for one of her Friday readings.

PHOEBE PALMER
Preacher, Writer, Mission Founder, and Theologian

How could anyone justify a woman's public preaching in light of the nineteenth-century consensus that a woman must keep silent in church? True, Margaret Fell had answered objections in *Women's Speaking Justified.*

147

Fry and the Five Pound Note

Prison reformer Elizabeth Fry is the new face of the English five pound note. Though undoubtedly a member of the great and good, is she a slightly obscure choice for this rare honour? [She] was selected to go on the five pound note and end a decade during which the only woman on our paper money was the Queen. The bank's Court of Directors opted for "the angel of the prisons" from a shortlist headed by novelist Jane Austen, poet Elizabeth Barrett Browning and Octavia Hill, founder of the National Trust.

BBC News, May 21, 2002

But that short booklet was published nearly two centuries earlier and by a long-forgotten Quaker. The time was ripe. In 1859, Phoebe Palmer published a hefty four-hundred-page volume, capturing the answer to that question in the title, *Promise of the Father*. Her thesis was her strongly held conviction that God's promise to pour out his Spirit on both sons and daughters was no less than biblical truth. These were the very words of the prophet Joel repeated again at Pentecost. That ministers and men in general had sought to prevent women's speaking and prophesying was to her a great travesty. She did not mince words in making her case:

> We believe that hundreds of conscientious, sensitive Christian women have actually suffered more under the slowly crucifying process to which they have been subjected by men who bear the Christian name than many a martyr has endured in passing through the flames.[2]

Such religious feminism had long been practiced—and in some cases preached—by women, from Hildegard to Katherine Zell and Margaret Fell. But Phoebe's most immediate influence came from Methodists such as Susanna Wesley, Mary Fletcher, and others. Her long and laborious defense of such ministry, however, began deep in the Old Testament. We should not be surprised that she references in her twenty-one chapters Deborah, Huldah, Philip's daughters, even Isaiah's wife. But that she cites

148

the second-century *Dialogue* between Justin Martyr and Trypho the Jew indicates the scope of her research.

Phoebe was born in New York City into a family of devout Methodists. In fact, her father had been converted through the preaching of John Wesley himself. She could not remember a time of not having strong religious faith, but the Wesleyan doctrine and practice of entire sanctification eluded her, and she feared at times for her own salvation. God for her was a fearsome deity who demanded absolute surrender.

When her first child died, she was convinced that God took him because she was too devoted to the little one. She sensed God speaking: "Thou must resign thy child." After the death of her second child, she wrote:

> I will not attempt to describe the pressure of the last crushing trial. Surely I needed it, or it would not have been given. . . . The Lord had declared himself a jealous God; He will have no other Gods before Him. After my loved ones were snatched away, I saw that I had concentrated my time and attentions far too exclusively, to the neglect of the religious activities demanded.[3]

Her fourth child, Eliza, died in a house fire: "Never have I passed through a trial so severe." But now Phoebe knew for certain that God meant business: "The time I would have devoted to her, shall be spent in work for Jesus." With this additional time she testified that she was transformed into "a monument of what the grace of God can effect on a once rebellious child of Adam," asserting, "O! this, I am sure, is a holy ambition, and authorized by Scripture."[4]

It was on a summer night in 1837, the year Queen Victoria ascended the English throne, that Phoebe, at her home in New York, having been influenced by her sister, Sarah, realized her "holy ambition," her "day of days": "My heart was emptied of self, and cleansed of all idols, from all filthiness of the flesh and spirit. . . . I saw that the High and Holy One would have me enter into covenant with Him, the duration of which would be lasting an eternity, absolute, and unconditional."[5]

Though she was married to Walter, the Lord now asked her, "betroth thee unto Me forever," which would mean giving up her husband, "one with which every fibre of [her] being seemed interwoven." How could

God require such a thing: "Did Abraham know *why* he was called to give up Isaac at the *time* he gave him up?"[6] But as God had stayed the hand of Abraham, he stayed his hand and gave Phoebe more children by her husband.

To understand Phoebe is to understand her seriousness about life. There appears to be no fun or humor or playfulness. She quickly moved beyond indescribable losses to her solemn call to holiness. Charles Edward White, her biographer, suggests that her severity in looks and dress and overall manner as well as her lack of emotion capture the essence of her character. It is no exaggeration to imagine her a spoilsport, a wet blanket, a killjoy, a party pooper, an overall straight-laced sourpuss. Twice she wrote (unanswered) letters to Queen Victoria reprimanding her for her Sunday activities such as yacht excursions—activity that could risk her very eternal destiny. Other women of this era, including Hannah Whitall Smith and Mary Slessor, revealed a much lighter side, as we shall see.

With her assurance of entire sanctification, Phoebe joined her sister, Sarah Lankford, in leading the celebrated Tuesday Meetings ("for the promotion of Holiness"). In 1840, after her sister had left the area, she became the teacher of this gathering, which soon filled her large home to standing room only, both men and women. With a move to a larger home, she was able to accommodate as many as three hundred, including ministers, even bishops, from various denominational backgrounds.

These meetings as well as her publication, *The Guide to Holiness*, paved the way for Phoebe's revival ministry. She left behind her surviving children with Walter and a maid, though he later joined her part-time. "Never have we witnessed such triumphs of the cross as during the past summer and fall," she reported in 1857. "Not less than two thousand have been gathered into the fold. . . . Hundreds of believers have been sanctified wholly, and hundreds have received baptism of the Holy Ghost, beyond any former experienced."[7] Her travels took her into Canada and on to the British Isles, where she (as well as Walter) preached sometimes four or five times a day. Meticulous records were kept, with an estimated twenty-five thousand decisions.

The tallied decisions were not for salvation only. Her plea was for sanctification as well. How, one might ask, could a person make an on-the-spot decision for entire sanctification? It is that issue that separates Phoebe from those who came before her. Whereas John Wesley had viewed sanctification as a process, she preached her "Altar Theology" whereby entire sanctification was bestowed instantaneously: "How soon may I expect to arrive at this state of perfection?" she asked her audience. "Just so soon as you come believingly, and make the required sacrifice, it will be done unto you according to your faith. . . . When the Savior said, 'It is finished!' then this full salvation was wrought out for you. All that remains is for you to come complying with the conditions, and claim it."[8]

The experience required three short steps: placing one's sacrifice or all on the altar, faith in God's promise of entire sanctification, and publicly testifying to the experience. The third step was the kicker. Who would be so bold—so arrogant, perhaps—to claim to be entirely sanctified? Her answer was that no evidence or particular holiness was necessary for verification. If someone were to question the testimony because of an apparent lack of holiness in the individual's life, all she need do is point the person to God and his promise. Case closed.

In addition to her Tuesday Meetings and her revival campaigns, Phoebe was involved in a wide variety of humanitarian endeavors, including temperance activities. Her best known outreach was her Five Points Mission in one of New York City's worst slums, a district the visiting Charles Dickens declared to be as filthy and decayed as anything in London—a no-man's-land filled with crime and debauchery of every description. Here Phoebe

Phoebe Palmer's Altered Theology?

Theological differences become apparent swiftly when the teachings of Phoebe Palmer on entire sanctification are contrasted with John Wesley's own. In stark contrast to Wesley's vision of a lengthy, often difficult effort concluding with sanctification, Palmer expressed sanctification as a state of being that all believers could achieve in an instant. This was a viewpoint that Wesley had specifically warned against, as can be seen in the *Minutes of the Methodist Conference* (1771).

Chad Elliott, "Altar Theology or Altered Theology?—Part Two" set up her mission, offering housing, health care, and schooling for the poorest of the poor.

After her death in 1874, Phoebe's widowed sister, Sarah, returned to lead the Tuesday Meetings as well as edit *The Guide to Holiness*. Two years later she married Walter Palmer, Phoebe's widower.

CATHERINE BOOTH
Mother of the Salvation Army

Criticism of Phoebe Palmer challenged Catherine Booth to investigate for herself the topic of women in public ministry. Phoebe, with her husband at her side, had been invited by supporters to minister in England and had received a warm welcome. But many respectable Brits were shocked by such impropriety—the audacity of an American woman presuming to preach from the pulpit, and to a mixed audience no less.

For Catherine, now married and approaching thirty, the subject of women's equality was not new. Indeed, she had raised the issue some seven years earlier before she agreed to marry William Booth. While they were courting, he had commented in a letter to her that while he had high regard for her he suspected that she had "a fibre more in her heart and a cell less in her brain"[9] than he. Such a statement, he should have realized, was neither a good pickup line nor one that would advance their courtship. Her response was unequivocal. She would never marry a man who did not regard her as his full equal. William backed down.

Catherine Mumford Booth is most remembered as the cofounder of the Salvation Army. Without her enormous influence, it is difficult to imagine where that organization would be today. She was born in Derbyshire, England, in 1829, eight years before Queen Victoria began her more than sixty-year reign. A precocious child, often sickly, she spent her childhood reading. Encouraged by her parents, she read the Bible many times over before she reached her teens. Her father was a lay Methodist minister and carriage builder who would later become an alcoholic and lose his faith.

Phoebe's preaching spurred Catherine not only to search the Scriptures but also to wonder if she might preach herself. She had been active in the temperance movement, but the thought of public speaking terrified her. By her own testimony she had from childhood been "one of the most timid and bashful disciples the Lord Jesus ever saved."[10] But then one Sunday after her husband had finished his sermon, she stood with no forethought and added her own short message. William was so taken by surprise that when she was finished, he had no further word except to announce that she would speak that evening. And thus her preaching career was launched.

It soon became evident that they had two entirely different preaching styles and audiences. William reached out to the down-and-out in East London, while Catherine preached to large crowds in London's well-heeled West End. She defended her ministry with appropriate Scripture texts, convinced that it was the devil who kept women from the pulpit: "The Spirit [at Pentecost] was given alike to the female as to the male disciple. . . . What a remarkable device of the devil that he has so long succeeded in hiding this characteristic of the latter-day glory!"[11]

Like Margaret Fell some two centuries earlier, she published a booklet justifying women's public ministry. She minced no words in *Female Ministry: Or, Woman's Right to Preach the Gospel*: "Judging from the blessed results which have almost invariably followed the ministrations of women in the cause of Christ, we fear it will be found, in the great day of account, that a mistaken and unjustifiable application of the passage, 'Let you women keep silence in the Churches,' has resulted in more loss to the Church, evil to the world, and dishonour to God, than any of the errors we have already referred to."[12]

Catherine's West End preaching supported the growing family, while William continued his ministry to the poor. Then in 1873, more than a decade after she had published *Female Ministry*, she began preaching in Portsmouth, which proved most successful in terms of numbers, sometimes drawing as many as three thousand people packed in a large music hall. She was a dynamic speaker. Her son Bramwell likened her to an attorney: "She reminded me again and again of counsel pleading with judge and jury for the life of the prisoner. The fixed attention of the court, the mastery of facts, the absolute self-forgetfulness of the advocate, the ebb and flow of feeling, the hush during the vital passages—all were there."[13]

Catherine's concern for the poor was no less than that of her husband, who focused particularly on men addicted to alcohol. Her passion was aimed at the terrible plight of prostitutes, many of them mothers who sold their bodies to feed their little ones—women whose husbands threw their wages away on cheap gin. Out of their joint efforts, the Salvation Army was born. From these early converts came their pool of volunteers, including transformed prostitutes. From the beginning women played an important role in the ministry. They worked in teams and were billed as the "Hallelujah Lassies."

For Catherine, the most difficult aspect of her all-consuming ministry was the consequent loss of family togetherness. At the time of her daughter's wedding, she wrote:

> Mothers will understand . . . a side of life to which my child is yet a stranger. Having experienced the weight of public work for twenty-six years, also the weight of a large family continually hanging on my heart, having striven very hard to fulfill the obligation on both sides, and having realized what a very hard struggle it has been, the mother's heart in me has shrunk in some measure from offering her up to the same kind of warfare.[14]

Her struggle in denying herself the joys of family life for the sake of the poor can be understood only in light of Jesus's words to forsake all for the gospel. Others before and after her had made such sacrifices. But to read her excruciating death is far more difficult. She died in 1890, after having undergone unsuccessful surgery for breast cancer. Refusing morphine on religious grounds, her agony was only relieved by death.

During the preceding months, however, she dictated hundreds of letters encouraging others, while suffering unspeakable pain herself, as William's diary entries attest:

> A large part of the breast has fallen off, and [Salvation Army Captain] Carr has cut it away and left the gaping wound which is simply one mass of cancer.
> She exclaimed again and again as she started with the stabbing pains, which like lightning flashes started in her poor bosom, "Oh, these fiery scorpions! These fiery scorpions!"

Evangeline Booth: Salvation Army Lassie and General

All of the Booth children went into ministry, Evangeline being the most prominent. For eight years she served as the commander in Canada, after that as the American commander (1904 to 1934), and finally as general of the Salvation Army, though over her brother's fierce objections, causing serious family discord. At fifteen she had become a Hallelujah Lassie, and she never lost her flare for the dramatic, drawing larger audiences than her mother ever had. Her name illustrates the networking among nineteenth-century women leaders. Having read Harriet Beecher Stowe's *Uncle Tom's Cabin*, Catherine named her baby after the girl heroine, Eva; William changed her name on her birth certificate to Evelyne. However, when she was an adult serving in America, she was persuaded by Frances Willard (founder of the Woman's Christian Temperance Union) to change her name to Evangeline (the full name of the fictional Eva).

Two nurses are required, seeing she is so very helpless, and the breast has to be repeatedly dressed to keep the fiery flame that burns night and day anything like down. . . .

My darling had a night of agony. When I went into her room at two a.m. she had not closed her eyes. The breast was in an awful condition. They were endeavouring to staunch a fresh haemorrhage. Everything was saturated with the blood.[15]

CARRY NATION
Hatchet-Wielding Temperance Reformer

She was a wild and crazy hatchet-wielding saloon smasher. That is how we remember her. Google her image, and you see her familiar pose. She thrived on publicity and was always poised for headlines. If she were alive today, every avenue of social media would be exploited to promote her causes. Yet as was true in her own day, she still remains difficult to pigeonhole. Was she the leader of some sort of right-wing, homegrown militia? Was she a radical in the tradition of John Brown? Or was she a do-gooder somewhere in the middle?

Almost anything that has been written about this woman has been exaggerated or falsified or simply misunderstood. She was not a manly Amazon who stood over six feet tall. She was by no means the first saloon smasher. She had friends and supporters in high places while she languished in small-town jails. She was a Protestant fundamentalist who had broad ecumenical leanings and was often seen going to Catholic mass. She was both a conservative prohibitionist and a liberal civil rights activist; she demanded women's rights and was deeply concerned for the poor, both black and white.

Carry was not widely regarded as a crazy fanatic in her day—at least not in Kansas and other western states. She considered herself first and foremost a Christian preacher. She was well-versed in the Bible and was photographed with it wherever she went—never with a hatchet alone but often with just the Bible. Although she was a shameless self-promoter, hawking her souvenir hatchets, her generosity was legendary, and she refused to lodge or dine in anything but cheap establishments.

Not until God called, she insisted, did she become a smasher. She awakened on the morning of June 5, 1899, to a "murmuring musical" voice saying, "Go to Kiowa," and "I'll stand by you." It was very clear that God was telling her to "smash" a saloon as others had done before her. "I threw as hard, and as fast as I could," she later recalled, "smashing mirrors and bottles and glasses and it was astonishing how quickly this was done. These men seemed terrified, threw up their hands and backed up

The Most Conspicuous Woman of Her Time

Carry Nation was a national phenomenon, possibly "the most conspicuous woman" of her time. . . . [She] did what few other performers did in her time—moved back and forth between Chautauqua, Broadway, vaudeville, burlesque, pulpit, and music-hall stages.

Fran Grace, *Carry A. Nation*

in the corner. My strength was that of a giant. I felt invincible. God was certainly standing by me."[16]

Carry's first husband was an alcoholic who left her behind to raise her baby. Most of her life, until that fateful summer day in 1899, was consumed with domestic and business activities, often on the move following the whims of her second husband, David Nation. Indeed, after settling in and establishing a successful boardinghouse in Texas, he insisted they move to Kansas and leave behind all her hard work.

There she joined in protests against alcohol and marched with other women as early as 1894. But before 1899 she was known primarily for her Sunday school teaching and her work as a doctor of osteopathy. True, she

Frances Willard: Suffragette and Social Activist

A lifelong Methodist, Frances Willard was a teacher, a two-time president of the Evanston College for Ladies, and the first dean of women at Northwestern University. But she is best known as the celebrated second president of the WCTU. Frances broadened the scope of the organization with her understanding that temperance alone was not enough to confront the issues that were tearing families apart. Under her leadership, the Union called for an eight-hour workday, free public education and school lunches, women's higher education and suffrage, welfare and sanitation programs for the poor, and laws against child abuse and rape. Though she has been identified by some as a lesbian, her nineteenth-century definition of a same-sex relationship would not necessarily have included sexual intimacies. In her autobiography, *Glimpses of Fifty Years*, she wrote:

> The loves of women for each other grow more numerous each day, and I have pondered much why these things were. That so little should be said about them surprises me, for they are everywhere. . . . In these days when any capable and careful woman can honorably earn her own support, there is no village that has not its examples of "two hearts in counsel," both of which are feminine.

had no respect for the moral-suasion concept of the WCTU (Woman's Christian Temperance Union), but she had not yet made a name for herself as a saloon smasher.

She used the Bible to justify her radical turnabout, sometimes comparing herself to the biblical Deborah. On other occasions she took her cue from Moses, who smashed the stone commandments, and from Jesus, who drove the money changers out of the temple. When her husband said somewhat in jest that she might be more effective wielding a hatchet, she took him up on it and found her own unique symbol. The hatchet quickly caught on and others joined her, including some well-known sophisticated women.

Carry's new activism and strong personality were not conducive to marriage, certainly not to a man who expected a woman to cater to his every need. His 1901 divorce petition stated that she was "guilty of extreme cruelty" by her neglect of him while she had been caring for "the poor and down-trodden."[17] Now, with her marriage over, she was entirely free to travel and speak. But as a divorced woman, her domestic life was put to the test and was found wanting. Her married daughter with young children was mentally unstable. Was that the fault of Carry—and, many asked, was Carry herself unstable?

Carry, however, never let controversy stop her, and slander seemed not to harm her cause. She would carry on to the very end, always emphasizing good works over smashing saloons. She died in 1911, at age sixty-five.

CONCLUDING OBSERVATIONS

For a historian, the decision on how to present individuals and events and who and what to include is always a struggle. History makes no sense if everything is presented in chronological order as it happens, thus topical grouping is a necessity. The same goes for a biographical history as this book purports to be. I am always pleased, therefore, when I discover that someone else has grouped individuals or events in similar ways. Such was true when I came upon this quote by Catherine Booth:

> Will any one venture to assert that such women as Mrs. Elizabeth Fry, Mrs. Fletcher of Madely, and Mrs. [Hannah Whitall] Smith have been deceived

158

with respect to their call to deliver the gospel messages to their fellow-creatures? If not, then God does call and qualify women to preach, and His word, rightly understood, cannot forbid what His Spirit enjoins. . . . Nor are the instances of the spirit of prophecy bestowed on women confined to by-gone generations: the revival of this age, as well as of every other, has been marked by this endowment, and the labours of such pious and talented ladies as Mrs. Palmer.[18]

If we take into account Catherine herself, three of the women included in this chapter are cited by her; Hannah Smith and Mary Fletcher have found their way into other chapters. The quote is taken from Catherine's book, *Female Ministry: Or, Woman's Right to Preach the Gospel*, first published in 1859. Catherine's primary concern here was preaching as opposed to across-the-board equality. Her feminism, like that of Lottie Moon and countless other Christian women, was self-sacrificing more than self-serving.

Indeed, very few Christian women prior to the late twentieth century imagined themselves contending for equal rights per se. They regarded God's call as far more significant than gender equality, though it is true that Catherine herself had more feminist inclinations, particularly in marriage, than did most of her contemporaries. Even women's suffrage (opposed by many Christian women) was stressed not as a right but rather as a responsibility for the purpose of voting for temperance.

This was true of Carry as well. To view her primarily as a strong-armed, hatchet-wielding performer fails to understand the profound connection between poverty, prison, and alcohol during this era. Her prohibitionist stance was prompted by her deep concern for the poor, particularly women and children.

QUESTIONS TO THINK ABOUT

Have you or anyone you have known ever gone bankrupt or struggled with poverty after enjoying relative wealth, as Elizabeth did? Have you ever fallen prey to someone else's reckless financial decisions, worse yet, a fellow Christian you trusted? Should a wife bear the shame of her husband's decisions that have hurt others?

How should we assess Phoebe Palmer and her belief that God was taking her little ones as punishment for her unbelief? From this are we to infer that God chastised her as a "rebellious child of Adam" for her devotion to her little girl? "There is something monstrous," one author writes, "in such holiness."[19] Do you agree?

If Christian ministry were defined more in terms of service and evangelism (as the Booths defined it) rather than authority and headship, do you think the debates over women in ministry and ordination would be less contentious? Do you know any women who have been denied ministry opportunities due to gender?

If you had been involved in the temperance movement of a century ago, would you have shunned Carry Nation or joined with her? Do you know any eccentric women like her involved in ministry today?

If you had the opportunity to interview just one of these women—Elizabeth, Phoebe, Catherine, or Carry—which one would you choose? Which one would you most eagerly welcome into your Bible study, book club, or potluck group?

10

Anne-Marie Javouhey and British and European Missionaries

Who is your favorite biblical character? I am sometimes asked that question when I am being interviewed on my books *The Biographical Bible* and *Dynamic Women of the Bible*. The word *favorite* is not the word I would use because it suggests the one I like best—like my favorite flavor of ice cream. But my favorite biblical character is the one I find most fascinating. King Saul sometimes holds that position for me. We meet him as a youth with everything going for him. He is handpicked by the prophet Samuel to be Israel's first king, but he thoroughly botches things up. He struggles with mental illness, and in the end, just after he has gone to a witch to contact the spirit of the deceased prophet Samuel, he's wounded in battle and commits suicide by falling on his sword. Would I want to hang around with Saul? Surely not, but his is the kind of story that biographers relish.

My favorite figures in church history are similar. For me it is more difficult to recount in an interesting way the life of a super-saint who has no identifiable flaws or failures. I want my characters to be real, not plaster saints of medieval hagiography. I've been faulted for writing too much about the sins of the saints, but others have found encouragement in how God has used flawed individuals. Often the flaws and imperfections combine with eccentricities. How true of Anne-Marie and Mary Slessor. Mary was a pioneer missionary to Africa who climbed trees when she was bored. Writing in her Scottish dialect, she chided the apostle Paul in the margin of her Bible for his insistence on wifely submission: "Nay, nay, Paul, laddie, that will not do."[1]

Anne-Marie Javouhey did far more than chide her bishop when they clashed over which one of them wielded final authority over her mission society. Amy Carmichael, a missionary to India, often considered too good to be true, clashed with a fellow missionary in such a way that two lives were nearly ruined. Gladys Aylward set out on a journey across two entire continents with pots and pans clanging from her baggage. In fact, she endured such an unbelievable series of events that her life story was turned into a movie starring Ingrid Bergman. Such conflicts and quirks intrigue me and fire up my curiosity to dig deeper. Mildred Cable traveled nearly as far on her trek through China on the Silk Road to the Gobi Desert beyond the Great Wall.

Anne-Marie was the first of these women to claim God's call to the far-flung fields of foreign missions, and she did not stop. One ship's captain declared her to be his "most seasoned sailor." Unlike the others featured in this chapter, who were Protestants and hailed from the United Kingdom, she was French and a devout Catholic as was Madeleine Sophie Barat. Unfortunately these missionary women have suffered from biographers who have given them super-saint status. But if remarkable holiness does not sum up their personalities, a strong will, an independent spirit, and more than a touch of eccentricity certainly do. They simply refused to be pushed around. Having sacrificed so much for overseas ministry, they were bound and determined to carry out their callings.

ANNE-MARIE JAVOUHEY
Founder of the Sisters of Saint Joseph

Venerated and beatified, though not yet canonized, the blessed and holy Anne-Marie Javouhey takes her place among thousands of other Catholic

The Missionary Call of God

For Amy Carmichael, the call was simple: the Lord said "Go ye," and she went. For others it was more complicated, but for all of them, the apostle Paul's missionary call to Macedonia had laid the foundation for missions abroad.

> Paul and his companions traveled throughout the region of Phrygia and Galatia, having been kept by the Holy Spirit from preaching the word in the province of Asia. When they came to the border of Mysia, they tried to enter Bithynia, but the Spirit of Jesus would not allow them to. So they passed by Mysia and went down to Troas. During the night Paul had a vision of a man of Macedonia standing and begging him, "Come over to Macedonia and help us." After Paul had seen the vision, we got ready at once to leave for Macedonia, con-cluding that God had called us to preach the gospel to them.
>
> Acts 16:6–10

saints or would-be saints. In many ways, however, this French nun stands alone and is far better served without the official designations that often distort more than they describe. She challenges us in her strong convictions more than in her so-called saintliness. Today it is tempting to take her side in the fierce struggle she waged with her bishop and simply dismiss his point of view. But there is surely no denying that from his standpoint she was no saint.

Born into a prosperous family, she was the fifth of ten children. From childhood, she had a resolute mind of her own, and during the French Revolution (which erupted when she was nine), she would stand guard to warn priests and nuns whose very lives were in danger. The whole of society seemed to be turning upside down, and she feared for the future of the church and dreamed of one day helping to reverse the losses. At nineteen, by way of a visionary call that included dozens of dark-skinned children, she received her marching orders. A voice spoke: "These are the children God has given you. He wishes you to form a new congregation to take care of them. I am Teresa [of Ávila]. I will be your protectress."[2]

This call to ministry is stunning, especially if we assume that she had not been contemplating such a ministry before the vision in the night. She had already become a novitiate with the Sisters of Charity, though she had not yet taken her final vows. But in less than a decade, having moved from convent to convent, she had founded the Sisters of Saint Joseph, and some years later would establish her base in an abandoned monastery at Cluny purchased by her father. Among those who served alongside her were three of her sisters. In the early years the nuns focused on the needs of the poor and on education in the aftermath of the revolution.

By the 1820s, however, she had launched missionary work in Africa, where she was involved in a variety of charitable endeavors in Senegal, Sierra Leone, and Gambia. Her most far-reaching endeavor began in 1828, when she was commissioned, with help from the French government, including the king and queen, to establish a settlement in Guyana (South America), to be known as Mana. Only months after she arrived, she wrote:

> Everything is progressing steadily towards good order—the work is moving forward, the lands under cultivation are visibly growing, religion is becoming stronger in the hearts of those who had only a superficial idea of it, and all this by means of good example. . . . We brought with us fifteen well-chosen workers for the most useful trades. . . . With the good Sisters, I am hoeing and planting beans and cassava; I am sowing rice, corn, etc., as I sing canticles, tell stories, and regret that our poor Sisters in France are not sharing our happiness.[3]

As carefree as she sounded, her assignment was daunting. Her job was to oversee a large tract of land—a safe haven for some five hundred slaves who had been taken by force from slave traffickers. Though she spoke of her task as being "a mother in the middle of a large family," the risks were high, and there was danger at every turn. Nevertheless, she oversaw the farming venture and health care and educational facilities, all of which were infused with her devout Catholic faith. In 1838, a decade after she arrived, she presided over a ceremony that gave nearly two hundred slaves their freedom.

Madeleine Sophie Barat: Nun for Whom a Toy Was Named

Anne-Marie was not the only wayward nun in France. Madeleine Sophie Barat, the same age as Anne-Marie, was the founder and director of the Society of the Sacred Heart. She battled the archbishop of Paris, who sought to wrest from her control of the order. She sought support from the presiding cardinal and Pope Gregory XVI. "Into what abyss they are plunging a work which," she wrote, "should be supported and protected wherever we are established." In the end, she was forced to back down, a move that may have abetted the decision to canonize her in 1925. Sophie the Giraffe, a French children's toy (and best-selling toy on Amazon), was named for her because it went into production on her feast day—May 25, 1961.

The success of her work was not appreciated by everyone, particularly Bishop d'Héricourt, a onetime military officer, whose diocese included her convent in Cluny. He maintained that he, as her bishop, was the head of the religious order, and that she had sought to "extricate herself from episcopal authority" by, among other things, appointing nuns without his approval. She regarded his claim to authority preposterous: "I am not only the Superior General of the Congregation of St. Joseph of Cluny; I did not merely cooperate in the foundation of that Order; I am its sole and solitary foundress. I am its Mother General as God is its Father, since it is I who created and have developed it."[4]

In her lengthy dispute with her bishop, she did not so much fear the loss of her seasoned nuns, many of whom were stationed abroad and loyal to a fault. But he threatened to close her convent in Cluny and return all the novices to their families. What he actually did was to inform them that their very salvation was at risk by having entered a religious order whose founder was in "open revolt against bishops and against the church." He likewise reminded other bishops that "episcopal authority sticks together" and that this was a time when "more than ever [they] had] to stay united."[5]

Like Bishop d'Héricourt, Anne-Marie herself was an authoritarian leader whose orders came straight from the Almighty: "God has made known to me what he wants me to do."[6] As to the bishop, she argued that he was her superior only in personal matters—that he was not the superior over her religious order. He agreed, at least on the former point, and took it upon himself to excommunicate her, thus denying her the Eucharist while her nuns were able to partake.

In the end she won the battle when the archbishop sided with her. But she was physically exhausted by the ordeal. With a tone of lighthearted sarcasm, she credited him as a benefactor of the sisters: "God made use of him to try us when as a rule we were hearing around us nothing but praise. That was necessary, for since our congregation was succeeding so well we might have thought we were something if we hadn't had these pains and contradictions."[7]

When she learned of his death, she wrote to one of her nuns: "We almost met, he and I, on that very day, before the judgment seat of God. So he's gone in ahead of me, that good Bishop. Well, that is correct; that is how it ought to be."[8]

Mary Mitchell Slessor
Missionary and Magistrate

Like her hero, the great missionary explorer David Livingstone, Mary Slessor was part of the vast and largely undocumented child labor force in the nineteenth-century Scottish textile mills. By the time she was fourteen, she had become the family's primary wage earner, working twelve-hour shifts and attending classes at night. Her paltry earnings intended to support the large family were squandered by her abusive alcoholic father. Life was grim. But Mary was by nature optimistic and carefree—and, like her mother, a devout Christian.

It was not until she was in her twenties that Mary's early childhood vision of following in the footsteps of Livingstone began to take form. Her father died in 1870 and three years later her older brother, who her mother had hoped would serve in Africa. With his death and the news of Livingstone's death in 1873, Mary was now confident that her time had come.

Ministry was surely not new to her. From her youth she had taught Sunday school and for some years had been actively involved in the work of the Queen Street Mission, which served the blighted slums of Dundee, marked by street gangs, open sewers, sickness, and poverty. Yet she left her mark. Years later an elderly resident spoke of her sacrificial ministry: "She sat down among the poor as one of themselves. . . . She stooped very low. She became an angel of mercy in miserable homes."[9]

This description of her fits precisely her forty years in Africa. She became an African perhaps more than any Western missionary before or since. When she arrived in Calabar (now Nigeria) in 1875, she quickly realized how utterly out of place she was. Missionaries were men accompanied by their wives—Victorian ladies—who worked with African women and children on the mission compound and met together each day for afternoon tea. Mary opted out, preferring to climb trees. She begged to leave the compound to move upcountry, and her request after some years was finally granted, despite objections that the region was too dangerous for a lone missionary, particularly a woman. Her first days of settling in must have made her wonder if she had made the wrong decision.

> In the forenoon I was left alone with the mud and the rain and the general wretchedness. . . . I looked helplessly on day after day at the rain pouring down on the boxes, bedding, and everything. . . . I am living in a single apartment with a mud floor and that not in the best condition. Moreover it is shared by three boys and two girls and we are crowded in on every side by men, women, children, goats, dogs, fowls, rats and cats all going and coming indiscriminately.[10]

Having left the missionary compound behind, she no longer felt pressure to fit in. In the years that followed, a visitor might find her attired in a short sack-like garment, barefoot, red hair chopped short, and without her false teeth—sometimes her skin covered with boils. The Africans accepted her with mixed emotions. She was confrontational, vehemently protesting such cultural practices as twin murder. Some such babies she was able to rescue and raise as her own.

Despite opposition, her perseverance paid off. Less than a decade after she had gone upcountry, Mary Kingsley, writing a travelogue, summed up her work:

This very wonderful lady has been eighteen years in Calabar; for the last six or seven living entirely alone, as far as white folks go, in a clearing in the forest near one of the principal villages of the Okoyong district, and ruling as a veritable white chief over the entire district. Her great abilities, both physical and intellectual, have given her among the savage tribe a unique position, and won her, from white and black who know her, a profound esteem. Her knowledge of the native, his language, his ways of thought, his diseases, his difficulties, and all that is his, is extraordinary, and the amount of good she has done, no man can fully estimate. Okoyong, when she went there alone . . . was given, as most of the surrounding districts still are, to killing at funerals, ordeal by poison, and perpetual internecine wars. Many of these evil customs she has stamped out. . . . Miss Slessor stands alone.[11]

That Mary was "ruling as a veritable white chief" was no accident. She had been appointed by the British government as a vice-consul in the region, acting as a judge in cases involving everything from marital disputes to theft and murder. Her style was drawn from her no-nonsense personality far more than conventional standards of law and justice. But her sense of fairness served her well. In a letter to a friend, she wrote: "I have always said that I have no idea how or why God has carried me over so many funny and hard places, and made these hordes of people submit to me, or why the Government should have given me the privilege of a Magistrate among them, except in answer to prayer."[12]

In this official capacity, she came in contact with bureaucrats who were fascinated by her living conditions and repartee with the Africans. Indeed, she had an unusually cordial relationship with British officials, who were often in the region and sometimes traveled far out of their way to visit and listen to her stories. They delighted in her sense of humor and teased her to their heart's content, she enjoying every minute of it. One of them later quipped that the whole consulate was given over to "Mariolatry." That fellow Brits enjoyed her quick-witted retorts, her laughter, and sense of humor was only natural, but Africans found her equally clever and were often observed having great fun with her.

Nevertheless, Mary felt at times a deep sense of loneliness. Single women who were assigned to work with her were not able to endure the privations. Nor was Charles Morrison, who had come to Calabar as a teacher. He courted her and presented her with an engagement ring. But due to health concerns he was not able to join her upcountry, and she was unwilling to leave her ministry. She broke the engagement, though not without sadness. "When you have a good thing or read a good thing or see a humorous thing and cannot share it," she wrote, "it is worse than bearing a trial alone."[13]

In 1904, having served in Africa nearly three decades, Mary moved with her seven adopted children to open up a new field of ministry among the Ibu peoples. That missionaries were following in her wake and picking up where she had left off was, to her, good news. Her daughter Jamie was now a young adult and worked faithfully alongside her. But disease and debilitation took a toll after forty years in the tropics. She succumbed at age sixty-six, surrounded by her African family in her simple thatched hut.

AMY CARMICHAEL
Mission Founder and Writer in India

In many respects Amy Carmichael was Mary Slessor's polar opposite. It would be difficult to imagine British officials teasing and bantering with Amy and her enjoying such frivolity. Nor would Amy ever offer Mary's confession: "I don't half live up to the ideal missionary life."[14] Both would become famous in their lifetimes, Amy as the most revered of Protestant saints.

Born in Ireland in 1867 into a wealthy family, Amy would later realize how fleeting the glitter of gold could be. At the time of her father's death when she was eighteen, it was learned that his flour mills were in serious financial straits. The good life was over. Having been reared a devout Presbyterian, Amy now focused almost entirely on spiritual endeavors and became part of the Deeper Life movement, which offered a perfectionist theology not so different from the Wesleyan emphasis on entire sanctification.

At twenty-five, despite serious health problems, she was convinced that she was called by God to be a missionary to Japan. There she suffered from a nervous condition and became convinced that God was calling her to Ceylon. After a short while there, she returned home all in the space of two years. In less than a year she then sailed for India, this time remaining until her death more than fifty years later, not once returning home.

Despite her poor health, Amy would see significant success in her mission work in India. During the next half century she established Dohnavur Fellowship, a mission compound with an orphanage, school, and medical center. She wrote more than thirty widely circulated books, and she founded the Sisters of the Common Life, a religious order of women pledged to celibacy. Within a decade, there were more than one hundred girls and young women housed at Dohnavur.

Throughout her ministry Amy was deeply fearful that her mission would be contaminated with worldly missionaries. "The saddest thing one meets is a nominal Christian," she wrote. "The church here is a field full of wheat and tares." Again, she wrote: "O to be delivered from half-hearted missionaries! . . . Don't come if you mean to turn aside for anything. . . . Don't come if you haven't made up your mind to live for *one thing*—the winning of souls."[15] Missionaries who worked with her were allowed to take a retreat each year but never to associate with anyone outside her mission. "The devil is awfully busy," she lamented. "There are missionary shipwrecks of once fair vessels."[16]

Her insistence on separation from the worldly, halfhearted Christians, however, did not preclude her going out of her way to snub such perceived individuals. On one occasion when she was on horseback, she could not conceal her contempt on seeing her enemies enjoying a walk: "Oh, that you could see us as we tear along," she wrote in a letter. "We are called the mad riders of Kotagiri." They had intentionally headed in the direction of the Anglican Mission compound, where she had spotted the retiring bishop, his replacement, and "various old ladies." She and those with her galloped directly toward them. They "parted with alacrity as we shot through, and we caught a fleeting glance at the gaze of astonishment and horror." She went on: "Once I ran over a man. I did not mean to—he wouldn't get out of the way and one can't stop short in mid-gallop."[17]

Some have found humor in such accounts; the man she ran over undoubtedly did not. She wrote to missionary candidates: "Bring to India a strong sense of humor and no sense of smell."[18] Amy was accused by other missionaries of walling herself up and separating herself not only from them but also from the Indian people themselves, never acknowledging her gratitude for being a guest in their land. She loathed Hindu religious rites.

Once while walking in the hills with Saral, a native coworker, she spotted stones piled by a tree, which Seral told her were idols. Amy was quick to respond: "To see those stupid stones standing there to the honor of the false gods, in the midst of the true God's beauty, was too much for us. We knocked them over and down they crashed. . . . It makes one burn to think of His glory being given to another."[19]

In some instances she appeared to be almost itching for battle against Hindus. In the case of a high-caste married woman who she hoped would convert to Christianity, she wrote: "If so, we shall be in the very thick of the fight again—Hallelujah!" In another situation she wrote: "Will God move in [her] heart so that she will dare her husband's fury and the knife he flashed before her eyes? If so, our bungalow will be in the very teeth of the storm, angry men all around it, and we inside, kept by the power of God."[20]

Nearby missionaries were troubled by such threats and openly criticized her. Hearing such censure only made her more determined. She was convinced that she was directed by God and that her actions should not be questioned. "Our Master . . . demands obedience. . . . Sometimes the Spirit of Jesus gave a direct command. . . . Sometimes an angel was sent, sometimes a vision. . . . In the end our God justifies His commands."[21]

Rarely was she challenged. When Saral suggested organizing a knitting class for Hindu women who then might be open to the gospel, Amy insisted that the gospel alone was power enough without the need for such frills. Saral, knowing all too well who wielded the power at Dohnavur, backed down. Stephen Neill did not.

In 1924, the Neill family arrived in India to work with Amy. They had heard of her work and offered their expertise to serve alongside her—all four of them, the parents who were both medical doctors, their daughter, and Stephen, a brilliant Cambridge graduate. The elder Neills realized within months that the situation was not workable and severed their ties with her. But Stephen stayed on. There was something so compelling about her, and the feelings were mutual.

He soon realized, however, that Amy's way was the only way to do things at Dohnavur. As with Saral, Amy accused him of wanting to introduce frills. No knitting, of course, but to organize sports teams so that the boys could play other teams outside the compound. But such, she was convinced, would contaminate them.

Stephen stayed on for more than a year until one night in late November 1925. Amy summed up the situation as "one of the saddest nights of my life." The incident came to a head, according to Amy, after "a dreadful time of distress. . . . Never such known before. I am beginning to sink. Lord, save me." The following year she confided in a friend: "I long over him still, miss him and want him and long to be one in affection. The stab is not even beginning to skin over. It's just red raw."[22]

From Stephen's vantage point the situation was even more upsetting, later alluded to in his autobiography: "During that first year . . . [was] brought into my life such darkness and suffering that it took me many years to recover from the injuries, and the scars are still there."[23] Even on

Mildred Cable: Missionary to the Gobi Desert

When J. Hudson Taylor founded the China Inland Mission in 1865, he ignored critics and welcomed single women into the work. In the decades that followed they poured into China, often outnumbering their male counterparts 2 to 1. Among them the Trio—Mildred Cable, Eva French, and Francesca French—who began their work together during the first decade of the twentieth century. For some twenty years they set up schools and centers for recovering opium addicts. But then they sensed a calling to the unreached peoples of the Gobi Desert. Their mission superiors nixed the idea, some, as Mildred later reported, suggesting that "there are no fools like old fools." But with Mildred egging them on, the Trio followed the Silk Road, conducting evangelism along the way to their desert destination, a most inhospitable region beyond the Great Wall. Despite incredible hardships, they traveled through the desert along caravan routes to village fairs, where they camped in tents and held outdoor meetings and distributed literature. They treated the sick, delivered babies, and taught people to read. Mabel wrote books on their wild adventures, inspiring the next generation to missionary service.

his initial introduction to her, he recognized "an impression of power," not permitting the "smallest disagreement." He had desperately wanted it to work out. "I gave my whole soul to Dohnavur," he claimed, but during that year he experienced things that "were so excessively painful that by January 1926 the darkness was complete."[24] He returned to England a broken man, his troubles still haunting him several years later. From the scanty sources available, this conflict was no doubt exacerbated by Neill's own hair-trigger temper.

In the years that followed he would serve as an Anglican bishop in India, interestingly in a region that included Dohnavur, a factor that no doubt prompted Amy to finally, once and for all, sever her ties with that church. Stephen went on to write many books and to hold prestigious teaching positions. Amy continued on in the work, seriously debilitated due to a fall. Indeed, she was an invalid during the last two decades before her death at Dohnavur at age eighty-three.

GLADYS AYLWARD
Small Woman with a Big Heart

So compelling was her story that it was fashioned into a Hollywood film in 1958, starring none other than the celebrated Academy Award–winning Ingrid Bergman. But Gladys Aylward, though flattered by the attention, was utterly mortified by how she and her ministry were portrayed. Indeed, how could this gorgeous, leggy blonde, nearly a head taller than she, possibly play her? Gladys, however, was largely unknown, and the viewing public was no doubt much more interested in Ingrid than in her. Though drawn from her biography, *The Small Woman* by Alan Burgess, the film skipped over her almost absurd determination to serve in China, a story so powerfully portrayed by Burgess.

She was in her late twenties when she set out for China on October 15, 1932, having been turned down as a missionary candidate by the China Inland Mission. That she had grown up in a poor family, had limited formal education, and worked as a house servant would not have disqualified her. Those in charge, however, may have wrongly suspected her IQ was deep in double digits when in fact she may have had a learning disability.

The rejection was painful, but she was not going to let it prevent her from serving in China, particularly after she made contact with Jennie Lawson, a missionary who needed her help. She had saved enough money for a train ticket that she was convinced would get her through Europe and on to her destination.

Gladys was not a light traveler. Her luggage, besides a bedroll and clothing and enough food for the lengthy journey, included pots and pans and a small stove. What was she thinking? Did she not know that this would be more than an autumn color tour? Did she not know about lax train schedules, especially beyond Western Europe? Did she not know that Russia was involved in an undeclared border war with China? Did she not know about the bitter Siberian winters? And what about her tickets? Would Russian agents even validate them? Of course not, but for the fact that Gladys absolutely insisted that, come hell or high water, she must get to her destination.

That the trains were filled with Russian troops, to her, seemed beside the point. No soldier was going to push her around. This was precisely how she reacted when they ganged up on her, all speaking and motioning at once that she must exit the train. She refused. And so, along with the soldiers, she was deposited in the war zone, with cracks of gunfire in the distance. Fortunately, the station from which they had departed was within walking distance. Burgess describes the scene:

> The Siberian wind blew the powdered snow around her heels, and she carried a suitcase in each hand, one still decorated ludicrously with kettle and saucepan. Around her shoulders she wore the fur rug. And so she trudged off into the night, a slight, lonely figure, dwarfed by the tall, somber trees, the towering mountains, and the black sky, diamond bright with stars. There were wolves near by, but this she did not know. Occasionally in the forest a handful of snow would slither to the ground with a sudden noise, or a branch would crack under the weight of snow, and she would pause and peer uncertainly in that direction. But nothing moved. There was no light, no warmth, nothing but endless loneliness.[25]

Eventually, after traveling through Manchuria and on to Japan, Gladys, with the help of the British consulate, was able to enter China, cross the mountains, and make her way to the home of the elderly Jennie Lawson. If she had imagined that she would be warmly welcomed, she was wrong. Jennie, entirely on her own since the death of her husband, was operating an inn for mule drivers, their beasts, and baggage. She was brusque and exhausted and wasted no time putting Gladys to work. Feeding mules, cleaning dirty beds, and serving meals to rough men was not the mission work Gladys had envisioned.

In comparison, her work as a live-in "parlor maid" in London certainly had its advantages. But it was too late to take back the insane decision she had made more than a year earlier. The bright side of her situation was that while she served meals, Jennie entertained the men telling Bible stories. And for some inexplicable reason, Gladys was learning by ear a language that she had found impossible to comprehend in written form. And when the words did not come, she supplemented with body language.

With the death of Jennie, however, Gladys was entirely on her own to operate the unprofitable inn. Jennie had received support from the homeland, but now Gladys was without funds, that is, until she became employed as a foot inspector by local Chinese officials. Even before the 1930s, the Chinese government had regulated against foot binding. The painful practice caused deformity and had a crippling effect on the women. But tiny feet were appealing to men. Big feet were simply not cool. So women, especially those in the villages, continued binding the feet of their daughters.

That Gladys would be hired to be a foot inspector might seem odd but for the fact that no Chinese women wanted the job. In this capacity, she could familiarize herself with the countryside and the language at the same time. In every village, despite her communication deficiencies, she told Bible stories as Jennie had done. People congregated around her, drawn to her personality and to her increasing—and amazing—expertise in the various dialects used in the area.

As the years passed, however, she began to hear rumors of war, and by the late 1930s, her little world in Shansi Province had become a military encampment. The mountains she had grown to love were now in the midst of a war zone, and no village was safe from Japanese bombs. She had become a Chinese citizen and had no intention of seeking evacuation. In fact, she wrote to her mother: "Do not wish me out of this or in any way seek to get me out, for I will not be got out while this trial is on. These are my people; God has given them to me; and I will live or die with them for Him and His Glory."[26]

During this time, she served as a spy behind enemy lines, gathered orphans under her care—and fell in love. His name was Linnan, a military officer. Considering their cultural differences, their relationship might have gone nowhere in peacetime. But common loyalty and goals and incredible acts of courage in the midst of war have a way of turning things upside down. Burgess writes of this in his biography:

> Few love affairs can have flourished in circumstances stranger than that of Gladys and Linnan. They met at odd moments in the mountains, in shattered villages, in bombed towns. They talked at odd moments between battles and births and baptisms, they exchanged scraps of news, had a meal together, talked of the future they would build in the new China. His concern, his gentleness, his tenderness toward her never wavered. They discussed marriage; he was eager that they marry at once. . . . It was Gladys who said, "No." The war had to be won first.[27]

After hiding for months in caves with dozens of refugee children including those she had adopted, Gladys determined that with the help of others she would get them out of the war zone to safety. To complicate matters, however, the Japanese had learned of her spying and had put a hefty price on her head, dead or alive. The journey through the mountains to the border was harrowing, and when the children were finally given a safe haven, Gladys herself collapsed from mental and physical exhaustion.

In many ways her collapse symbolized what was happening across a vast region of China. Homes and families and livelihoods had been destroyed—as had a budding love affair. War had taken a terrible toll, and never again would life go on as it had.

Gladys returned across the border into China and for a time worked with other *foreign* missionaries. But she was not foreign; she was Chinese. So she left to work with a church in Chengtu, where she served as a Bible woman, a role always filled by uneducated Chinese women. She did not see herself above such a dignified, and yet lowly, position.

She most likely would have remained in China the rest of her life but for pleas from her parents, who, though in good health, were getting on in years. Indeed, her mother had gotten a new lease on life since her daughter had become a missionary. Not every British mum has a daughter running a muleteer inn, serving as a foot inspector, then a spy, and finally a heroic guide through the mountains. She arranged for speaking engagements for her daughter, always with the same title: "Our Gladys in China."

When Gladys arrived home, her mother-agent had paved the way, and she quickly became a celebrity, a role that made her uncomfortable. Yet the invitations came—from the BBC, to appear before Queen Elizabeth, and to travel the world. The Burgess biography and the film *The Inn of the Sixth Happiness* would solidify her fame—when all she had ever wanted was to be a missionary to China.

CONCLUDING OBSERVATIONS

The issue that separated Anne-Marie and her bishop was that of authority: Who is ultimately in charge—the founder of the mission or her religious superior? In the end, she outmaneuvered him and won. Google her name. Dozens of sites appear. Where are sites devoted to him? In fairness I wanted to read his side of the story but alas was stymied by online black holes. Dare we conclude that Bishop Bénigne-Urbain-Jean-Marie du Trousset d'Héricourt resides only in the dustbin of history?

The matter of authority also intersected with the ministry of Mary Slessor. Unlike Anne-Marie, she was not hounded by a bishop, but she was hindered by the restraints and societal expectations placed on women. She had no aspirations of leading a mission organization. Rather she set out on her own to evangelize Africans and in the process was appointed a vice-consul. Here she effectively wielded power that she had never sought.

Amy Carmichael was an authority figure to those who worked with her at Dohnavur. She demanded that those under her submit to her rule. Stephen Neill spoke of the "power" she wielded and her demand for obedience. She defended any such power, believing her authority came directly from God.

Although Gladys Aylward was possessed of incredible determination, she did not seek authority in her own right or aspire to a leadership position as did Amy. True, she ran the muleteer inn for a short time, served as an official foot inspector, and led a party of children out of China. But in the end she was content to serve as a lowly Bible woman.

QUESTIONS TO THINK ABOUT

Are men more likely than women to seek positions of authority? What insights do Anne-Marie, Mary, Amy, and Gladys offer on issues of power, authority, and leadership? Do these terms fit your personality and aspirations?

Does the Bible teach male headship (or leadership) in ministry? Does the issue of male headship relate to Anne-Marie's conflict with her bishop or with Amy's conflict with Stephen Neill?

Which woman would you most want to study further? Which one do you find most interesting? Most heroic?

If you were assigned to work under or alongside one of these four women, which one would you choose?

Do most people who defy odds as Gladys did to become a missionary succeed, or is it typically better to accept the decision of the experts, in her case, the mission board?

Have you or anyone you know struggled with learning disabilities? Does the success of others who have overcome the odds help such individuals cope with life?

For what trait would you most want to be remembered? Would you rather be remembered as being holy or a woman of great accomplishments?

11

Harriet Beecher Stowe and Nineteenth-Century Poets and Writers

The nineteenth century was a time when women writers flourished. We remember their names and writings today in popular culture, particularly in television, theater, and film. Jane Austen has fared particularly well in recent years with such Hollywood films as *Sense and Sensibility* (1995, starring Emma Thompson), *Emma* (1996, starring Gwyneth Paltrow), and *Pride and Prejudice* (2005, starring Keira Knightley). Charlotte Brontë's *Jane Eyre* has also tempted the film industry over the years, as has sister Emily Brontë's *Wuthering Heights.*

But nineteenth-century women writers extend far beyond England and Jane Austen and the Brontë sisters, and their works encompass much more than fiction only. Elizabeth Barrett Browning, Mary Shelley, and Christina Rossetti were English poets. Fredrika Bremer was a Swedish novelist and Rosa Campbell Praed, an Australian novelist. Margaret Fuller, an American journalist and feminist writer, was among dozens more who would be listed among the century's notable writers. Many of these women were born into

Jane Austen and the Brontë Sisters

Move along, Jane Austen. Hollywood is hot for the Brontës again.

Filmmakers' long affair with the divine Miss Austen is finally waning, after two decades of movies made from her elegant novels with their well-mannered characters, placid plots and witty repartee.

But enough with the endless circling of the Pump Room at Bath—time to get hearts racing! Time to bring back those wildly Romantic Brontë characters—plain Jane Eyre and moody Mr. Rochester, doomed Cathy Earnshaw and vengeful Heathcliff—to rend their garments, wail disconsolately and stagger across windswept moors.

Maria Puente, "New Films Move the Brontes Back into the Hollywood Frame,"
USA Today

prosperity and never married, factors that allowed them sufficient leisure time to devote to their passion.

Among them were committed Christians, some of whom made their faith a central feature of their writing or wrote specifically for Christian audiences. Others interacted significantly with writers outside the Christian community. Hannah More was an evangelical social activist who focused her attention on Sunday schools and education, but she was also involved in the antislavery movement, which frequently brought her in contact with William Wilberforce. At the same time she was known for her poetry and her morality plays. Among those in her literary circle were Samuel Johnson and Edmund Burke. Had she written a tell-all memoir, she might have piqued curiosity with the account of her six-year engagement to William Turner. When he broke it off, she suffered a mental breakdown, and he was assessed a generous annual annuity for her upkeep—enough to allow her the leisure of a literary life.

The most notable female Christian writers in America during this era, except for Emily Dickinson, are remembered mostly for their popular appeal. Harriet Beecher Stowe's *Uncle Tom's Cabin* helped turn the tide against slavery in the years prior to the Civil War, but it was never acclaimed as a literary masterpiece. The same could be said for Fanny Crosby. Her beloved hymn lyrics, however, had staying power and served to bring unity among Christians who might otherwise have been separated by doctrinal differences. Such is also true of Hannah Whitall Smith, whose best-selling devotional book has sold millions of copies since it was first published in 1883.

All three of these women were celebrated for their writing in their own lifetimes. Not so Emily Dickinson. Though generally unknown as a poet in

God's Silence and Hiddenness

Does Emily Dickinson belong in a book on Christian women—in a chapter on Christian writers? If Job belongs with the great patriarchs of old (a whole book of the Bible devoted to him), then surely Emily belongs here, despite her doubts and questions, which are often the theme of her provocative poems. Hannah Smith also struggled with doubts, though she did not write of them openly. Indeed, Christian writers have feared to openly express religious doubts. Not so Job.

> If only I knew where to find him;
>   if only I could go to his dwelling!
> I would state my case before him
>   and fill my mouth with arguments.
> I would find out what he would answer me,
>   and consider what he would say to me.
> Would he vigorously oppose me?
>   No, he would not press charges against me.
> There the upright can establish their innocence before him,
>   and there I would be delivered forever from my judge.
>
> But if I go to the east, he is not there;
>   if I go to the west, I do not find him.
> When he is at work in the north, I do not see him;
>   when he turns to the south, I catch no glimpse of him.
>
> Job 23:3–9

her own day, she has since become a literary giant—and one whose words in recent years have been more and more quoted by evangelical Christians.

HARRIET BEECHER STOWE
Literary Abolitionist

The daughter of Lyman Beecher, a fiery Connecticut Calvinist preacher and abolitionist, Harriet was raised primarily by her sister Catherine, eleven years her senior. Their mother was sickly and had died when Harriet was five, and soon thereafter Catherine established the Hartford Female Seminary, where Harriet herself, at sixteen, became a teacher. Several years later the family moved to Cincinnati, Ohio, where her father became the first president of Lane Theological Seminary. By this time Harriet was a budding writer. She was invited to join the local Semi-Colon Club, whose members included Judge Salmon P. Chase, who would one day become a Supreme Court justice.

In her midtwenties, she married Calvin Stowe, a professor at the seminary, and in the years that followed, she gave birth to seven children and suffered two miscarriages. Though burdened with family cares, she found time for writing short stories primarily on family matters and domestic concerns. Her husband supported her. "My dear, you must be a literary woman," he penned in a letter to her. "It is so written in the book of fate."[1]

In 1850, more than a dozen years into their marriage, Calvin accepted a faculty position at Bowdoin College in Brunswick, Maine. At this same time, Harriet began to take up the cause of abolition. Her younger half sister, Isabella, pleaded with her: "Hattie, if I could use a pen as you can, I would write something that would make this whole nation feel what an accursed thing slavery is."[2]

It was a tall order to influence a "whole nation," but Harriet was up to the job. The actual idea for her book came while she was listening to a sermon based on Jesus's words: "Inasmuch as ye have done it unto one of the least of these my brethren, ye have done it unto me." Later she wrote: "My heart was bursting with the anguish excited by the cruelty and injustice our nation was showing to the slave, and praying God to let me do a little and to cause my cry for them to be heard."[3]

Within months Harriet was writing a serialized version of *Uncle Tom's Cabin*, and in 1852 the completed book grabbed the nation's attention, selling some three hundred thousand copies within a year. The fictionalized story of Uncle Tom and Eliza, a young mother, portrayed the anguish and evils of the institution of slavery far more effectively than did well-argued essays or lectures. Harriet was soon a celebrity with speaking engagements throughout America and Europe. Later when she met President Lincoln in 1862, he would utter his now famous words: "So you're the little woman who wrote the book that led to this great war!" Or did he? Some scholars today argue the quote is apocryphal.

Hannah More: Writer, Social Activist, and More

Long before Harriet had become famous for *Uncle Tom's Cabin*, Hannah was utilizing the power of her pen to abolish the slave trade in the British Empire. Though a daughter of a mere schoolmaster, she became known in literary circles for her intellect and wit, having been strongly encouraged by her mother. Her father, on the other hand, as Karen Swallow, her biographer, points out, discouraged her. Unlike her mother, her father was alarmed by "how quickly Hannah picked up the rudimentary lessons in Latin and Greco-Roman history that the teacher in him couldn't resist imparting even though they were improper subjects for girls." She was equally taken by mathematics, but her father quashed her budding curiosity. As a result, she wrestled with her "conflicted attitude toward female education and ambition for the rest of her life." A friend of William Wilberforce, she worked tirelessly as a social activist, particularly in Sunday school efforts during a time when poor children had no access to schooling. Through her wide-ranging ministry, children and their parents learned to read by studying the Bible and Sunday school literature. Her social activism and literary capabilities went hand in hand. She was a novelist, a poet, and a playwright, whose productions were seen at London's Royal Theater. She died in 1833, at age eighty-eight, and is remembered as a philanthropist and much more.

Despite her other books and the soaring sales of *Uncle Tom* (some two million copies within five years), Harriet did not earn enough to maintain the home she and her husband had built in Hartford. With the sale of that house, they purchased a smaller home that just happened to be across the road from another writer, Samuel Clemens (aka Mark Twain), who would also have financial problems in later years.

For Harriet, however, money woes were certainly not her first concern. Her adult children struggled with serious problems, not the least of which was morphine addiction. Likewise, she and Calvin had for many years had a rocky marriage. Long separations, particularly due to his travels, did not help matters, nor did Harriet's aversion to sex due to fear of more pregnancies. In a letter to Calvin, more than a decade into their marriage, she alluded to some of their issues:

> One might naturally infer that from the union of two both morbidly sensitive and acute, yet in many respects exact opposites—one hasty and impulsive—the other sensitive and brooding—one the very personification of exactness and routine and the other to whom everything of the kind was an irksome effort—from all this what should one infer but some painful friction. . . . In reflecting upon our future union—our marriage—the past obstacles to our happiness—it seems to me that they are of two or three kinds. 1st those from physical causes both in you and in me—such on your part as hypochondriac morbid instability for which the only remedy is physical care and attention to the laws of health—and on my part an excess of sensitiveness and of confusion and want of control of mind and memory.[4]

For Calvin's part, their lack of a physical relationship was the greatest problem between them, and his expectations were high when he returned home. Travel, pregnancies, and Harriet's fear of more pregnancies left him seriously frustrated, as he penned to her in a letter: "It is almost in fact eighteen months since I have had a wife to sleep with me. It is enough to kill any man, especially such a man as I am."[5]

To his credit, Calvin did not appear to be threatened by his wife's popularity. He was a biblical scholar and promoter of public education in his own right. Soon after her bestseller was published he wrote her a letter that offers insight on their marriage relationship: "Money matters are entirely in your hands, and no money is spent except in accordance with your judgment and that saves me a great deal of torment and anxiety."[6]

Both Calvin and Harriet, despite poor health, would live on into old age, he dying at eighty-four, and she a decade later at eighty-five. The saddest aspect of her final years related to her dementia. Only a year or two after Calvin died, due to an "incurable mental malady," she began "writing *Uncle Tom's Cabin* over again," according to an article in the *Washington Post.* "She imagined that she was engaged in the original composition, and for several hours every day she industriously used pen and paper, inscribing long passages of the book almost exactly word for word . . . unconsciously from memory."[7]

Fanny Crosby
Blind Hymn Writer

It's a small world. One of Fanny Crosby's dearest friends was the hymn writer Phoebe Knapp (daughter of Phoebe Palmer), a wealthy woman some fifteen years younger than she. Fanny often visited her at her New York mansion, where she enjoyed talking with another of Phoebe's friends, Harriet Beecher Stowe. It was Phoebe who wrote the tune for one of Fanny's most memorable hymns. Fanny was visiting the Knapp home when Phoebe played a tune she had composed. As the story goes, she asked Fanny, "What do you think the tune says?" Fanny, without hesitation responded: "Blessed assurance, Jesus is mine." Between 1870 and her death in 1915, Fanny Crosby wrote some eight thousand hymns, many of which are still found in hymnals and continue to be sung today, including "Blessed Assurance," "Pass Me Not, O Gentle Savior," "Safe in the Arms of Jesus," "Jesus, Keep Me near the Cross," "Rescue the Perishing," and "To God Be the Glory." Though blind, she wrote of one day seeing—seeing "the bright and glorious morning" and viewing "His blessed face, and the luster of his kindly beaming eye."

She would later say that she had the good fortune of being blind, a condition she insisted had developed when she was two months old, the result of a hot mustard poultice administered to cure her illness. It is more likely, however, that she was born blind. Perhaps it was her good fortune.

With normal sight, she might never have become a hymn writer. Before her first birthday, her father died. From that point on, she was raised primarily by her grandmother while her mother worked. At age fifteen she left home to live at the New York Institution for the Blind, first as a student and later as a teacher. All the while, from girlhood through adulthood, she wrote poetry, publishing her first collection, *The Blind Girl and Other Poems*, in 1844.

Though raised by a pious Christian grandmother, Fanny did not date her conversion until 1850, when she was thirty years old. She had struggled to break through to God for some time. She attended revival meetings, but nothing happened, as she later wrote in her autobiography:

> Some of us went every evening, but although I sought peace, I could not find the joy I craved, until one evening—November 20, 1850—I arose and went forward alone. After prayer the congregation began to sing the grand old consecration hymn of Dr. Isaac Watts:
>
> > Alas and did my Saviour bleed?
> > And did my Sovereign die? Would
> > He devote that sacred Head
> > For such a worm as I?
>
> And when they reached the 3rd line of the last verse: "Here, Lord, I give myself away; 'Tis all that I can do." I surrendered myself to the Saviour, and my very soul was flooded with celestial light. I sprang to my feet, shouting "Hallelujah."[8]

As open as she was about her religious experience, Fanny remained mostly silent on her personal life. Eight years after this religious experience, she married Alexander van Alstine, a colleague and former student who was also blind. At thirty-eight, she was eleven years older than Van, as he was known. Of him she wrote: "He was a firm trustful Christian, a man of kindly deeds and cheering words. Our tastes were congenial, and he composed the music to several of my hymns. At different times he was organist in two of the New York Churches; he also taught private classes in both vocal and instrumental music. We were happy together for many years."[9]

A Broken Marriage

In 1858 Crosby entered a marriage in which she and her spouse, Alexander van Alstine, apparently soon thereafter opted for utterly separate lives. She retained her maiden name (she said at his insistence), and for many years they had separate addresses. She was not with him during his last illness; others tended him. She provided no marker for his grave in a Queens, New York, cemetery. . . . [It was] a most unusual married life.

Edith L. Blumhofer, *Her Heart Can See: The Life and Hymns of Fanny J. Crosby*

For most of their married life, however, they lived separately. Another very private matter was the birth of their only child. Of that she later wrote: "God gave us a tender babe, [but soon] the angels came down and took our infant up to God and His throne."[10] In the years that followed the death of her infant, Fanny focused her attention on poetry, particularly the cause of the Civil War, writing one patriotic song after another, some of them with a tone of mockery, as was true in her "Song to Jeff Davis":

> Now, Jeff, when thou art ready,
> Lead on thy rebel crew,
> We'll give them all a welcome—
> With balls and powder too!
> We spurn thy constitution!
> We spurn thy southern laws!
> Our stars and stripes are waving,
> And Heav'n will speed our cause.[11]

In 1864 Fanny teamed up with William Bradbury, a move that launched her ministry as a hymn writer. For the next four decades until her death in 1915, she wrote as many as seven hymns a day. She was driven, though she testified that she always prayed for inspiration before she began writing. Whether inspired or not, many people were critical of her sentimental and sometimes syrupy lyrics. And it is significant that out of her eight thousand hymn lyrics, fewer than forty would become well known and widely sung.

One of the most popular hymns she wrote was "Pass Me Not"—called for at every meeting of the 1874 Moody-Sankey Campaign in London. Indeed, it was credited with saving more souls than any other hymn. But Fanny did not believe that hymn writing should be her only means of saving souls. In fact, she regarded her rescue mission work at several different locations in New York City as her primary ministry. She found housing near a mission in a low-rent neighborhood and spent little on herself, giving generously to the poor.

When she was in her nineties, she moved to Connecticut to live with a niece. Her admirers made pilgrimages simply to see and talk with the old lady who wrote hymns. It was their good fortune when she would sit at the piano and play for them a favorite, often adding a bit of unexpected rhythm and flare.

EMILY DICKINSON
God-Intoxicated Poet

Whether or not Emily was a bona fide Christian has, over the generations, been a matter of debate. Whether she was a bona fide poet has not. She would never, however, enjoy the popularity of Fanny Crosby, ten years her senior and whose hymns were already gaining popularity during Emily's lifetime. But Emily's religious understandings were rooted in the Puritan Calvinism of Jonathan Edwards as opposed to the sentimental Victorian religion that undergirded Fanny's spiritual life and influenced her hymn writing. "Sinners in the Hands of an Angry God" still reverberated in sermons and in the collective consciousness of Emily's family and neighbors. Fanny was influenced more by nineteenth-century revivalism. Fanny had postponed her emotional conversion experience until she was thirty. Emily, prompted by philosophical uncertainties, postponed hers altogether.

Twice, however, Emily was nearly caught by the revival fires, the first time in 1846, while she was a student at Amherst Academy, the second time while back home in 1850.

> I never lost as much but twice,
> And that was in the sod;

Twice have I stood a beggar
Before the door of God!

Angels, twice descending,
Reimbursed my store.
Burglar, banker, father.
I am poor once more.[12]

Regarding the Amherst revival, to a friend she wrote: "I was almost persuaded to be a Christian. . . . I can say that I never before enjoyed such perfect peace and happiness as the short time in which I felt I had found my savior. But I soon forgot my morning prayer or else it was irksome to me. One by one my old habits returned and I cared less for religion than ever." In 1850, she wrote to another friend: "How strange is this sanctification, that works such a marvellous change [but left her] standing alone in rebellion and growing very careless."[13]

Who was this nineteenth-century poet who wrestled so with religious revivalism and with God? Perhaps the one word that best describes her is *honesty*. She spoke aloud—in poems and letters—the doubts that others sometimes felt, and she refused to feign an experience just because others were claiming it. Born into a prosperous family in Amherst, Massachusetts, she was the middle of three children. She never married, and except for spending a school year at Mount Holyoke Female Seminary, she lived her entire life in the family home. In her youth, she was described as a vivacious redhead, but she would spend her adult years largely in seclusion.

Possessed of a brilliant mind, she struggled with matters that are today in the forefront of religious discussions. Many of the questions and issues raised in her poetry and letters relate to the difficulty in correlating religion with new discoveries in science. Her own education included serious academic offerings, though never without religious underpinnings. If geological findings pointed to an ancient earth, well and good, God was all the greater.

But science began to change in 1859, with the publication of Charles Darwin's *The Origin of Species*. Emily spoke of such knowledge as so dangerous that "God's right hand . . . is amputated."[14] Elsewhere she mused in a letter: "We thought Darwin had thrown the Redeemer away."[15] She was giving vent to the incredible emotional toll that Darwin's theory had taken on those who held fast to God while acknowledging scientific discoveries. The overriding issue was how to read the Book of Nature alongside the Bible.

More than by any particular scientific finding, Emily was troubled by God's distance and very existence. There was no way, it seems, that she was able to silence the voices inside her that constantly questioned everything she was supposed to take for granted. Like the prophet Job, she wondered where God was hiding and why God was silent. Others claimed to hear his voice, but for her there was deafening silence. Yet like Job she could not succumb to any form of atheism, as is evident in one of her most often-quoted poems:

> I know that He exists.
> Somewhere—in Silence—
> He has hid his rare life
> From our gross eyes.[16]

That Emily was wracked with doubts only served to stimulate her creative genius. Indeed, without her strong religious foundation and critical questioning, her poetry would be spiritually vacuous. Take away from the Bible the book of Job (as well as whole chapters in Psalms and Ecclesiastes), and it is shorn of some of its most provocative and powerful passages. Emily's uncertainty stands alongside, and in contrast to, Fanny Crosby's certainty. If Fanny wrote with certainty, "Praise Him, Praise Him," Emily could write with ambiguity, "I worshipped—did not pray." By doing so, she allowed herself to come to terms with God's hiddenness. Indeed, when God is absent in personal prayer, it is no trifling thing to worship in awe.

> My period had come for Prayer—
> No other Art—would do—
> My Tactics missed a rudiment—
> Creator—Was it you?
>
> God grows above—so those who pray
> Horizons—must ascend—
> And so I stepped upon the North
> To see this Curious Friend—

His House was not—no sign had He—
By Chimney—nor by Door
Could I infer his Residence—
Vast Prairies of Air

Unbroken by a Settler—
Were all that I could see—
Infinitude—Had'st Thou no Face
That I might look on Thee

The Silence condescended—
Creation stopped—for Me
But awed beyond my errand—
I worshipped—did not "pray"—[17]

In other poems, Emily almost appears to mock God, or more accurately perhaps the God of Jonathan Edwards and his Puritan forebearers. In her seemingly flippant tone, one can almost imagine her seeing Edwards's spider dangling over a fire by a thread—as God reprimands happiness that competes with the eternal joys of heaven.

Of God we ask one favor,
That we may be forgiven—
For what, he is presumed to know—
The Crime, from us, is hidden—

Immured the whole of Life
Within a magic Prison
We reprimand the Happiness
That too competes with Heaven.[18]

To lose one's faith was surely not something about which to be flippant, and Emily was not. Nor would she have been flippant about losing one's estate. As a child she may have heard about the Panic of 1837, then as an adult, the Panic of 1857. People lost money and sometimes their entire estates. Bad enough, but one could make a financial comeback. Far worse was the loss of faith, which cannot be regained ("but [only] once—can

191

be"). Such belief that consists of theological propositions (or clauses) is lost forever if even one link in the chain is annihilated, the result being "beggary"—words from her pen so concise and exact.

> To lose one's faith—surpass
> The loss of an Estate—
> Because Estates can be
> Replenished—faith cannot—
>
> Inherited with Life—
> Belief—but once—can be—
> Annihilate a single clause—
> And Being's—Beggary—[19]

Did Emily lose her faith? Did she ever have it? Will we see her in heaven one day? Did she even believe there was a heaven? From the first lines of the following poem, it would seem so. But then she takes it all back. Is she chiding those who speak of heaven so blithely when in fact they do not want to go there—at least, not yet? Do they also want to "look a little more at such a curious earth"? And if they actually believe in heaven, why does it often seem like such a humdrum matter? Why does it not, as Emily suggests, take their breath away?

> Going to heaven!
> I don't know when. . . .
> And yet it will be done
> As sure as flocks go home at night
> Unto the shepherd's arm! . . .
> If you should get there first,
> Save just a little place for me
> Close to the two I lost! . . .
>
> I'm glad I don't believe it,
> For it would stop my breath,
> And I'd like to look a little more
> At such a curious earth!
> I'm glad they did believe it

Whom I have never found
Since the mighty autumn afternoon
I left them in the ground.[20]

HANNAH WHITALL SMITH
Evangelist with an Unhappy Life

If all the ideas and beliefs and poetry of Fanny Crosby and Emily Dickinson were to be stirred together in a bowl and baked for one hour, the mixture might just come out of the oven as an inedible upside-down cake, a metaphor for Hannah's dysfunctional family. Her happy Christian spirituality was infused with a family DNA of disabling doubt. Hannah might have been just another nineteenth-century evangelist but for her 1875 bestselling book, *The Christian's Secret of a Happy Life* (still in print today, long since having passed ten million in sales).

The underlying thesis of the book was not new. Many Christians before Hannah had argued for passivity as opposed to striving for perfection or personal improvement. Like others she used a biblical metaphor to make her point:

> In order for a lump of clay to be made into a beautiful vessel, it must be entirely abandoned to the potter, and must lie passive in his hands. And in order for a soul to be made into a vessel unto God's honor, "sanctified and meet for the Master's use, and prepared unto every good work," it must be entirely abandoned to Him, and must lie passive in His hands.[21]

Born into a prosperous New Jersey Quaker family, Hannah was an independent, precocious child who was determined to let neither gender nor religious restrictions hold her back. Her marriage at age nineteen to Robert Pearsall Smith, also from a long line of influential Quakers, set the stage for her active decades of ministry. Both became Bible teachers, after having shifted their allegiance from the Quakers to a more generic form of evangelicalism, though Hannah would later return to her Quaker roots.

Robert, a preacher and writer in his own right, did not appear to be threatened by Hannah's preaching or her success as an author. They sometimes worked as a team, other times traveling solo. When Robert was abroad in 1875, he wrote to his son, "All Europe is at my feet."[22] Hannah was more Bible teacher than flamboyant evangelist. His personal spirituality was also far more emotionally charged than hers. During a camp meeting he had an unforgettable baptism of the Holy Ghost. Hannah described it: "Suddenly from head to foot, Robert was shaken with what seemed like a magnetic thrill of heavenly delight, and floods of glory seemed to pour through him, soul and body."[23]

Hannah attempted to bring about a similar experience for herself, but to no avail. Indeed, after several attempts, she concluded that she was no more than "a dry old stick." No doubt referencing Robert as an example, she later concluded that people should be wary of "emotional blessings." Their emotional and personality differences could also be seen in their marriage. She was strong in the face of adversity; he was weak and prone to nervousness. "My ideal of marriage is an *equal partnership*, neither one assuming control over the other," she wrote. "Any marriage other than this is to my mind tyranny on the one hand and slavery on the other."[24]

But Hannah did not attempt to build an egalitarian marriage. "I think marriage is a frightful risk," she confessed. More than that: "I do not like men," a feeling that seemed to include her son, Logan. She conceded that she "felt in her heart . . . that a boy could never be as valuable and interesting a human being as a girl." Girls were better than boys: "Daughters are wonderful luxuries . . . well worth a bad husband, at least mine are."[25]

That she had a bad husband is well documented. While he was abroad, Hannah received a telegram informing her that he was ill in Paris. She later learned that he had been dismissed from a conference in England. The headlines said it all: "Famous Evangelist Found in Bedroom of Adoring Female Follower." Robert fell into deep depression and eventually lost his faith. In fact, so *lost* that he became involved in a long-term romantic affair right under Hannah's nose with, in her words, "a polished female friend."[26]

Although her book expressly implied that she had found the secret to a happy life, it is difficult to imagine Hannah as happy. That only three of her eight children survived to adulthood brought great sorrow and repeatedly tested her faith. "At least I am not now in such a totally hopeless spiritual state as I was last year," she wrote early in her marriage.[27] But she hung on to her faith, even as family members dropped out. Logan would later say that he lost his faith at age eleven, and his sisters would follow after, Mary losing her faith while in college and Alys soon after her marriage to Britain's most prominent atheist philosopher, Bertrand Russell. It should not be surprising that their marriages would fail as well.

As pained as Hannah was by the wholesale loss of faith, she found solace in her belief in universalism. When Robert died, she was convinced that he had been "safely gathered," as would her children one day:

> As a mother, I will never cease to love my children, no matter what they do. God, our loving God, has a heart of mother-love infinitely greater than mine. He never withholds his love from any sinner, no matter how black-hearted or unrepentant the person may be. His love is completely unconditional. Oh, it is too much. I cannot bear to hear a preacher of the gospel say such limited and untruthful things about the Love of God.[28]

This doctrine of restitution (or universalism) was very controversial and caused some conference leaders to cancel her speaking engagements. She emphasized, however, that she had not pulled the doctrine out of thin air. She was a Bible teacher (a proof texter, some would say). She argued that Christ had died "for our sins: and not for ours only, but also for the sins of the whole world" (1 John 2:2 KJV). The passage she reiterated most often, however, was from the apostle Paul, Philippians 2:10–11: "That at the name of Jesus every knee should bow, of things in heaven, and things in earth, and things under the earth. And that every tongue should confess that Jesus Christ is Lord, to the glory of God the Father" (KJV).

No doubt her secret to a happy life was based in part on her interpretation and application of these verses. In the end, all would be well.

CONCLUDING OBSERVATIONS

I once wrote a poem titled "Fanny Crosby and the Psalms":

> "Redeemed, how I love
>   to proclaim it."
> *O God, do not keep silent*
>   *be not quiet.*

"Rescue the perishing
  care for the dying."
*O God, you have
  cast us off.*

"Draw me nearer,
  nearer blessed Lord."
*Why do you stand
  afar off, O Lord?*

"Blessed assurance
  Jesus is mine."
*My God, my God
  why have you forsaken me?*

"Pass me not O Gentle Savior
  hear my humble cry."
*O, my God, I cry in the daytime
  but you do not hear.*

"And I shall see him
  face to face."
*How long will you hide
  your face from me?*

"I shall know him
  I shall know him."
*He who sits in the heavens
  shall laugh.*

Fanny Crosby is a romantic. The psalmist is a realist. And I love them both, but Fanny Crosby has influenced my spiritual life far more than the psalmist. With my husband it is an even draw. John was born and raised in the Christian Reformed Church. He sang the psalms from his earliest memories. The hymn book for church services was the psalter. No other one would do. Interestingly, though, Fanny Crosby's hymns and all the other great Victorian hymns were sung in Sunday school.

Despite Fanny's unblemished outward Christian life, her marriage, for all practical purposes, was broken as were Harriet's and Hannah's. Emily, perhaps wisely, remained single.

It is interesting that Emily's poetic lines often parallel the psalms. What faith she had in God did not come easily. But I suspect that in the chill of her doubts she bloomed as beautifully as does my favorite autumn flower, the purple gentian. I resonate with her as she reflects on her own wintery spirituality—a spirituality conditioned by both nature and nurture, by both her psychological makeup and her surroundings. Like her, I can never be the rose of summer, but through God's grace I will bloom in frosty weather.

> God made a little Gentian—
> It tried—to be a Rose—
> And failed—and all the Summer laughed—
> But just before the Snows—
>
> There rose a Purple Creature—
> That ravished all the Hill—
> And Summer hid her Forehead—
> And Mockery—was still—
>
> The Frosts were her condition—
> The Tyrian would not come
> Until the North—invoke it—
> Creator—Shall I—bloom?[29]

QUESTIONS TO THINK ABOUT

Using the metaphor of a flower, are most of the Christians you know more like a summery rose or a frosty gentian? Is one preferable to the other? Which flower best fits Fanny and Hannah? Which flower best fits you?

If you were a poet would you rather write popular verse and be remembered for what many consider dated hymn lyrics or for polished poems that are still included today in literature textbooks? Has either Fanny or Emily influenced your own life?

Of the two women Fanny Crosby and Harriet Beecher Stowe, who do you believe made the greatest and most long-lasting contribution in her writing? Would you rather write a onetime bestseller or a series of beloved hymn lyrics?

Is Hannah's longing for a glorious onetime spine-tingling spiritual experience a common expression among Christians today? Have you or anyone you know sought to reach such a spiritual high?

How should Christians regard Hannah's universalism—her likening God to a mother who would never consign a child to hell no matter how disobedient the child was? Have beliefs about hell become less well-defined and more metaphorical in recent decades? What do you believe about hell? Do you assume that most people you encounter in your daily life are headed there?

If these four women were somehow brought together today for an extended period of time, what would they have in common besides their writing? How do you think their relationships would develop?

12

Susannah Thompson Spurgeon and Ministers' Wives

In May 1990, a furor broke out at Wellesley College. "A seemingly harmless invitation," according to the *New York Times*, "has ignited a dispute that has roiled the campus and raised questions around the country about the nature of feminism." The invited commencement speaker was Barbara Bush, wife of President George Herbert Walker Bush. Students were "outraged" that a woman who had "dropped out of Smith College after two years to marry, and has been best known as a supportive wife and mother" would be perceived as a role model for the class of 1990.[1]

The following year, in 1991, the commencement speaker was Madeleine L'Engle. There were no protests.

As we rate women for their accomplishments, how do we rank Barbara and Madeleine? When I googled Barbara there were more than fifty million results (though admittedly hers is a common name). Madeleine's unique name gave me fewer than a million results. Both rate substantial Wikipedia articles. Madeleine, like Barbara, was a wife and mother, but Madeleine's renown as a writer and speaker clearly stood apart from her husband, Hugh Franklin, an actor.

Madeleine's *A Wrinkle in Time* was the 1963 winner of the Newbery Medal, the most prestigious prize an author can receive for children's literature. The book's protagonist is a frizzy-haired girl named Meg who accomplishes incredible things and continues to serve even today as a role model for girls. I knew Madeleine better for her *Crosswicks Journals*, however, and was disappointed to read after she died in 2007 that her memoirs were perhaps almost as fictional as were her novels.

So how do we rate the role models of our lives? Must they be honest and must they stand apart from their celebrated spouses?

In many ways the feminism of today is more nuanced than it was a quarter century ago. Perhaps Barbara's speaking at Wellesley would not now raise ire. But I contemplate the issue in this chapter. Someone might

A Wife of Noble Character

There is only one passage of Scripture devoted exclusively to the wife. She is married to a prominent man, as are the women in this chapter. The passage is no doubt a composite of perfection, though it is often held up as a standard for the submissive wife. It is quickly apparent, however, that this ideal woman is strong and forceful, anything but a shrinking violet whose work is behind the scenes, whose life is in the shadows.

> A wife of noble character who can find?
>   She is worth far more than rubies.
> Her husband has full confidence in her
>   and lacks nothing of value.
> She brings him good, not harm,
>   all the days of her life.
> She selects wool and flax. . . .
> She considers a field and buys it;
>   out of her earnings she plants a vineyard.

question how women married to famous men fit into the broader context of the book. Would any of them have been noted women in their own right? Perhaps not. Nevertheless, within Protestant circles since the Reformation, beginning with Katie Luther, the minister's wife has filled a very important role.

When I first filled that role in a small church in 1972, I realized quickly that the expectations were high. Although I was a full-time graduate student, I was eager to become involved in the ministry. I took on a Sunday school class for middle school girls, jointly coordinated the high school youth group, led a women's Bible study, and often joined my husband in home and hospital visitation. But when I was asked to also lead an Awana club, I declined, though offering to serve as a substitute. For some my lack of full involvement was not enough. They were critical, but I held my ground.

Today in many churches the minister's wife is almost invisible. But such was not the case in previous generations. Expectations were high, and God forbid if she had a career or was a full-time graduate student. So we invite

> She sets about her work vigorously;
>   her arms are strong for her tasks.
> She sees that her trading is profitable,
>   and her lamp does not go out at night. . . .
> She opens her arms to the poor. . . .
> Her husband is respected at the city gate. . . .
> She makes linen garments and sells them. . . .
> She is clothed with strength and dignity;
>   she can laugh at the days to come.
> She speaks with wisdom,
>   and faithful instruction is on her tongue.
> She watches over the affairs of her household
>   and does not eat the bread of idleness.
> Her children arise and call her blessed;
>   her husband also, and he praises her.
>
> Proverbs 31:10–13, 16–18, 23–28

a selection of these wives who served in the shadow of celebrity preachers to join the parade of women in this volume: Susannah Spurgeon, Sarah Edwards, Eunice Beecher, Emma Moody, Daisy Smith, and Ruth Peale.

They all struggled in fulfilling their roles. Like Barbara Bush they were secondary to famous men, often put in a position of defending their husbands. Like Madeleine, their stories were often fictionalized. And like me, the expectations were typically greater than they were willing or able to fulfill.

Susannah Thompson Spurgeon
Powerhouse Invalid

The first time Susannah Thompson listened from her pew to the nineteen-year-old prodigy preacher, she was scornful. "So this is his so-called eloquence! It does not impress me. What a painful countrified manner! Will he ever quit making flourishes with that terrible blue silk handkerchief! And his hair—why, he looks like a barber's assistant!"[2] He was an overrated amateur devoid of class. What was his appeal? And why had he been invited to preach at London's prestigious New Park Street Chapel? And why did she even show up to hear him?

Just shy of her twenty-second birthday, Susannah had a quick wit and a keen intellect. She was adept at assessing any man in the pulpit, including the "old-fashioned dapper" senior deacon. He was a "lawyer and wore the silk stockings and knee-breeches dear to a former generation." As a hymn leader, he was situated in front of the pulpit: "He was a short, stout man, and his rotund body, perched on his undraped legs and clothed in a long-tailed coat gave him an unmistakable resemblance to a gigantic robin; and when he chirped out the verses of the hymn in a piping, twittering voice, I thought the likeness was complete!" Yet she "stood very much in awe" of the old deacon.[3] Not so the boyish Charles Haddon Spurgeon.

Through mutual friends, Susannah soon became acquainted with Charles on a personal level. Their first public appearance together was December 19, 1853, and the following June, their courtship began. Several months later, in January 1855, he wrote to her: "I am glad you are not here just at this moment, for I feel so deeply that I could only throw my arms around you and weep."[4] They were married one year later on January 9, 1856, when she was twenty-three. On September 20, less than nine months later, Susannah give birth to twin boys.

By this time Spurgeon's popularity had soared to such a height that New Park Street Chapel could no long hold the crowds. Surrey Gardens Music Hall was a much larger venue, and the first service there was scheduled for the evening of October 19, 1856. Some ten thousand people packed the auditorium, and before the service had hardly gotten under way, someone in the crowd apparently shouted "Fire!" and there was a stampede for the door. Eight people were trampled to death and many more seriously injured. Rather than closing the service, Charles carried on. According to one account, "vile preaching above the cries of the dead and dying, and louder than the wails of misery from the maimed and suffering, resounded from the mouth of Mr. Spurgeon."[5]

The account went on to tell about "mangled corpses" that were carried away amid the "clink of money" as the "collection-boxes" were passed.[6] When he realized how tragic the situation was, Charles was truly anguished. The stories in the press were not favorable, and he fell into depression. Nevertheless, crowds continued to flock to hear his preaching, and soon a new church building had been constructed.

Throughout her married life, Susannah had suffered various maladies, and by age thirty-three she was an invalid, having undergone serious surgery (though never specified in her writing). Her twins, not yet ten, spent time with their mother primarily at her bedside. She rarely got out of the house even to attend church. Invalidism among women in the Victorian era was not uncommon, nor has it been fully understood. Women, of course, were regarded the weaker sex and were more given to fainting spells than men. It is significant to note, however, that Susannah, though older than her husband, outlived him by more than a decade.

Despite her physical ailments and invalidism, Susannah initiated a book fund that she with the help of others would carry on for the remainder of her life. The initial purpose of the fund was to enhance the libraries of poor country ministers, but the recipients eventually included missionaries and almost any minister who made a request. The vast majority of books shipped out were Spurgeon's own writings, which included frequent

Spurgeon's Oddities

We have been several times to Mr. Spurgeon's chapel, and for the life of us we can discover little more than this to account for the crowds that follow him. In the man himself, and in his preaching, there is really nothing remarkable, excepting his oddities. His doctrine is not new; on the contrary, it is nothing more than old Calvinism revived in its most uncompromising form. He is not an orator, scholar, nor a man of genius; and he is the very worst reasoner we ever heard. But he is lively—says strange, odd, daring things, which keep the attention brisk, amuse the hearers, and give them something to talk about.

London Illustrated Times, October 11, 1856

mailings of his sermons as well as his magazine, *The Sword and the Trowel*. Large amounts of money were donated to the fund, and through her highly organized effort, Susannah did more than anyone else to spread the fame of her husband. With no Facebook or Twitter, her method was the most effective social media of the day.

One of the endearing traits of her husband, at least in the minds of his many supporters, was his spontaneous and sometimes shocking remarks. On a Sunday night in 1874, he had preached a sermon on so-called little sins that could bring a person down. At the end of his preaching before he closed the service, he invited a visiting minister from America to say some words. The minister picked up where Charles left off, using the habit of smoking as an example and how he had finally conquered that sin in his own life. Instead of simply closing the service with a hymn and prayer, Charles returned to the pulpit and told the congregation that he did not regard smoking as a sin and "hoped to enjoy a good cigar before going to bed."[7] The incident was not without controversy, and soon shops stocked cigar boxes embellished with his likeness.

Newspapers were not necessarily kind to the Spurgeons. There were stories of extravagant spending, particularly when they moved from one house described as a mansion to another that was even more ostentatious. One visitor offered details:

Many a millionaire might well have envied his home. This was at Westwood, on what is known as Beulah Hill, in Sydenham, which is one of London's fairest suburbs. Here he had a large and handsome mansion, situated in a spacious park; so that, although within a few minutes' ride of the teeming streets of London, it was as rural and as secluded as though in the heart of a wilderness. Passing the lodge gates, the visitor found himself amid an expanse of well-kept lawns, diversified with shrubbery and groves. A small lake was near the house, and elsewhere was a fountain containing many goldfish, of which pets Mr. Spurgeon was exceedingly fond.[8]

Clearly Charles did not shy away from controversy and, in fact, on occasion initiated it. Such was the case in the late 1880s with the Down-Grade Controversy, the term taken from articles in his magazine claiming that the Baptist Union was downgrading orthodoxy, but the real concern seemed to be a widespread lack of enthusiasm for old-line Calvinism. The backlash was swift, with a demand that he name the individuals, if indeed

Sarah Edwards and a Sunday Scandal

Long before Susannah expressed anger over criticism of her megachurch minister husband, Sarah was struggling to fit into a congregation that was openly antagonistic toward her husband, Jonathan Edwards, one of America's most noted theologians and revivalists. In fact, after twenty-three years as pastor of his Northampton church, he was voted out by the congregation. With no other ministry available, he moved his family to an outpost to do mission work among Native Americans who were more hostile (and dangerous) than his congregation had been. One of the many criticisms of the Edwardses related to the Sunday births of six of their eleven children. That Sarah and Jonathan had a strong and loving relationship was not questioned, but how and when they expressed their love apparently was. It was widely believed in Colonial New England that a baby was born on the same day of the week that it had been conceived, and some ministers actually refused to baptize babies born on Sunday and thus conceived in sin. Sexual intimacy was not deemed an appropriate activity on the Sabbath, particularly for a minister.

they were propounding heresy. He refused, and his reputation was damaged as a result. After his death when Susannah was writing his biography, she stated that "his fight for the faith . . . cost him his life."[9]

During her final years, Susannah spent time editing her husband's personal papers and turned them into a volume she called his autobiography. She insisted that no defense of him was needed now that he had gone home to be with the Lord, where there were no more "heartless attacks" or "unjust cruel words," where "the points of the arrows are all blunted" and "the stings of these scorpions are all plucked out."[10] If she had ever assumed that reporters would have given her husband a pass, she was seriously mistaken. He had invited publicity and had certainly not shied away from controversy. Susannah never could have imagined that generations after her husband's death most of the criticism would have been forgotten and that his writings would be spread today through Facebook and Twitter.

EUNICE BEECHER
Humiliated Preacher's Wife

If Susannah was upset by the newspaper accounts critical of her husband, how must Eunice Beecher have felt? Susannah and Charles were no doubt aware of the news reports spreading scandal about one of America's most noted preachers. In fact, the very year that Charles was being mocked for his cigar smoking, Henry Ward Beecher was making headlines for the scandal of the century. Henry, son of the renowned minister Lyman Beecher and brother of Harriet Beecher Stowe, had been the pastor of the large and prestigious Plymouth Church of Brooklyn for more than a quarter century.

Eunice was the daughter of Dr. Artemas Bullard of West Sutton, Massachusetts, her birth coinciding with the outbreak of the War of 1812. She became acquainted with Henry, more than a year younger than she, while he was a student at Amherst College. They became engaged soon after they met, but for various reasons he delayed the wedding for seven years, by some accounts because he had fallen for other young women in the meantime. When he finally did decide to tie the knot, he gave Eunice very little warning and then expected her to pack up and move to Lawrenceburg, Indiana, shortly thereafter. He had answered a pastoral call to a tiny church in that town without making living arrangements. So their first home was a spare bedroom in the home of a church elder.

When they did find a place of their own, it was above a barn, and Eunice was forced to take in boarders to make ends meet. Two years later Henry accepted a call from another tiny church in Indianapolis. In his eight-year tenure, the congregation grew from thirty to three hundred, and Henry thrived. But Eunice missed her New England family and was busy having babies, fighting malaria, and working as a seamstress to meet expenses. She was accused of being cranky, while the boyish Henry socialized with the townspeople and spent more money than they could afford on books. When he accepted a call to Plymouth Church in Brooklyn, New York, in 1847, she was ecstatic. It meant a much higher standard of living and servants, which she needed with her sixth child on the way.

Besides preaching, Henry was a social activist and wrote columns regularly for various newspapers. Eunice did not object to his antislavery stance, but when he began touting women's rights she strongly disagreed. "I have no sympathy for the new woman," she wrote. "What is the ability to speak on a public platform or the wisdom that may command a seat on a judge's bench compared to that which can insure and preside over a true home?"[11] She strongly objected to his involvement with Elizabeth Cady Stanton and Susan B. Anthony, whom she believed would destroy the family with their campaign for women's suffrage.

As was true in Lawrenceburg and Indianapolis, Eunice did not become a beloved minister's wife. She was accused of making Henry's life a living hell and of being a jealous and suspicious wife. Perhaps for good reason. Even while in Indianapolis, she had heard rumors of his attraction to other women. Now in New York, rumors snowballed. She had realized years earlier that Henry took great pleasure in spending time with women, but not her. The two of them were on different wavelengths. Her concerns were the children and family issues. His were theological and social issues of the day. She was a conservative, holding tight to traditional values, while he was hankering for more freedom and touting a liberal agenda.

His engaging interaction with feminists of the day more than irritated Eunice, but it was his relationship with Libby Tilton that truly angered her. Libby was a Sunday school teacher who also ministered to destitute women and their families living in tenement housing. More than twenty years younger than Henry, she was the mother of two young children and the wife of Theodore, one of Henry's close associates. Henry often stopped by their home to visit—even when Theodore was away on lecture tours. He found Libby to be a good listener and a great admirer of his writings and preaching. She confided in him, and, as Henry would later tell, she "gave an account of what she had seen of cruelty and abuse on the part of the husband that shocked me."[12]

Likewise, Henry would later insist that he simply engaged in pastoral counseling. Yes, perhaps there were some hugs and maybe kisses, but it was all part of the consolation a father figure would offer to a woman young enough to be his daughter. Libby, however, told a very different story, first to her husband, who then reported it to others. Henry's response was to accuse Theodore himself of sexual misconduct and Eunice, now in her late fifties, joined in the effort to besmirch Theodore's name. At the same time Henry sought reconciliation, but by the spring of 1871 reporters had gotten wind of the story and turned it into tabloid fodder.

The scandal quickly began to take a toll on Eunice, who was described by one acquaintance as "white haired" and a "dozen years older" than when this woman had last seen her. "My heart has been full of pity for her," she continued. "Her face is written over with many volumes of human suffering." Henry turned his back on Eunice, which only added to her misery. He moved all his personal papers to his sister's home and sent her to Havana or Florida, presumably to relax and relieve her mind of the gossip. All the while he wrote pitiful letters to her, one lamenting, "My life is almost over."[13]

In the meantime, Plymouth Church set up a committee to investigate, and in 1874 Henry was exonerated, even though Theodore had testified that Henry had committed adultery with Libby. The following year Theodore brought a case against Henry in Brooklyn. Eunice, now home in New York, was in court every day. In the end the jury failed to reach a verdict. Technically Henry was off the hook, but most people, including his own parishioners, thought him guilty. Later Libby, separated from her husband, confided in a letter that she had lied when she testified in court that she had not committed adultery with Henry.

Nevertheless, Henry held on to his prestigious pastoral position at the church and was frequently in the pulpit. Publicly Eunice stood by her man, but privately she was enduring anguish. "I live in the past over and over, and every little while when talking most cheerfully," she confided to a friend, "such a flood of fiery indignation sweeps over me that I am constantly on the watch lest I lose my self-control and show it." Here again, her indignation seems to have been directed more at Libby than Henry. He left on lecture tours while putting their daughter-in-law in charge of the household and sending Eunice to Florida, a matter she deeply resented.[14]

It is very bitter to go away from you, worse now than years ago, because while under this mysterious cloud, whatever it may be, and feeling its cruelty, I am in danger of that which will be far worse than death, that my love and trust in you may grow cold or waver. . . . If your heart has not changed woefully, you would not—you could not subject me to the torture of the last four years.[15]

Emma Moody: The Engine Driving D. L. Moody

She was a shy fifteen-year-old Sunday school teacher when she met the twenty-year-old successful Chicago shoe salesman. More than that he was the one who had organized this successful Sunday school among poor children of the tenement neighborhoods. He had an easy way with words, and soon they were engaged. That he would one day become a world-renowned evangelist would not have entered her mind. His grammar and pronunciation were almost laughable, and he often looked like he had slept the night before in his clothes. But this British-born lass soon polished him up. He became America's most celebrated evangelist and preacher of the late nineteenth century, while she reared the children. More than that, Emma was a first-rate teacher actively involved in personal evangelism whose expertise was the pride of her husband. She endured hardships throughout their marriage, particularly the loss of their home and church during the Chicago fire of 1871, and later observing the waywardness of their two sons.

Eunice was intuitive enough to realize that her marriage to Henry was essentially in name only. Despite her insecurities she carried on as best she could. In fact, she continued her writing, which she had begun after moving to New York. At age forty-seven, more than a decade after they had settled there, she had published her first book. Then in 1875, in the midst of the scandal, her second book was released, *Motherly Talks with Young Housekeepers*, and three years later *How to Make Homes Happy*. The title was ironic considering her inability to make her own home happy.

Henry died at seventy-three; Eunice lived on for more than a decade. When she was eighty, she published an article in the *Ladies' Home Journal*, which might have made a greater impact than anything either she or her husband had ever written. It appeared at a time when severe corporal punishment was widely practiced. Her examples and words of caution were words that parents needed to hear. This article was for all practical purposes her final message. She told how she had once been severe in her physical discipline, but the deaths of one child after another had a profound effect on both her and Henry: "Little Georgie's loss was a very severe trial, and through the sorrow we were led to a milder interpretation of parental duties." Then after the twins died she wrote that they never again "resorted to corporal punishment."[16]

DAISY BILLINGS SMITH
Pushed-Aside Popular Preacher

Daisy's husband, Oswald J. Smith, was an internationally celebrated minister who founded the Peoples Church in Toronto in 1928 and served as senior pastor for thirty years; he then passed the torch on to his son Paul, who carried it for another thirty-five years. According to Wikipedia, Oswald accomplished great things in his ninety-six years. "Over the course of eighty years he preached more than 12,000 sermons in 80 countries, wrote thirty-five books (with translations into 128 languages), as well as 1,200 poems, of which 100 have been set to music." The article also cites his strong enthusiasm for overseas missions and his role as "a leading force in Fundamentalism in Canada."

His "gracious and generous helpmate" is barely mentioned except for her "sublimating her career to his."[17] That statement in many ways uniquely sums up her life. Neither Susannah nor Eunice had a career to sublimate. Daisy did, and she suffered on that account. From her youth growing up in a poor family in Ontario, she longed to be a missionary. Before graduating from high school, she began working in a factory to save money to pay for expenses at Nyack Missionary College in New York, where she enrolled in 1908. There she worked in the laundry for room and board.

She was single-minded in her commitment to ministry. When she received a letter from a young man who confessed he was "falling in love" with her, she responded that her "only goal [was] to study God's Word, to be better equipped to preach it somewhere to those who have never heard." In his original letter her suitor had complimented her on her "marvelous deep speaking voice," adding that she was "going to make a great preacher."[18]

On graduating, she and Ada, her roommate, set out for West Virginia to begin ministry in Roaring Fork, a small coal town. When they arrived late at night, they were shown to a dilapidated shack furnished with bedbug-ridden sagging cots. Waking up with bites and rashes, they heard a knock at the door. A destitute woman informed them that her baby had died in the night. Daisy returned with the woman to a pitiful hovel where a very young girl was sitting on a bench holding the dead infant. The mother took the tiny body and handed it over to Daisy and left with the girl. No books or school courses had trained Daisy for this. She washed the body, found some clothes, a blanket, and a box, and waited for the woman to return. When she did, they dug a grave and lowered the box into it. Daisy prayed, read Scripture, and offered words of consolation.

In the two years that followed, the two missionaries reopened a church and began services, Ada playing the old pump organ and Daisy preaching. When they left, due to the terminal illness of Ada's mother, one of their coal-miner converts agreed to carry on with the ministry. Roaring Fork, however, had offered Daisy an opportunity to fulfill the young man's prediction that she was going to make a great preacher. Preaching invitations poured in, and soon she was asked to join Pastor J. D. Morrow on the staff of Dale Presbyterian Church. Her work there primarily involved outreach to the poor, but preaching was what she enjoyed the most.

With added growth, Morrow invited Oswald to join the staff. Daisy was assigned more work off-site, while Oswald took over her preaching and congregational duties. Many people were unhappy with the change, not the least of whom was Daisy. She resented his intrusion but realized that she had been out*manned*. Oswald assumed it was his place to do the preaching, but he recognized Daisy's remarkable gifts. Having just gone through a broken engagement, what he later described as the greatest sorrow of his life, he began wooing Daisy. She was in her midtwenties, approaching "old-maid" status. She knew what she was doing. She traded preaching for a wifely supporting role.

The headlines said it all: "Assistant Pastor of Dale Presbyterian Church Weds Its Popular Deaconess." Soon after the wedding, Morrow took an extended leave of absence. Oswald, true to his nature, immediately set about changing things. Without consulting the church board, he hung in front of the church a large banner with red lettering: GET RIGHT WITH GOD. He changed the style of music without informing the music director. The focus was now entirely on "soul saving." The church was in turmoil. Daisy, once so popular, was almost undone. Members of the congregation who had loved to hear her preach now avoided her. She felt alone and even abandoned by her husband, who spent late-night hours with those eager to be involved in his special prayer groups.

When Morrow returned, he was distressed by the situation, accusing Oswald of putting the church in debt. Oswald resigned, thus ending three stormy years of ministry. With no other opportunities, Oswald decided to move to British Columbia to do mission work among lumberjacks. Here the pregnant Daisy was often alone for days on end with their baby. With that ministry faltering, he uprooted the family again and returned to Toronto, where he left Daisy and their two sickly babies with her financially strapped family while he tried his hand at an itinerant ministry.

Eventually Oswald did find a measure of success but not enough to support Daisy in even modest circumstances. He was convinced that God was calling him to an international ministry. In 1924, he sailed to Europe, leaving Daisy behind in Toronto with three little ones. During the long absences, she became depressed and filled with self-doubt. "Why, O, why is God taking you away from me," she wrote. "I only wish I were worthy of you. . . . I fall so short of my own ideal for myself as wife and mother, and often wish, really and truly, that I were taken away so that before you are old you might have a more ideal woman."[19]

In 1927, Oswald accepted a ministerial call to Los Angeles, but before they arrived by auto, he had a change of heart. He called back home to cancel the furniture movers, only to learn that it was too late, so he agreed to stay at this new church for a year. Having kept his word to the very day, he then moved the family back to Toronto, where he found himself once again persona non grata in his previous church circles. Thus at forty he established his own church—the People's Church. He was a dynamic evangelistic speaker, and soon the seats were full. "For some time I did not take much interest in the work," he later wrote. "Very often I left others in charge and travelled." Daisy stayed home. The once-strong young woman who had preached so confidently in Roaring Forks and Dale Presbyterian was beaten down. "I try to be brave," she lamented to her husband, "but I feel so defeated by it all."[20]

When the children reached their teens, Oswald expected Daisy to leave them home and join him. She responded to him in a terse letter: "You never wanted me with you before, and I'm not going now. The children still need me."[21] In the years that followed when the children were on their own, she sometimes did accompany her husband, all the while his fame increasing while she supported him behind the scenes.

Ruth Peale
The Power behind Positive Thinking

Had she not been married to Norman Vincent Peale, one of the fore-most ministers of the twentieth century, Ruth would be one more pastor's wife remembered only by close family and friends. Her life spanned the twentieth century, 1906–2008, and deserves telling from beginning to end. But her significance, at least for the purposes of this volume, lies in her authorship of a fascinating book, *The Adventure of Being a Wife*. Unlike Eunice Beecher, she was not hesitant to speak of marital problems. Nor was she tempted to turn her husband into a saint as Susannah Spurgeon had sought to do.

For fifty-two years Norman served as senior pastor of the Marble Collegiate Church in Manhattan. From that base he built his empire, which included organizations that to some seemed more secular than sacred, among them the Horatio Alger Association and the American Foundation of Religion and Psychiatry. He came of age as a minister when radio and TV were seemingly begging for sermons, particularly those that offered audiences a positive slant on life. But the work for which he is remembered most was his best-selling book, *The Power of Positive Thinking*. For that and for other contributions he had made, President Reagan awarded him the Presidential Medal of Freedom.

One might imagine that being married to the authority on positive thinking, Ruth would have been blessed with a serene and optimistic husband. Nothing could be further from the truth. She wrote honestly of two people enduring each other's flaws in marriage: "For example, I have to put up with his volatility and unpredictability where plans and appointments are concerned. He, on the other hand, has to live with my lack of flexibility and tendency to become bogged down in details."[22]

These problems continued throughout their marriage. The problem of Norman's mother continued for decades as well. His mother had strongly objected to their marriage, and she insisted that she and Norman's father accompany them on their honeymoon to a cabin in the Adirondack Mountains. When they traveled abroad, she accompanied them. Norman had no backbone to prevent her joining them. He was indecisive and weak willed.

But a far greater issue throughout their marriage was Norman's serious bouts of depression, sometimes long periods of black despair. "When he gets depressed," Ruth wrote, "he sees only the negative side of everything. Sometimes I think he writes about positive thinking because he understands so much about negative thinking." Indeed, it was Ruth who kept his head above water when he was drowning in despair. "I considered it part of my job as a wife to understand all this, to evaluate it unemotionally, and then do something about it."[23]

Doing something about it sometimes entailed a severe scolding. When Norman was in the depth of self-pity on one occasion, he quoted her saying to him: "You are not only my husband. You are also my pastor, and in the latter department I'm frank to say I am becoming increasingly disappointed in you. I hear you from the pulpit talking about faith and trust in

God's wondrous power. But now I hear in you no faith or trust at all. You just whine your defeat."[24]

In her willingness to be open and honest about marital difficulties, Ruth was ahead of her time. She placed no value on feigned spirituality or pretense of any kind, particularly about any such ideal as perfection in marriage. If a marriage was devoid of differences and if there were no disagreements and disputes, she suspected it was not alive and growing. Her outspoken reflections are as refreshing as they are telling:

> Countless times, talking with a married couple I've just met, I've heard them say to me, "Oh, yes, we've been married fifteen years (or twenty, or thirty) and we've never had a cross word between us." I always smile and nod happily, but what I'm really thinking is, "How dull! How boring! What a drag a marriage like that would be."[25]

CONCLUDING OBSERVATIONS

Ministers' wives, like politicians' wives, are expected to follow the counsel of Tammy Wynette's hit song, "Stand by Your Man." How often we see the politician at the microphone (his wife discreetly standing at his side), apologizing for infidelities or other sorts of wrongdoing. Even though women are in far greater numbers entering politics and ministry, we always picture a wife supporting her husband more than the reverse. It is true today, as it has been historically.

Susannah was a natural at playing second fiddle to her husband, though her initial assessment of him gave no hint of her being a wallflower, much less a preacher's wife. But she found her place and had a critical role in making his sermons and writings known far beyond those who were part of his congregation. And when he was publicly criticized, she was his strongest defender. She blamed his opponents for his early death and posthumously edited his autobiography, not surprisingly a very sympathetic account that helped to establish his future prominence in evangelicalism.

Eunice also defended her husband, but she was publicly standing by her man while desperately trying to cope with the pain her flamboyant, unfaithful husband had inflicted on her. Susannah had married the up-and-coming preacher of her own church, while Eunice and Daisy Smith found out the hard way how difficult it was to follow their husbands from place to place and raise little ones without a steady income. Daisy's story is perhaps far more common than we realize. She was forced to set aside her dreams and her remarkable gifts for the sake of her husband's ministry. Her private anguished letters are critical to understanding the larger picture of Christian ministry and the toll it can take on individuals and families.

Ruth was amazingly honest about her bipolar minister husband, and she was open about their problems and personal differences, hoping that others would realize that marriage—whether to a preacher or a politician or anyone else—is hard work, particularly when a mother-in-law is overbearing and a husband is seriously depressed.

QUESTIONS TO THINK ABOUT

Do you think the ministry of Charles Spurgeon might have been enhanced had he been married to a woman who was not only a supporter but also a constructive critic? Do you know of situations when a wife would have done well to strongly encourage her husband to make important changes in his work or relationships?

Can you put into words how Eunice must have felt when she heard the news that Libby had accused Henry of having an inappropriate relationship with her? How should a woman respond in such instances? Do you personally know of similar situations?

Does a husband's ministry or career take priority over that of a wife? Is there something Daisy might have done to hold on to her ministry and curtail her husband's rash decisions to uproot the family? Does her frustration ring true with women today?

Can you relate to Ruth Peale's problems with her overbearing mother-in-law? Are mother-in-law troubles overplayed? Do you know women with serious mother-in-law issues? What kinds of solutions are advisable?

If you could pick one of these ministers' wives to speak at a women's retreat, who would be your first choice? Which one would you most enjoy having an intimate one-on-one afternoon with?

13

Aimee Semple McPherson and Pentecostal Preachers

She is the founder—the controversial founder—of the Foursquare Church. I've known about her ministry and have studied her fascinating life on and off for decades. But for this study I needed an update. I typed *foursquare* into Google. The first items that came up, however, related to social media, not to a church. Foursquare, according to Wikipedia, is "a location-based social networking website for mobile devices."[1] I didn't know. No surprise. My only mobile device is a twenty-dollar Walmart phone with a prepaid card for eight dollars a month. Someday, I tell myself, I'll get a smartphone.

I am by no means on the cutting edge of technology. Aimee Semple McPherson, founder of the Foursquare Church, was. Today that church continues to utilize the latest technology. From its website we read that the church-wide "Conversation" to "Reimagine Foursquare" will be a local event. How so?

> As you prepare for your local Town Hall meeting, download the framework for the Reimagine conversation. . . . Can't make the stop in your district? We have you covered. We will be streaming live from two locations, including one in Spanish. You'll still have the chance to ask questions and offer your feedback.[2]

Aimee would have been proud of the technological progress her church has made. If today's social media had been available in her day, she would have been in the forefront. But it might have backfired on her. Foursquare, Wikipedia goes on to inform us, has the capability to track people down. "Location is based on GPS hardware in the mobile device or network location provided by the application, and the map is based on data from the OpenStreetMap project."

If Aimee had taken her smartphone with her when she disappeared back in 1926, law enforcement and the meddlesome media would have tracked her down. The mystery would have been solved in no time. But with no GPS tracking devices, no one knew if she had drowned while swimming in the ocean, her body swept out to sea, or if perhaps she had been kidnapped. Or was she enjoying a little R&R with a lover in a hideaway?

When she walked out of the desert just across the Arizona-Mexico border a month later, she told authorities she had been kidnapped. She told them she had been dropped off in the middle of nowhere and had walked some twenty miles across the hardscrabble terrain, no food, no water—no smartphone. To local officials, she looked fresh, clean, and well dressed for such an ordeal, but that was her story and she was *stickin' to it*.

In her absence, the newspapers had a field day of speculation, and it certainly didn't stop with her reappearance. But Aimee carried on with her ministry despite a long, drawn-out court battle. In subsequent years she continued to preach, and the church continued to grow. But Aimee would always be the butt of jokes. In fact, further online searching took me unexpectedly to lyrics by folk singer and songwriter Pete Seeger, the late Pete Seeger who died in January 2014. The song is a nine-verse spoof at Aimee's expense. Verse six parodies Aimee and her lover holed up in a cottage, cavorting on a worn-out bed. (If *I'd had a hammer*, I might have been tempted to conk my dear Pete over the head and ask him why he didn't use his creative genius in giving us more great songs like "Where Have All the Flowers Gone?" and "If I Had a Hammer.")

Aimee was far more than merely a joke. Before her alleged kidnapping, she was the most noted American evangelist of her time, a household name. She was likewise one of the first on the West Coast to build a grand megachurch, Angelus Temple. I visited the church on a weekday afternoon many years ago. The auditorium was empty. I tried to imagine Aimee standing at the pulpit. I could almost hear her voice, as I had heard it on taped recordings. She could hold a crowd. As I walked through the vestibule, I noticed what appeared to be glassed-in trophy shelves. Here were mementos people at her healing services had left behind: crutches, casts, neck braces, pill bottles, and everything imaginable that might no longer be needed by someone who had been declared whole.

Who was this woman? Nothing about her seems certain except that she will forever remain elusive. Her numerous biographers tell widely conflicting tales, and her story simply doesn't die. She was preceded and followed by other Pentecostal women evangelists, including Maria Woodworth-Etter, Florence Crawford, Susie Villa Valdez, Rosa de Lopez, Pandita Ramabai, and Kathryn Kuhlman. But Aimee stands alone.

Hebrews Hall of Faith

By faith Abraham, by faith Noah, by faith Jacob, by faith Moses, by faith Rahab. Here is a list that includes a coward, a drunk, a deceiver, a murderer, a prostitute. Confessions accompany none of the sins they committed. Should we be surprised if a modern Hall of Faith included Maria, Pandita, Kathryn—and Aimee?

> By faith the prostitute Rahab, because she welcomed the spies, was not killed with those who were disobedient.
>
> And what more shall I say? I do not have time to tell about Gideon, Barak, Samson and Jephthah, about David and Samuel and the prophets, who through faith conquered kingdoms, administered justice, and gained what was promised; who shut the mouths of lions, quenched the fury of the flames, and escaped the edge of the sword; whose weakness was turned to strength; and who became powerful in battle and routed foreign armies.
>
> Hebrews 11:31–34

MARIA WOODWORTH-ETTER
Trance Evangelist

She was known as the trance evangelist. As many as five hundred people fell into trances during one single meeting. Traveling with a huge tent, she went from town to town, healing and even raising the dead—that is, if her accounts are to be taken at face value. Indeed, whether her accounts are reliable is the main issue confronting scholars who would study her. Unlike the wide array of sources on other religious figures of the era, there is very little published material on her life and ministry—very little that is not taken from her own writings or those of her devoted followers. That she was the most widely traveled and influential woman evangelist of the late nineteenth and early twentieth century is well established.

Maria (pronounced like Mariah Carey) was an Ohio farmer's wife, mother of six, who painfully witnessed, one by one, the deaths of the first five. She was in her midthirties by the time she began her revival ministry, initially preaching in nearby small churches. Barely a dozen years later, she had traveled three times coast-to-coast, drawing large crowds despite hostility toward women preachers. Her unique style was compelling. Curiosity seekers and the faithful alike packed the tent. God spoke to her in visions, she testified, while she was in a trance. A vivid panorama of hell (and heaven) had prompted her to begin her evangelistic ministry:

> Then the Lord, in a vision, caused me to see the bottomless pit, open in all its horror and woe. There was weeping and wailing and gnashing of teeth. It was surrounded by a great multitude of people who seemed unconscious of their danger; and without a moments warning, they would tumble into this awful place. I was above the people on a narrow plank-walk, which wound up toward heaven; and I was exhorting and pleading with the people to come up onto the plank and escape that awful place. Several started. There was a beautiful bright light above me, and I was encouraging them to follow that light and they would go straight to heaven.[3]

Because Maria's husband had not sensed a call to ministry and did not wish to leave the farm, she mostly traveled without him. Then when she was forty-seven, she accused him of unfaithfulness and sued for divorce.

A decade later in 1902, she married Samuel Etter even as the invitations to speak declined. She had been wary of the new emphasis on speaking in tongues. Though people in her services fell to the floor in trances, she had regarded tongues speaking to be extreme. By 1912, however, she was back on the big-tent circuit, and if not embracing the new tongues of fire at least accepting them as a valid response to her fiery preaching.

The content of her sermons was drawn largely from her visionary trances. But soon the actual trances also became an awaited moment in her meetings. She would suddenly freeze in a trance, at times lasting for minutes, occasionally for hours. Indeed, so shocking was her demeanor that members of the audience would leave to bring others in just to look at her and sometimes fall into trances themselves. This aspect of her ministry was exaggerated in the telling. Decades later televangelist Kenneth Hagin claimed he had witnessed a three-day trance. His story was repeated word for word by others who denounced such activity as coming straight from Satan.

> She was in her 70's preaching in a tent which was full when right in the middle of her sermon with her hand uplifted to illustrate a point, and her mouth opened, the power of God came upon her. She froze in that position and stood like a statue for three days and three nights. . . . She had no bodily functions for three days and nights. She stood there. According to the newspaper account, it was estimated that more than 150,000 people came by to see her in the three day period. The third night, the Spirit of God released her. She thought it was the same night and the same sermon and she went on preaching at the same place in her sermon.[4]

Whatever the duration of these trances, she insisted she was experiencing "the power" of the Holy Spirit. Opponents referred to her as the "voodoo priestess" who hypnotized her listeners. They sometimes sought to put a stop to her ministry, more than once attempting to have her locked up on charges of insanity and fraud.[5]

Throughout her itinerant ministry, Maria kept a detailed record. In 1922, two years before her death, she published *Marvels and Miracles God Wrought in the Ministry for Forty-Five Years*. Chapter 15 is subtitled "Plots to Destroy My Life, in Imminent Danger of Death." Here she wrote:

Maria Ministering with Cherokee Evangelist

The December 9, 1922, issue of the [Assemblies of God] *Pentecostal Evangel* reported on the district's formation. . . . Watt Walker, a Cherokee evangelist who previously traveled with healing evangelist Maria Woodworth-Etter, was one of the featured speakers at the founding of the North Central District. Walker was chosen to serve on the North Central District's first Credentials Committee. It is significant that a Native American was elected to serve on the committee that voted to approve new ministers.

"This Week in AG History—December 9, 1922," Assemblies of God website

I have been in great dangers; many times not knowing when I would be shot down, either in the pulpit, or going to and from meeting. . . . But I said I would never run, nor compromise. The Lord would always put His mighty power on me, so that He took all fear away, and made me like a giant. . . . If in any way they had tried to shoot, or kill me, He would have struck them dead, and I sometimes told them so.[6]

As a fiery revivalist, Maria was often hailed in superlative terms. Indeed, fellow evangelist A. H. Argue described her meetings in Chicago as the "mightiest visitation from God of these latter days."[7] During the early years of her ministry, she established more than a dozen churches, and in 1918 she put her mark on a large church in Indianapolis, the Maria Woodworth-Etter Tabernacle, still carrying on today as the Lakeview Church.

SUSIE VILLA VALDEZ AND ROSA DE LOPEZ
Hispanic Evangelists

There are very few historical accounts of Hispanic evangelical women who were active in ministry. Many Hispanic women served with Catholic nuns and became nuns themselves. But very sparse is the historical record of Hispanic women outside the Catholic Church who were involved in evangelistic outreach. Perhaps due to machismo in Hispanic—particularly

Mexican—culture, such options were unavailable except in rare instances. Some Hispanic women broke through the barriers and served effectively as evangelists and social activists. That they were typically married, sometimes to supportive men, did not hinder their efforts. Even they, however, are barely footnotes in the history of evangelicalism.

After her conversion at the Azusa Street revival in 1906, Susie left behind her job as a seamstress and became a singing evangelist to destitute women and families living in the Los Angeles slums as well as to farm laborers in the migrant camps of the San Bernardino Valley. Her son Adolfo Valdez later reflected on his mother's work:

> I remember her hard but rewarding spiritual-social work with prostitutes and skid-row alcoholics done in the Lord's name. . . . My mother visited the slums, playing her guitar and singing sacred songs in the poorly lit streets for anyone who would listen. . . . She heard the troubles of many lonely and depressed people and usually introduced them to Christ. Around midnight she would walk . . . home, often arriving as late as 2 AM.[8]

Rosa de Lopez ministered with her preacher husband, Abundio, at the Azusa Street revival as well as in the open-air Mexican Plaza District. Together they made a joint statement attesting to their Pentecostal fervor. They publicly affirmed that they had been forgiven, sanctified, and baptized with the *Holy Ghost and fire*.

In 1908, Rosa discovered what she believed to be a life-threatening tumor. Fearing her life and ministry were nearly over, she and her husband sought out Maria Woodworth-Etter. Rosa was seeking a miraculous healing so that she might carry on in the ministry. And so it was. Maria's *Apostolic Faith* newspaper reported on the ministry of Rosa, which continued to grow as Spanish-speaking congregations were established in the years that followed.

PANDITA RAMABAI
Founder of Mukti Mission in India

The twentieth-century Pentecostal movement is often said to have begun on New Year's Eve 1901 in Topeka, Kansas, when Agnes Ozman, a student at Bethel Bible School, spoke in tongues as others were constrained to do

Florence Crawford: Founder of Apostolic Faith Church

Among those powerfully influenced by William J. Seymour and the Azusa Street revival was Florence Crawford. She wasted no time in launching her own evangelistic tour to Oregon, Washington, Minnesota, and Canada. Then she settled down in Portland, making the city headquarters for her Apostolic Faith Church with an auditorium seating some three thousand people and a comprehensive mission that served those in need. Before her death in 1936, the movement had spread to other states, and missionaries were commissioned to foreign countries. Publishing became her forte—books, tracts—and her testimony:

> I was raised in a home of unbelief. When I was a little girl, before my feet could touch the floor from the chair, I sat at the table with noted infidels. . . . I used to shake my feet against the chair, and something way down in my heart would say, "I know there is a God." . . . One night as I was dancing in a ballroom . . . I heard a voice speak out of Heaven and say, "Daughter, give me thine heart." . . . Some years later, this Christian woman . . . told me of a colored man preaching down in Azusa Street. . . . It was . . . an old barn-like building with only an old board laid on two chairs for an altar; there were no windows . . . the floor was carpeted with sawdust; the walls and beams blackened with smoke. Finally a big colored man arose to his feet and said, "Hallelujah!" It just went into my soul. . . . One week after I was sanctified, as I sat in my chair at one of the services, a sound like a rushing mighty wind filled the room, and I was baptized with the Holy Ghost and fire. . . . This tongue that never spoke another word but English began to magnify and praise God in another language. I was speaking Chinese.
>
> Amos Morgan, "'Mother Crawford':
> A Profile of Reverend Florence Louise Crawford"

likewise. But that was a relatively isolated incident. It was not until the Azusa Street revival of 1907 that the movement began to explode. And it was only after that when Maria Woodworth-Etter became part of the movement. Prior to Azusa Street, however, there were other tongues-speaking revivals, the word of which was spread by a supportive writer and reporter, Frank

Bartleman, an early Pentecostal leader who publicized extensively how the movement was "rocked in the cradle of little Wales," after which it was "brought up" in India, and finally became "full grown" at Azusa Street.[9]

At the time, Pandita Ramabai would not have realized the enormous part she had played in nurturing a worldwide revival. She had heard about revivals in Australia and Wales and prayed that a similar revival might occur at her Indian orphanage at Mukti. Soon others joined her in prayer that continued for months, climaxing in an "outpouring" of the Spirit. "Little girls," wrote one observer, "were lost for hours in the transport of loving Jesus and praising Him." Others reported that thousands were converted amid weeping, tongues-speaking, and miracles.[10]

The miracle stories were quickly passed along, as was the account of a dry well during a severe drought at Mukti. "Each of the two wells had all its contents used up every day," Pandita recalled. "But there came a fresh supply in the morning to each well, and it lasted all day." Perhaps even more significant than such miracles was the increase in evangelistic outreach. Pandita organized many of the girls into bands and sent them out to neighboring villages.[11]

The Mukti Mission, founded by Pandita in 1889, was very controversial in India. Hindus accused her of turning little girls into Christians with no concern for their religious heritage. She insisted that she taught both Hindu and Christian scriptures and gave the girls freedom to choose their path. Missionaries in turn pounced on her for propagating pluralism. She often felt as though she had been abandoned by virtually everyone except the girls, many of whom were very young widows who had no other place to live.

Controversy was not new for Pandita. Born in 1858 into a privileged high-caste Brahmin family, she grew up amid cultural disputes. Her father was a reformer and a recognized Sanskrit scholar. He advocated education for girls and homeschooled his young daughter in Hindu tradition and languages while encouraging her to cultivate an open-minded search for truth.

Following an economic downturn and a loss of wealth, her father began a religious pilgrimage with the family in tow. When her parents became ill and died, Pandita continued traveling with her brother and then decided it was her duty to pick up where her father had left off. "I am a child of a man who had to suffer a great deal on account of advocating Female

Education," she later wrote. "I consider it my duty, to the very end of my life, to maintain this cause and to advocate the proper position of women in this land."[12] After her brother died, she married a lower-caste lawyer, creating a scandal that did not subside with his death.

Adding to that disgrace was her widowhood. But she was determined to carry on with her call for female education and the prohibition of child marriages. She was one of the early Indian feminists of her day and as such was seeking counsel from anyone who might help her.

Enter Sister Geraldine, an Anglican nun. Their relationship blossomed, and Geraldine invited Pandita to visit her homeland of England and to study the Bible. Once again Pandita stirred controversy, befriending a Christian—and before long becoming a Christian herself. Had Geraldine understood Pandita at all, she should have realized that her new convert would not easily conform to her creeds and conditions. "I am, it is true, a member of the Church of Christ," she wrote to Geraldine, "but I am not bound to accept every word that falls down from the lips of priests or bishops." She minced no words: "I have just with great efforts freed myself from the yoke of the Indian priestly tribe, so I am not at present willing to place myself under another similar yoke by accepting everything which comes from the priests as authorized command of the Most High."[13]

Geraldine, apparently unschooled in cross-cultural contextualization, was offended—so offended that she told Ramabai she was disappointed that she had played a part in her conversion. Ramabai would have none of it: "I regret that I have been the cause of making you feel yourself wrong for the part you acted in my baptism." Indeed, her biting sarcasm spilled out: "I wish I knew that your Church required a person to be quite perfect in faith, doubting nothing in the Athanasian Creed, so that he had left nothing to be learnt and inquired into the Bible after his baptism."[14]

But the Anglican sister was not about to let the matter drop. She accused Pandita of "clinging to caste prejudice which ought to have been thrown to the winds" because of her refusal to eat such things as pudding made from eggs. Pandita saw right through Geraldine's sense of cultural superiority. Pandita, to be sure, was a proud Indian. "I confess I am not free from all my caste prejudices, as you are pleased to call them," she fired back. "How would an Englishwoman like being called proud and prejudiced if she were to go and live among the Hindus for a time but did not think it necessary to alter her customs when they were not hurtful or necessary to her neighbors?"[15] Case closed.

To the very end Pandita was a firebrand. Hindus strongly opposed her Christian mission. Christian missionaries criticized her for her respect for Hindu scriptures and making them available to the girls at her school. Even her revival work was often misunderstood. But she refused to be swayed by others and almost seemed to relish the opposition: "I am having a right good time in the storm of public indignation that is raging over my head."[16] Yet even during her lifetime she was honored as a reformer and revivalist as well as a Bible translator. And after her death she was recognized with awards and accolades.

AIMEE SEMPLE MCPHERSON
Pentecostal Superstar

From nuns and abbesses to prison reformers and missionaries, women made incredible sacrifices to spread the gospel. They were as persistent as they were persevering. They pushed against gender and religious restrictions. Their accomplishments were enormous. But fashion was not their forte—except in one case. There had never been a prominent woman in ministry, with the possible exception of Queen Esther, as dazzling and glamorous as Aimee. Indeed, amid the spotlights in Los Angeles, she rivaled the most alluring actresses of her day.

Her Canadian childhood and young adult years offered no clues to her later fame, but such is often the case. In some respects her celebrity parallels that of silent film star Mary Pickford, two years younger than she and also Canadian. Both were reared in poor families with strong Methodist influences. And both were captivated by the new entertainment of the day—the movies. And both, before settling in Los Angeles, would tour across country by automobile with their mothers, Mary to act in third-rate theater troupes and Aimee to preach in trashy storefronts and beat-up tents. Both settled in Southern California, married three times, divorced, and were secretly involved with other men while publicly expanding their popularity and fame. And both combined glamor with a sense of humor.

Aimee launched her revival ministry in Los Angeles in 1919, and within a few short years she had become the star of the revival circuit, picking up steam at the very time that the flamboyant "fire and brimstone" revivalist Billy Sunday had passed his peak. There was plenty of terrain for both Aimee and Billy, but to compete in the sport of revivalism Aimee needed more than a gospel message, patriotism, and glamor. Gimmicks were critical. Billy, a former baseball player, was acrobatic in his presentation but seemed almost dull alongside her. She had every trick imaginable up her sleeve. On one occasion, dressed as a traffic cop, she appeared onstage astride a motorcycle.

But Aimee, unlike Billy and most other revivalists, was determined to be more than a traveling preacher. She was a driven woman, almost unstoppable. In 1922, three years after she launched her revival ministry, she founded her own denomination, the International Church of the Foursquare Gospel. The following year she built her own church, Angelus Temple, which seated some five thousand, and in 1924, she began a far-reaching radio ministry. In comparison to many preachers of the day, she offered a more welcoming and loving approach to the gospel with fewer hell-raising scare tactics. With the help of media consultants, she honed her skills. And the money poured in.

A Show-Woman Extraordinaire

Aimee was a show-woman extraordinaire. Her services featured music, show choirs, talking birds, farm animals, healings, and her famed "theatrical sermons," which combined biblical teachings with pageantry. With her lilting voice, Aimee was the star of these productions, "radiating health, optimism and magnetism . . . she dances and claps her hands like a happy little girl in the pulpit and she starts the singing with all the carefree exuberance of a joyous child." She could play any part, dressing as a farm girl to tell the story of her life or as a policewoman for a sermon inspired by a recent speeding ticket. "In this show-devouring city," reported *Harper's* magazine in 1927, "no entertainment compares in popularity with that of Angelus Temple."

Hadley Hall Meares, "America's First Megachurch," *Curbed LA*, April 21, 2014

228

A significant aspect of her ministry was healing. People came by the thousands to be rid of their canes and crutches and casts. There was no malady, physical or psychological, that was not allegedly healed by God, through the touch or reach of this Pentecostal queen. But she touched more than illness. She ministered to the whole body—to whole families—and was known for her emphasis on social welfare. Her touch was not confined to the needy in her congregation only. The hungry and poor from miles around knew they could come to Angelus Temple for help, no questions asked, leaving with their dignity intact.

In the minds of many, Sister Aimee was above reproach. She could do no wrong. So when the news broke that she had gone missing, the apprehension was palpable. She was larger than life, and her followers could not imagine carrying on without her. They loved her, but at a distance. Indeed, with all her success, Aimee had developed few close friends. Her mother was often in the picture, but the two had a rocky relationship at best. Few people, if any at all, knew that beneath the surface, she struggled with depression and loneliness.

The date was May 18, 1926, the setting, a beach between Ocean Park and Venice along the waters of Santa Monica Bay. It was there where Aimee, according to her secretary Emma Shaeffer, had gone into the surf for a swim while she herself ran errands. When she returned, Aimee was nowhere to be found. The news was unsettling. By this time Aimee was an internationally known celebrity. Her mother, preaching at Angelus Temple that evening, told the crowd that Aimee had drowned—had gone to be with Jesus. Her followers were beside themselves, holding vigil along the beaches while searchers in small planes flew overhead and ones in watercraft dotted the bay.

The story quickly took on a life of its own. Neither did it die down when Aimee appeared on June 23, having allegedly walked some twenty miles through the desert after being released by kidnappers near the Mexico border. How could that be when she was wearing a perfectly clean dress and shoes? Or was she bedraggled and dirty? There was no demand for ransom. The story simply did not make sense. The news reports and rumors were contradictory. Was the kidnapping claim a ruse? Did she actually run away with the married Kenneth Ormiston, her radio manager? Reports of sightings proliferated, sometimes in very different locations at nearly the same time. Why hadn't anyone reported to law enforcement and collected the widely advertised reward money?

In an odd turn of events, Ormiston admitted that he had actually run off, not with Aimee, but with an unidentified woman who was not his wife. So where then was Aimee? The rumor mill was churning out an endless cycle of accusations that ranged from a secret abortion to plastic surgery. And no wonder. Her story of the kidnapping and torture was contradictory and full of holes. The Los Angeles district attorney did not take the matter lightly, and Aimee was charged with perjury. After all, her story was not merely fodder for tabloids. Two people had died in the Santa Monica search effort, and the cost to law enforcement was enormous.

In 1927, the court case was dropped. But Aimee's reputation was forever damaged. Four years later she did further damage to her name when she remarried and then after three years divorced again. When she died a decade later in 1944, just before her fifty-fourth birthday, the rumor mill churned out accusations of suicide.

Those who imagined that her ministry and the denomination she founded would collapse with such scandals were wrong. Growth continued not only in California and throughout America but worldwide. Despite her flaws and failures, her followers would defend her as their founder and leader, if not a full-fledged saint. Testimonials of her healing power and her concern for the poor would outweigh scandal. Actor Anthony Quinn's word spoke for many:

> During the Depression . . . the one human being that never asked you what your nationality was, what you believed in and so forth, was Aimee Semple McPherson. All you had to do was pick up the phone and say, "I'm hungry," and within an hour there'd be a food basket there for you.[17]

KATHRYN KUHLMAN
Woman in Angel White Chiffon

At the time of Aimee's death in 1944, Kathryn Kuhlman had been preaching for some sixteen years. Like Aimee and Maria, she started out as an itinerant evangelist, often going from one small church to another, but moved on to the big time, making effective use of media. Her radio broadcasts were widely aired, and she advanced into the television age with her own syndicated show, where she promoted her best-selling books. Like Aimee, she loved to dress in exquisite white chiffon gowns and pricey jewelry, and she had a taste for fine dining and first-class travel. As was true of both Aimee and Maria, Kathryn's divorce was saturated with conflicting accounts.

Kathryn first became involved in ministry as a tenth-grade teenager by giving her testimony at revival meetings while traveling with her sister and brother-in-law, an itinerant evangelist. After that she joined with Helen Gulliford to serve five years in a mission church in Boise, Idaho, often traveling and conducting revivals. From there, she and Helen moved on to Pueblo, Colorado, and then Denver, where she held services for months at a time in vacant buildings, often featuring local musicians who were eager to test the waters.

For Kathryn, this era of her life was distinguished most notably by poverty. She and Helen often spent days cleaning the vacant building before posting handmade signs to advertise their meetings. Their accommodations for a time were a scrubbed-down chicken coop. But Kathryn had dreams of the stage and the bright lights. She networked with traveling evangelists, an effort that would launch her own revival ministry.

While in Denver in 1937, she first became acquainted with Burroughs Waltrip, a handsome itinerant evangelist, husband, and father of two children. The following year he divorced his wife and married Kathryn, despite the strong objections of Helen and other associates who angrily left the ministry. Forced out of Denver, Kathryn and Burroughs moved to Iowa and then began traveling from town to town, but the scandal-soaked social media moved faster than they did and their ministry tanked. In 1944, Kathryn left him, and four years later, he divorced her. Though stymied by stories of her failed marriage, she moved to Pennsylvania and soon reestablished herself through a radio ministry, which opened other doors for her. It was in this setting that she began her healing ministry.

She was hounded by a host of detractors throughout her ministry— those who opposed women preachers, those who claimed her healings were bogus, those who pointed to her divorce, those who thought she was cozy

231

Dominican Brother Remembers Kathryn

In January of 1971 two of us decided that we would make the trip from Oakland, California, to Los Angeles to attend one of Kathryn Kuhlman's monthly miracles services held at the Shrine Auditorium. . . . [She] came on stage with both hands raised high above her head. She was not young but was in good physical shape and the slim-fitting white dress with puffy chiffon sleeves gave her the appearance of an angel floating back and forth across the stage. The audience was ecstatic. Applause and singing filled the entire auditorium. . . . Some folksy talk followed. . . . The choir sang another song. Her black soloist, Jimmy MacDonald sang a special piece that was one of her favorites and her pianist, Dino Kartsonakis played his own ivory-breaking rendition of a familiar hymn on the concert grand that ended in a flourish with his hands flying over the keys. The grandeur was emphasized by the addition of the pipe organ, and choir. The audience broke into a standing ovation led by Miss Kuhlman who was clearly the mistress of ceremonies.

Brother Daniel Thomas, O.P., "Kathryn Kuhlman and the Miracle Years"

with Catholics (even reveling in her private audience with Pope Paul VI), those who sued her for breach of contract, and many others. Yet during the mid-twentieth century, she became the most celebrated female evangelist in North America. Aided by a team of musicians and lively music, Kathryn attracted people from miles around who came to be healed and "come under the power."

Like Aimee, she was in the limelight and was often accused of living a double life. And like Aimee, she healed others but struggled with an assortment of ailments herself. In 1975 she died at the age of sixty-eight after undergoing open-heart surgery.

CONCLUDING OBSERVATIONS

In contemplating these female evangelists, I wonder if there are any inferences we can draw from their lives. A brief survey such as this does not offer a valid statistical sampling, but we learn by making comparisons and contrasts. Maria, Aimee, and Kathryn carried with them the baggage of failed marriages at a time when divorce was not nearly as common as it is today. The same was true of Carry Nation, who was on the evangelistic circuit before and concurrently with Maria Woodworth-Etter. Pandita Ramabai continued in ministry for many years without such scandal. That she hailed from a very traditional Indian culture may have been a significant factor. Likewise, she was not tempted to become a stage celebrity as the others were.

Each of the four major women in this overview had a distinguishing style. Maria was known for her trances onstage during which time she typically froze with her hand raised and received visions that often provided content for her sermons. A cynic might wonder if that time provided an opportunity for her to gather her thoughts and proceed with the sermon. Aimee Semple McPherson utilized high drama and flair to draw crowds, and she was known for her healing powers and humanitarian outreach. Katherine Kuhlman was also celebrated for healing, as well as for her lilting voice and long white dresses.

Pandita did not have the bearing or the stage presence possessed by the others, nor the flattering fans. Those who knew her recognized first her keen mind. She was not one to be pushed around, nor did she fawn over missionaries and the culture and lifestyle of the West. But she too had a charismatic flair, and she could count miracles as numerous as any other Pentecostal evangelist on the circuit or in a settled ministry.

Of Susie and Rosa we know too little to take away lasting impressions. Perhaps one day their stories and those of other Hispanic women in ministry will be available in more detailed accounts.

QUESTIONS TO THINK ABOUT

Have you ever imagined yourself as an evangelist speaking to large crowds? What kind of evangelism do you regard as most effective: stadium crowds listening to a celebrity speaker, or one of many varieties of friendship or personal evangelism?

Do you believe that celebrity evangelists encounter more sexual temptations than do pastors or Christians working in offices, in academia, or in other fields? Would you compare the failed marriages of celebrity stage evangelists with those of Hollywood or Broadway actors?

How do you assess miracles, particularly those claimed by well-known evangelists? Have you ever known anyone to go into a trance onstage? How might you have regarded Maria? Have you ever witnessed a mass healing service? Have you or anyone you know professed to be healed by someone who drew crowds based on miraculous cures?

Had you been a missionary to India, would you have joined with other missionaries in being critical of—or at least very concerned about—Pandita's calling herself a Hindu (or culturally Indian) Christian? Do you see yourself as a culturally American Christian (or whatever your own nationality is)? Do you ever think about how much Western Christianity is influenced by culture in general and consumerism in particular?

Are you more inclined to be accepting of great healing miracles (and raising someone from the dead) or more skeptical? Would you be inclined to accept Aimee's account of her kidnapping, or would you be suspicious?

If you were able to spend a day with Maria, Pandita, Aimee, or Kathryn, which one would you choose? Which one would be most at ease at your church potluck or in a Bible study or book club?

14

Corrie ten Boom and Celebrated Speakers and Missionaries

Imagine life without books. I could survive, and maybe even thrive, without movies, television, lectures, even newspapers, but not without books. My husband reads to me early every morning and again every night before we turn in. He's a master of pronunciation and accents, and I'm the beneficiary. We have together refought the Revolutionary War, lived alongside Jayber Crow in Port William, Kentucky, joined the Guernsey Potato Peel Pie and Literary Club, spent millions of rubles and slogged through Russia with Catherine the Great, laughed ourselves sick with Ignatius Riley and his *Confederacy of Dunces*, and even joined Jezebel in plotting against Elijah.

Books have changed my life. The Bible, of course. I cannot comprehend what my life would be like if it were not for the profound influence that volume has had on me. But other books have also influenced me—one in particular that I read for course preparation in the late 1970s. I was asked if I would teach History of Missions. None of my doctoral course work in history had even touched on missionaries. The professor who was retiring commented that it was an important topic to teach, but it was too bad the subject matter was so boring.

For anyone teaching by the book, his words rang true. The texts were filled with facts and figures and dates. How could I ever teach this course? Then I picked up *Through Gates of Splendor* by Elisabeth Elliot, which tells the story of the deaths of five missionaries, including her husband Jim. The young men were killed after they entered the territory of a remote Ecuadorian tribe then known as the Aucas. I was left with more questions than answers, but no single volume has ever had a more profound impact on me.

My course became a biographical history of missions, which soon opened the door for my writing a book, *From Jerusalem to Irian Jaya: A Biographical History of Christian Missions*, and decades more of teaching and further writing in the field of missions. What direction would my life have taken, I ask myself, if it were not for the powerful pen of Elisabeth Elliot? Whether writing of the Auca tragedy or of the struggles of single female missionaries, Elisabeth had a way with words and a knack for irony that easily struck envy in the mind of this budding writer. In that respect she was a role model for me—though certainly not in every facet of her writing and teaching.

She was what I would term a hard-liner on traditional roles for women. In 1988, when I was a visiting professor at Trinity Evangelical Divinity School, she came to campus and one evening spoke to a large group of women, primarily seminary student wives. I learned only later when I listened to the tape how she had responded to a particular question: "Should a wife remain in a home where she is being physically abused by her husband?" In response, she pointed to 1 Peter 2 that speaks of slaves who were beaten. From there she moved to the next chapter, emphasizing that women *in the same way* ought to submit to their husbands. "I don't think that requires," she continued, "a woman necessarily to stay in a home where she is literally being physically beaten to death. But on the other hand, it might."

I cringed when I heard those words. I personally had stayed too long in a marriage where I feared "being physically beaten to death." With the wise counsel of Trinity's president Ken Meyer, I got out in time. Does the Bible require a woman to stay in such a marriage? Not necessarily, Elisabeth said. "But on the other hand, it might." With a room full of young married women, statistics would tell us that more than a few had been seriously abused. Some of them might have heard only those words: *on the other hand, it might.* But I've long ago realized that I can learn from people with whom I disagree. I view Elisabeth's writing as an opportunity not only for inspiration but also for intellectual engagement. Here we interact with Corrie ten Boom, Henrietta Mears, Mother Teresa, and Helen Roseveare, as well as with Elisabeth.

Suffering in the Service of Christ

In this chapter we discover, among other things, how women endured great suffering, particularly Corrie and her sister Betsie, but also Mother Teresa, Elisabeth, and Helen. From their own stories and their biographers' writings, we know how deeply they participated in the sufferings of Christ. Henrietta is the exception. On the surface, she suffered very little, a reminder, however, to each of us that some who appear to have it all together are actually deep down struggling with depression or other forms of invisible suffering.

> Dear friends, do not be surprised at the fiery ordeal that has come on you to test you, as though something strange were happening to you. But rejoice inasmuch as you participate in the sufferings of Christ, so that you may be overjoyed when his glory is revealed. If you are insulted because of the name of Christ, you are blessed, for the Spirit of glory and of God rests on you. If you suffer, it should not be as a murderer or thief or any other kind of criminal, or even as a meddler. However, if you suffer as a Christian, do not be ashamed, but praise God that you bear that name. For it is time for judgment to begin with God's household; and if it begins with us, what will the outcome be for those who do not obey the gospel of God?
>
> 1 Peter 4:12–17

CORRIE TEN BOOM
Holocaust Survivor

One of the striking aspects of Corrie's fascinating life is that it hardly seems to begin until she is fifty years old. Her story is primarily that of an old woman, the very opposite of that of the other most noted heroine of the Nazi occupation of the Netherlands, the young girl Anne Frank. Corrie was in her midthirties when Anne was born.

We come to know them both through their writings. Corrie tells of her years of great sacrifice and of horrendous hardship in a concentration camp. Her miracle stories are balanced by her own temptation not to forgive her onetime ruthless prison guard. She is a modern-day saint—almost too good to be true. Not so, Anne Frank. She was a strong-willed Jewish girl who, amid Nazi terrors all around her, wrote of issues with her mother: "I need my mother to set a good example and be a person I can respect, but in most matters she's an example of what *not* to do." Again she wrote: "Although I'm only fourteen . . . I have my opinions, my own ideas and principles, and although it may sound pretty mad from an adolescent, I feel more of a person than a child, I feel quite independent of anyone."[1]

It is difficult to imagine Corrie writing such words as a teenager. She much later reflected on her close identity with Jews: "There, in Amsterdam in that narrow street in the ghetto they met many wonderful Jewish people. They were allowed to participate in their Sabbaths and in their feasts. They studied the Old Testament together."[2] But though in close proximity, they were worlds apart in many respects.

Following in the footsteps of her father and grandfather, Corrie was a watchmaker, the first licensed woman watchmaker in the Netherlands. But she is known today for her family's hiding Jews and her own Nazi concentration-camp horrors. Her family, including her parents, three siblings, and three aunts, all lived together in cramped quarters above the shop in Haarlem.

The Ten Boom family's involvement in the Dutch underground began in 1942, when they helped neighbors who were forced to leave their homes. Through their Reformed Church and business connections, they networked with trusted friends to provide temporary housing. Despite their crowded space, they hid as many as seven people at a time behind false walls and other secret spaces. But less than two years later, the Gestapo was on their steps. Those hidden managed to escape. But Corrie, her sister Betsie, and their father were arrested. The old man died in custody a short time later.

Corrie and Betsie were taken to the infamous Ravensbrück concentration camp, where tens of thousands would die. It was a hellhole where women fought for every blanket and particle of food and clothing. The sisters found themselves caged in with what seemed to be wild animals beaten down by Nazi guards. But together they vowed to make the best of their dire circumstances. They began reading Scripture and praying, inviting others to join. After a time their influence on barracks 28 began to make a difference.

Corrie later told how she had smuggled a small bottle of much-prized medicine into the barracks. When Betsie became ill, she gave her some each day. But others found out and were soon begging for the miracle medicine for themselves. Tempted to hoard, she reluctantly shared it with others at Betsie's urging:

> It was hard to say no to eyes that burned with fever, hands that shook with chill. I tried to save it for the very weakest—but even these soon numbered fifteen, twenty, and twenty-five. . . . And still, every time I tilted the little bottle, a drop appeared at the tip of the glass stopper. It just couldn't be! I held it up to the light, trying to see how much was left, but the dark brown glass was too thick to see through.[3]

The sisters were convinced that God had miraculously increased the liquid in the tiny bottle even as he would see them through this awful ordeal. They tried to remain optimistic, sharing with each other about their dreams of freedom. Betsie wanted to set up a home for refugees, but like so many others, she did not survive the starvation diet and the filthy, disease-ridden, overcrowded conditions of the concentration camp. She died before Christmas in 1944. Corrie was released less than two weeks later.

After the war, word of the sisters' suffering quickly spread. Corrie was invited to speak at nearby churches, then in larger venues, and finally around the world, traveling to more than sixty countries, from Israel and India to America and Vietnam. During a visit to Germany in 1947, Corrie later told how a man came up to greet her after her talk. She immediately recognized him as one of her cruel guards: "And I, who had spoken so glibly of forgiveness, fumbled in my pocketbook rather than take that hand. He would not remember me, of course—how could he remember one prisoner among those thousands of women? But I remembered him and the leather crop swinging from his belt. I was face-to-face with one of my captors and my blood seemed to freeze." He introduced himself as a guard at Ravensbrück, not knowing she recognized him. He explained that since those days he had become a Christian, and he wanted her forgiveness.

> And I stood there—I whose sins had again and again to be forgiven—and could not forgive. Betsie had died in that place—could he erase her slow terrible death simply for the asking? It could not have been many seconds that he stood there—hand held out—but to me it seemed hours as I wrestled with the most difficult thing I had ever had to do.[4]

HENRIETTA MEARS
Teacher Extraordinaire

In her *New York Times* review of the film *Fargo* (1996), Janet Maslin writes:

> The Coens [brothers Joel and Ethan] are at their clever best with this snow-bound film noir, a crazily mundane crime story set in their native Midwest . . . merrily evoking the singsong drabness of Midwestern life. . . . The violence is so quick it appears cartoonish. . . . Yet the film makers' absurdist humor and beautifully honed storytelling give it a winning acerbity, a quirky appreciation of the sheer futility captured on screen.[5]

Henrietta was born in 1890 in Fargo, North Dakota, and grew up in Minnesota, the actual setting of most of the film. I suspect that if she had been born a generation later, she would have made a point to see the film and would have relished its absurdist humor. She was dead serious about Bible teaching, but her quick wit and self-deprecating sense of humor and satire were only a clever quip away.

She was schooled in the fundamentalism of the early twentieth century, but she cleverly mocked her own deadly serious explication of the Bible and that of others. Her most often-repeated spoof was her retelling of the familiar nursery rhyme "Old Mother Hubbard." Her varied audiences typically consisted of serious-minded university students who felt honored to sit under her teaching. But on occasion, to bring some lighthearted fun into the room, she would play the part in a whimsical costume with an odd assortment of accessories, gripping a phone book that substituted for the Bible.

After reading the rhyme to the end, she invited her listeners to go back to the beginning to draw out the fuller meaning of the text. She dug into each word and phrase seeking a deeper understanding of the *old* woman and the *poor* dog and even how the woman *went* to her cupboard. The *wenting* and the *cupboard* were begging for in-depth exegesis, and the text as a whole was a sad commentary on life itself. Her skit was an obvious spoof on certain preachers. Henrietta's zany humor was a real hit, and the students howled with laughter.

Having grown up in Minneapolis from the time she was eight, Henrietta enrolled at the University of Minnesota and after graduating taught in a public high school for more than a dozen years. Her first year of teaching was in a nearby small town, where she taught chemistry and served as principal. The following year she transferred to another nearby school, again as principal and chemistry teacher. Here she organized and coached a football team. In her spare time she taught Sunday school and Bible classes. After leaving that school, she returned to Minneapolis, where she taught chemistry at Central High School for the next decade.

Her return to Minneapolis set the stage for the next decades in two significant ways. She teamed up with her sister Margaret in their living arrangement and evangelistic outreach that would continue for more than thirty years, and she also committed herself to teaching Sunday school as a second vocation. She took on a small class of uninterested girls that over the years grew into the hundreds, and many of the young women entered ministry themselves.

Word of her Sunday school success soon spread to other states and around the country. Then a call came from the large and prestigious Holly-wood Presbyterian Church. She accepted, and for the next thirty-five years she served as the director of Christian education. Revitalizing the Sunday school was her primary assignment, but she would expand that role into teaching young adults, publishing, and establishing a retreat center.

That she built a Sunday school of a few hundred kicking and screaming children of church members to some six thousand eager students is the stuff of legend in itself. Finding suitable educational materials, however, posed a problem that would somersault into Gospel Light Publications and become a worldwide ministry. Initially, Henrietta wrote the materials herself, but as the company grew others joined her, and the company would later expand into book publishing and other areas. Her Forest Home Retreat Center, purchased in 1938, would also exert a wide influence.

Beyond her grand success in Sunday school, publishing, and conference sponsorship, Henrietta's most lasting legacy was perhaps felt among individuals she influenced on a personal level, particularly young men. Among her protégés were Bill Bright (founder of Campus Crusade for Christ), Dawson Troutman (founder of the Navigators), Richard Halverson (chaplain of the US Senate), and Billy Graham, who said her impact on him was greater than that of any other woman with the exception of his wife.

She observed these young men enter ministry, marry, and raise families, while she remained single. She later told of a young man who had

Tragedy and the Birth of Forest Home

A tropical system centered on the San Bernardino Mountains brought rain that year on January 30th. Beginning February 27th a second series of storms dumped 50 inches of rain in some mountain locations over six days. . . . Forest Home Resort had been for sale for $50,000, but the trout fishing operation and structures had been severely damaged in the flood. In July 1938 Henrietta Mears purchased Forest Home, 320 acres with 52 cabins, dining and dance halls, tennis and badminton courts, a soda fountain and coffee shop for $30,000 and the current Forest Home was born. In the valleys below, hundreds had died, thousands were homeless, 100 bridges were gone in San Bernardino, and it would take years to rebuild and regain the prior progress.

Shannon Wray, "The Life of the Canyon," *Bear Facts*, Winter 2011 shown particular interest in her when she was young, but his lack of a strong Christian commitment was unacceptable to her. That she and her sister Margaret had developed a tight partnership did not bode well for marriage, nor did her strong personality and career success. Her humor easily diffused threats to the male ego, but as a wife she might have been intimidating. Her own rationale for not marrying was as simple as it was comical—that she had never found anyone who could match the qualities of the apostle Paul.

Henrietta loved living in style in a beautiful home, wearing high fashion, pricey jewelry, big hats, and bobbed hair as did the flappers of the 1920s. She recognized the fun she could have with fashion and her own quirky personality, and she laughed the loudest when her boys dressed in drag and mimicked her. She would have never been mistaken for an earlier version of Mother Teresa.

MOTHER TERESA
Twentieth-Century Doubting Saint

"Darkness is such that I really do not see—neither with my mind nor with my reason—the place of God in my soul is blank—There is no God in me—when the pain of longing is so great—I just long & long for God. . . . The torture and pain I can't explain."[6] These words were written by Mother Teresa in the early 1960s, more than three decades after she began her mission work in India, and more than thirty-five years before she died.

Only her confessors and closest friends had any idea that she struggled so with doubts. "Where is my faith?" she asked on another occasion. "Even deep down there is nothing but emptiness and darkness. If there be a God—please forgive me." Still again, she wrote that "the reality of darkness and coldness and emptiness is so great that nothing touches my soul."[7]

There was nothing in her childhood or early adult years that would have signaled the crises of faith Mother Teresa would later endure. She was born Agnes Bojaxhiu in1910, the youngest of three children. Life was easygoing in the Albanian village of her childhood until she was nine, the year her father died. Though left impoverished, her mother was buoyed by her devout faith and opportunities to serve in the community. Agnes drew on her mother's faith and was inspired by stories of missionary sisters who had gone to India, many living in poverty in thatched huts with danger on all sides.

It was no surprise then when Agnes, at age nineteen, informed her mother that she wished to be a missionary. Her mother gave her blessing, and her daughter sailed for India a short time later. At twenty-one, she took her vows to become a Loreto sister and was assigned to teach in a girls' school. Several years later she was appointed headmistress.

She might have carried on with that work until her death, but for what she was convinced was the voice of God while traveling to her annual retreat:

> This is how it happened, I was traveling to Darjeeling by train, when I heard the voice of God. . . . I was sure it was God's voice. I was certain that He was calling me. The message was clear I must leave the convent to help the poor by living among them. This was a command, something to be done, something definite. I knew where I had to be. But I did not know how to get there.[8]

That she heard this call was as natural as it was supernatural. That she would spend her life in a cloistered convent educating girls from India's prosperous families was not what she had envisioned for her missionary vocation. But to follow her call into the streets was regarded as ludicrous by some of her superiors who thought she was too frail for such strenuous work. She was persistent, however, and only two years later was authorized to form a new religious order, the Missionaries of Charity. Three of her students volunteered to join her. From the beginning, she determined that this would be a convent without walls: "Our Sisters must go out on the street. They must take the tram like our people, or walk to where they are going. That is why we must not start institutions and stay inside. We must not stay behind walls and have our people come to us."[9]

In the decades that followed, the Missionaries of Charity grew at a steady pace. When she left India for the first time in 1960, there were more than one hundred sisters in the order. Now the world was getting to know her as she traveled through Europe and America. People were taken with her, dressed in her blue and white Indian sari, a worn gray sweater over her shoulders and sandals on her bare feet. Who was this tiny woman who was defined by her ministry to the poorest of the poor? Everywhere she went reporters followed, people volunteered, and money flowed into her coffers.

Soon there were thousands of Missionaries of Charity stationed around the world and not in underdeveloped countries only. New York City and San Francisco became centers of outreach. As the spotlight turned on her various ministries, critics raised issues. It was true that she was in many respects a poor administrator. Yet she alone remained in control. She was a dictator, some charged. Others challenged her rigid stance against birth control and family planning in India and in other countries where babies and young children were dying of starvation.

In December 1979, a year before her seventieth birthday, Mother Teresa accepted the Nobel Peace Prize, which brought even greater focus on her selfless missionary service. When asked how she identified herself, she responded: "By blood and origin, I am all Albanian. My citizenship is Indian. I am a Catholic nun. As to my calling, I belong to the whole world. As to my heart, I belong entirely to Jesus."[10] She remained active in ministry until her death in 1997, at age eighty-seven.

An Outsider's Support of Mother Teresa

Their life is tough and austere by worldly standards, certainly: yet I never met such delightful, happy women, or such an atmosphere of joy as they create. Mother Teresa, as she is fond of explaining, attaches the utmost importance to this joyousness. The poor, she says, deserve not just service and dedication, but also the joy that belongs to human love. . . . The Missionaries of Charity . . . are multiplying at a fantastic rate. Their Calcutta house is bursting at the seams, and as each new house is opened, there are volunteers clamoring to go there. As the whole story of Christendom shows, if everything is asked for, everything—and more—will be accorded; if little, then nothing.

Malcolm Muggeridge, *Something Beautiful for God*

ELISABETH HOWARD ELLIOT
Missionary and Writer

In *No Graven Image*, Margaret Sparhawk is a fictional character who sacrifices the pleasures and delights of an American middle-class life to serve as a missionary among the Quichuas in Ecuador. Without medical training, she seeks to offer basic treatments to the sick and injured. She has become acquainted with Rosa and her children, and when Pedro injures his leg, she offers to give him a shot of penicillin. However, he dies, probably from a reaction to the antibiotic. Had she left him alone, he no doubt would have survived.

> O ineffable, sardonic God who toys with our sacrifices and smashes to earth the humble, hopeful altars we have built for a place to put Your name! Do you mock me? Why did You let him die? Why did You let me kill him? O God! I came to bring him life—*Your* life—and I destroyed him in Your name.[11]

If readers are hoping to find resolution at the end of the book, they are disappointed. Margaret does not pack up and return home—at least not yet—but her once secure calling is shaken, as is her faith. The book was so controversial that some Christian booksellers refused to display it on their bookshelves. But it certainly was not the only controversial book written by the hand of Elisabeth Elliot.

In many respects fictional Margaret is Elisabeth herself. Like Margaret, she had gone to South America as a single woman and struggled with loneliness and was not taken as seriously as were the missionary men. In *These Strange Ashes*, she tells how she was one of four single missionaries stationed together, each hoping to escape their plight through marriage—preferably to a single male missionary. In the meantime, they struggled desperately with boredom in the jungle. Elisabeth recounted her "dimestore" dreams—the longing to just wander the aisles and make a little purchase of nothing more than scotch tape or a nail file. She distracted herself with every imaginable household task just to avoid the hard work of language learning. Days dragged into weeks and months.

Then she was faced with two very serious setbacks. The first was the death of a tribal woman whom the four women had tried to save in childbirth: "It was a life and death matter, and if God had spared Maruja's life, the whole Quinones tribe might have been delivered from spiritual death. In my heart I could not escape the thought that it was God who had failed." Sometime later when Macario, her faithful and indispensable language informant, was murdered, she questioned her calling: "Had I come here, leaving so much behind, on a fool's errand? . . . How was I to reconcile His permitting such a thing with my own understanding of the missionary task?"[12]

If these incidents pulled the very rug of divinity out from under Elisabeth, the worst was yet to come. Her escape from her life among the Colorado Indians came with her marriage to Jim Elliot. They had known each other at Wheaton College when he envisioned himself as an unmarried missionary giving his entire life to evangelizing those who had never heard the gospel. Now they would work as a team. They might have carried on with their work in the jungle of Ecuador for decades, like most missionaries unknown to the outside world, but for Operation Auca.

Operation Auca, a rash ploy to enter the lands of very territorial native warriors who had killed outsiders before, ended with the tragic death of Jim Elliot and four other young missionaries. In my biographical history of missions and in other writings I have been critical of their approach, arguing that it should not be seen as a model for mission outreach to native peoples. It was a hastily conceived strategy so risky that two of the men flew out each night because the natives were known to attack in the predawn hours. Because of the obvious danger the venture was top secret, details of which were transmitted by coded messages. No one outside the small group was informed, not the most seasoned missionaries in the area, not even their mission superiors.

Fearing the outsiders, the native warriors speared all five of the men to death on January 8, 1956, only a few months after their entry into the territory had been secretly devised. Within days, however, it became the most publicized missionary news story of the twentieth century. In 1957 Elisabeth told the story in her book, *Through Gates of Splendor*. But Operation Auca would not be the end of the story. Rachel Saint, sister of Nate Saint, one of the five killed and the pilot of the operation, was a Wycliffe missionary nearby who had been learning the tribal language with Dayuma, a woman who had left the Auca territory. In September 1958, Dayuma visited her people and then invited Rachel and Elisabeth, with her young daughter, Valerie, to come and live in the tribe, which they did.

The story of Operation Auca and its aftermath is complicated and controversial. Elisabeth realized that herself. "For those who saw it as a great Christian martyr story," she later reflected, "the outcome was beautifully predictable. All puzzles would be solved. God would vindicate Himself. Aucas would be converted and we could all 'feel good' about our faith." However, that is not the way it happened. "The truth is that not by any means did all subsequent events work out as hoped. There were negative effects of the missionaries' entrance into Auca territory. There were arguments and misunderstandings and a few really terrible things, along with the answers to prayer."[13]

Elisabeth, who suffered from Alzheimer's in her later years, was an outspoken and controversial writer. In the process she managed to offend—and inspire—evangelicals and others on almost any issue her quick mind and cunning pen tackled. She refused to be ignored.

HELEN ROSEVEARE
Missionary Medical Doctor

The story is chilling. The setting, a mission compound in a Congo jungle. The year 1964, long after sundown on October 29. Americans would celebrate their scariest holiday two days later, but what happened that pitch-black night was far worse than any imagined Halloween horrors. Helen was an unmarried missionary medical doctor who had turned her back on a bright future in England to bring health care to some of the world's most needy people.

The Congo was in the midst of a violent civil war, and for some months the compound had been occupied by Simba rebels. Helen had been strongly counseled to evacuate the country, but she insisted that the people needed her medical services now more than ever. She heard gunfire, but that had become the norm. She was sleeping in her small bungalow, doors and windows bolted shut. Then without warning, her door was kicked down. In barely a nanosecond, terror shot through her like high-voltage electric current. She had to run, to get out, to escape, to flee to the tangled jungle.

They found me, dragged me to my feet, struck me over head and shoulders, flung me on the ground, kicked me, dragged me to my feet only to strike me again—the sickening, searing pain of a broken tooth, a mouth full of sticky blood, my glasses gone. Beyond sense, numb with horror and unknown fear, driven, dragged, pushed back to my own house—yelled at, insulted, cursed. . . . My God, my God, why have you forsaken me?[14]

After that awful incident she was taken to a convent where other women, including nuns, had been imprisoned by the rebels. There the horror of that night of rape was repeated over and over again. Amid the terror, she was able to minister to other women and on one occasion to push a rebel soldier away from a trembling teenage girl who had just been brought in and to volunteer to go out into the night herself to suffer unspeakable brutality.

During a time when the "taboo subject" of rape was rarely written about and surely not spoken of in polite company, Helen was unusually honest about the trauma she endured. "At that time we were not taught in missionary training school how to face up mentally to where rape fits into the picture," she later recalled. "The strange thing is, of course, that the actual sexual experience of rape does stir you. You suddenly find yourself sexually awakened. And it was terrible because right in the suffering, in all the awfulness of prison life, beatups and everything, this other thing came too."[15]

Born in 1925 in Cornwall, England, Helen enjoyed privilege as the daughter of a highly acclaimed mathematician who had been knighted for his outstanding service during World War I. After graduating from an exclusive girls' boarding school, she went on to Cambridge for a degree in medicine. Few missionaries had come to the Congo with such stellar credentials, but she quickly realized that education and background counted for little. Blatant gender bias was the norm. She was assigned a region, however, where she was her own boss and was able to set up a medical center with the help of Africans. She fought back when she was ordered to relocate to an old leprosy complex, but to no avail. So again she set up a training school and an outpatient clinic.

Helen was driven. Her accomplishments were legendary. She moved with a long stride and at a furious pace, preferring to work without other missionaries interfering. But, as such, she was a threat to the male mission executives. So several years after she arrived in the Congo, a young male doctor who had just arrived on the field was assigned to take over her work and serve as her supervisor. It was an outrage. All her arduous labor of building a successful endeavor was now in the hands of a novice. She was distraught. He even took over her Bible class for the nursing students. Then he fired her van driver, who knew all the rutted, winding two-track trails. She knew she had been beaten, emotionally as well as professionally. She requested home leave and returned to England.

Back home, however, she realized that her heart was still in Africa. But she was convinced that as a single woman she could never accomplish what needed to be done. She would find a husband, preferably a surgeon. And so it was; she snagged the perfect man. But when the innocent doctor realized she was grooming him for the Congo, he got cold feet.

She had purchased new clothes, permed her hair, and even resigned from the mission in an effort to win him. The breakup was a very trying time, as she later confessed: "Well, in the end I jolly near mucked up the whole furlough. I couldn't find a husband in the mission, so I got out of the mission. God let me go a long way, and I made an awful mess. Then God graciously pulled me back and the mission graciously accepted me back."[16]

When she returned to the Congo in 1960, the independence movement was becoming more violent. She nevertheless continued her work and took over the now-abandoned medical center she had built years earlier. The young doctor who had taken her place had fled the country with his family. In the following years she carried on with the work, particularly the work of training young men as nurses, many of whom were then licensed by the government. Then the work stopped suddenly in late October 1964, when she was taken into captivity after having been assaulted and raped. Two months later American and Belgian troops rescued her and others. Only then did she learn that many missionaries and countless Congolese had been brutally killed.

On returning home, Helen was too mentally and physically broken to even imagine going back to the Congo—that is, until letters began arriving from her students begging her to help them put their war-torn nation back together. How could she? But just over a year later she was back directing cargo planes as they ferried everything from food to building materials into remote landing strips. Within a year she was back at her base and rebuilding her school and clinic. But life would never be the same. New students with a spirit of independence and nationalism were unwilling to defer to the demands of an authoritarian white woman teacher.

Yet she stayed on for seven more years. The ending, however, was perhaps in some ways almost as painful as the brutality she endured at the hands of rebel soldiers.

> When I knew I was coming home from the field and a young medical couple were taking my place at the college and an African colleague was taking over the directorship of the hospital, I organized a big day. It was to be a welcome to the two new doctors, a handover to my colleague, graduation day for the students in the college, and my farewell. A big choir had been practicing for five months. I got lots of cassettes to record everything and films to snap everything. Then at the last moment the whole thing fell to bits. The student body went on strike. I ended up having to resign the college where I'd been the director twenty years.[17]

Why did she decide to waste her life in Africa in the first place? She was a brilliant physician who could have practiced in London or anywhere else in the British Isles. Now she was back home depressed and disgraced. She might have blamed others, but instead she blamed herself. Perhaps she was too strong willed and dictatorial. She might have been more forgiving of her students who were finding their way amid the new spirit of freedom. Her openness and honesty opened the door for invitations to share her story, and in the decades that followed she traveled the world speaking at conferences and colleges, swaying audiences with her humility and humor—and her unmistakable British accent.

Concluding Observations

Anyone who has ever endured the anguish of being fired—or given a terminal appointment or let go or laid off—knows that at the time the news is devastating. But for Dr. Helen Roseveare and many of us, we come to realize that it is possible to journey beyond such potholes and discover there is smooth pavement ahead. Helen was very familiar with impassable two-track roads through the Congo forests and the pitiless perils lurking in the midnight jungle. But the most difficult-to-navigate depression in the road appeared suddenly and where she least expected it—so suddenly that she might have been altogether derailed in her life journey. Instead, she pulled herself out of the mud, trudged home, took a new direction, and revved her engine, cheered on by compassionate crowds.

Elisabeth and Mother Teresa might also be categorized as celebrity missionaries. Like Helen they were both unusually honest in relating personal issues they encountered as missionaries who were supposed to serve as saintly role models. Elisabeth was plagued with idleness while questioning her calling. Mother Teresa struggled with doubts so dark as to obscure the very reality of God. Despite expectations to the contrary, Elisabeth reflected on Operation Auca and its aftermath not in pious platitudes but with hard-nosed integrity.

Corrie ten Boom in some ways became the ultimate celebrity saint for evangelicals, though the first five decades of her life are dim. But during her years of public ministry, there were no scandals or setbacks or serious censure. She reported many miracles, not the least of which was her willingness to forgive. Henrietta Mears was a force to be reckoned with who may have had little awareness of the power of her personality. She covered her dominating disposition as well as her faults and foibles with her quick wit and humor.

QUESTIONS TO THINK ABOUT

How do you relate to Helen Roseveare in her loss of her position as director and teacher of the school she founded? Have you ever been fired from a job? Is it easier to tell people openly that you were terminated or to accept an opportunity to resign and tell people that is what you did?

What can we learn from Helen's account of being raped? Are there both pros and cons in making public what is often a very private violent crime?

Do you think that most people today make a real sacrifice to serve in Christian ministry? Do you personally know of anyone making a sacrifice comparable to that of Mother Teresa, Elisabeth, or Helen when they serve in cross-cultural missions?

Are you surprised to know that such a revered spiritual giant as Mother Teresa struggled with faith-threatening doubts? Do you think it is important for people to reveal the deepest doubts about God? Do you know people who have anguished over doubts about God's very existence?

Should Christians expect God to honor their sacrificial ministry by protecting them or those they depend on from violence, sickness, and death as Elisabeth seemed to expect? When someone says God saved her when she missed her connection on the plane that crashed after takeoff, how should we respond? Is such a statement implying that while God purposely saved her, he purposely did not save all those who died?

Do you like to think of those in Christian ministry as saintly individuals? Is that how you perceive Corrie ten Boom and the others?

Epilogue

When we consider Matthew's genealogy of Jesus or Hebrews 11 (the biblical Hall of Faith), or when we consider all the other women and men who walk out of the pages of the Bible, we, without even trying, recognize our sameness with this unseemly lot.

> We . . . meet sundry folk
> even more exotic than ourselves.
> "By adventure"—
> by happenstance—
> we have fallen into fellowship.[1]

Try as they may, most of them fall far short of what we—and they—have idealized as the holy Christian life. We do them no service when we gloss over their flaws and failures. It is no different when we look about us in church, or when we gather at the city park for a grand family reunion. We see those about us as we see ourselves if we are honest.

Should it be any different when we open the pages of our Christian heritage? Should we be surprised when women of faith have feet of clay? For too long good Christian biographers have tried to convince us that these women were mostly sweet ladies, more than that, saints and heroines. But we have learned that neither Hildegard nor Teresa of Ávila were saints in a conventional way. Nor were Amy Carmichael, Fanny Crosby, or even Mother Teresa. Indeed, messy spirituality permeates the Bible and the record of Christian history.

As such, these women offer road maps and signal detours on our own journey—a journey that looks backward to help us avoid the rough terrain ahead. But through their sacrifice and self-denial and passion, they also offer the inspiration of mountain vistas and the sparkling energy of river rapids. We have fallen into fellowship, and they join us on our journey, our own pilgrimage of faith.

Notes

Introduction

1. Madame Guyon Quotes, *Women of Christianity*, http://womenofchristianity.com/quotes/madame-guyon-quotes/.

2. Jerome, Letter 127, available at New Advent, http://www.newadvent.org.

3. Christina Nehring, "Heloise & Abelard: Love Hurts," *New York Times*, February 13, 2005.

4. Helen Taft Manning, "Address at Memorial Service for M. Carey Thomas," quoted in Helen Lefkowitz Horowitz, *The Power and Passion of M. Carey Thomas* (New York: Knopf, 1999).

Chapter 1: Thecla and Early Martyrs, Monastics, and Saints

1. Quoted in Peter Conn, *Pearl S. Buck: A Cultural Biography* (Cambridge, UK: Cambridge University Press, 1996), 20.

2. All quotes taken from the *Acts of Paul and Thecla*, available at New Advent, http://www.newadvent.org/fathers/0816.htm.

3. All quotes, unless otherwise specified, are from *The Martyrdom of Saints Perpetua and Felicitas*, available at http://www.ssfp.org/pdf/The_Martyrdom_of_Saints_Perpetua_and_Felicitas.pdf.

4. Joyce E. Salisbury, *Perpetua's Passion: The Death and Memory of a Young Roman Woman* (New York: Routledge, 1997), 92.

5. Mary Reed Newland, "Catholic Activity: Story of the Martyrdom of Sts. Felicity and Perpetua," Catholic Culture.org, http://www.catholicculture.org/culture/liturgicalyear/activities/view.cfm?id=248.

6. This and following citations from Methodius, *Banquet of the Ten Virgins*, trans. Rev. William R. Clark, available at http://mb-soft.com/believe/txua/methodiu.htm.

7. Jerome, letter 127, available at New Advent, http://www.newadvent.org/fathers/3001127.htm.

8. Quoted in Christopher A. Hall, *Reading Scripture with the Church Fathers* (Downers Grove, IL: InterVarsity, 1998), 44.

9. Ibid.

10. Jerome, letter 108, available at New Advent, http://www.newadvent.org/fathers/3001108.htm.

11. Quoted in *The Letter Collection of Peter Abelard and Heloise*, ed. David Luscombe, trans. Betty Radice (New York: Oxford University Press, 2013), 103.

12. Jerome, letter 23, to Eustochium, available at Christian Classics Ethereal Library, http://www.ccel.org/ccel/schaff/npnf206.v.XXII.html.

13. Quoted in Richard B. Lyman Jr., "Barbarism and Religion," in *The History of Childhood*, ed. Lloyd deMause (Lanham, MD: Rowman & Littlefield, 1974), 86.

14. Quoted in Marianne Dorman, "St Jerome and the Holy Women of Rome," http://marianne dorman.homestead.com/JeromeandPaula.html.

15. Gregory of Nyssa, *Life of St. Macrina*, available at The Tertullian Project, http://www .tertullian.org/fathers/gregory_macrina_1_life.htm.

16. Ibid.

17. Ibid.

18. Ibid.

19. Quoted in "The Life of Our Holy Mother Saint Mary of Egypt," http://www.abba moses.com/stmarylife.html.

Chapter 2: Hilda of Whitby and Medieval Nuns and Abbesses

1. Peter D'Epiro, *The Book of Firsts* (New York: Random House, 2010), 265.

2. Bede, *The Ecclesiastical History of the English People*, Oxford World Classics (Clarendon: Oxford, 1999), 212–13.

3. Bede, *Ecclesiastical History of England*, ed. A. M. Sellar, book 4, chap. 24, available at Internet Sacred Text Archive, http://www.sacred-texts.com/chr/bede/hist110.htm.

4. Alban Butler, *The Lives of the Primitive Fathers, Martyrs, and Other Principal Saints* (Edinburgh, 1799), 339.

5. Lina Eckenstein, *Women under Monasticism* (1896; repr., Project Gutenberg, 2013), http://www.gutenberg.org/files/42708/42708-h/42708-h.htm.

6. Rudolf, "The Life of Saint Leoba," trans. C. H. Talbot, in *Soldiers of Christ: Saints and Saints' Lives from Late Antiquity and the Early Middle Ages*, ed. Thomas F. X. Noble and Thomas Head (University Park: Penn State University Press, 1995), 259.

7. This and the following quotations, unless otherwise noted, are from Rudolf of Fulda, *Life of Leoba*, available at Internet Medieval Sourcebook, http://legacy.fordham.edu/halsall /sbook.asp.

8. Ibid.

9. Ibid.

10. All quotes from the letters of Abelard and Héloïse are from *The Letter Collection of Peter Abelard and Heloise*, ed. David Luscombe, trans. Betty Radice (New York: Penguin, 1974).

11. Ruth A. Tucker, "Heloise and Abelard's Tumultuous Affair," *Christian History* no. 30 (1991), http://www.christianitytoday.com/ch/1991/issue30/3028.html?start=3.

12. A letter from Clare of Assisi to Agnes of Prague (1253), Epistolae: Medieval Women's Letters, http://epistolae.ccnmtl.columbia.edu/letter/572.html.

13. G. K. Chesterton, *Saint Francis*, chap. 3, Saints.SQPN.com, http://saints.sqpn.com /saint-francis-by-g-k-chesterton-chapter-iii/.

14. Philip Hughes, *A Popular History of the Reformation* (New York: Image Books, 1960), 19.

Chapter 3: Hildegard of Bingen and Catholic Mystics and Scholars

1. Hildegard von Bingen, *Scivias*, quoted in Sabina Flanagan, "Hildegard von Bingen," http://www.hildegard.org/documents/flanagan.html#scivias.

2. Ibid.

3. Ibid.

4. Hildegard of Bingen, *Liber Subtilatum*, quoted in "The Life and Works of Hildegard von Bingen (1098–1179)," http://www.isi.edu/~lerman/music/Hildegard.html.

5. Quoted in "Work as Abbess," Land der Hildegard, http://landderhildegard.de/her-life /work-as-abbess/richardis-of-stade/.

6. Quoted in Barbara Newman, *Voice of the Living Light: Hildegard of Bingen and Her World* (Los Angeles: University of California Press, 1998), 13.

7. Quoted in "Work as Abbess."

8. *Scivias*.

9. Quoted in Dan Doriani, *Women and Ministry* (Wheaton: Crossway, 2003), 156.

10. Julian of Norwich, *Revelations of Divine Love*, available at Christian Classics Ethereal Library, http://www.ccel.org/j/julian/revelations/.

11. Quoted in Nicholas Watson and Jacqueline Jenkins, eds., *The Writing of Julian of Norwich* (University Park: Penn State University Press, 2006), 428.

12. Benedict XVI, General Audience, November 24, 2010, http://w2.vatican.va/content/bene dict-xvi/en/audiences/2010/documents/hf_ben-xvi_aud_20101124.html.

13. Quoted in Ruth A. Tucker and Walter L. Liefeld, *Daughters of the Church* (Grand Rapids: Zondervan, 1987), 158.

14. Catherine of Siena, *Dialogue*, quoted in "God the Giver of All Gifts—Catherine of Siena," Crossroads Initiative, http://www.crossroadsinitiative.com/library_article/1244/God _the_giver_of_all_Gifts____Catherine_of_Siena.html.

15. Gregory of Tours, *The History of the Franks* (New York: Penguin, 1974).

16. *The Book of Margery Kempe*, quoted in Alison Torn, "Margery Kempe: Madwoman or Mystic—A Narrative Approach to the Representation of Madness and Mysticism in Medieval England," in *Narrative and Fiction: An Interdisciplinary Approach*, ed. David Robinson, Noel Gilzean, Pamela Fisher, Tracey Lee, and Pete Woodcock (Huddersfield, UK: University of Huddersfield, 2008), 79–89, available at University of Huddersfield Repository, http://eprints.hud.ac.uk/4830/2/Chapter_9_Alison_Torn.pdf.

17. Ibid.

Chapter 4: Katherine Schütz Zell and Protestant Reformers

1. Roland Bainton, *Women of the Reformation in Germany and Italy* (Minneapolis: Augsburg, 1971), quoted in "The Hidden Tradition: Women of the Reformation, Part II," RPM Ministries website, http://www.rpmministries.org/2008/05/the-hidden-tradition-women -of-the-reformation-part-ii/.

2. Ibid.

3. Ibid.

4. Ibid.

5. Ibid

6. Ibid.

7. Ibid.

8. Ibid.

9. Ibid.

10. Quoted in Diane Severance, "You Wouldn't Want to Argue with Argula," Christianity .com, http://www.christianity.com/church/church-history/timeline/1201–1500/you-wouldnt -want-to-argue-with-argula-11629897.html.

11. Ibid.

12. Ibid.

13. Quoted in Ruth A. Tucker and Walter L. Liefeld, *Daughters of the Church* (Grand Rapids: Zondervan, 1987), 186.

14. Ibid.

15. Quoted in Olympia Morata, *The Complete Writings of an Italian Heretic* (Chicago: University of Chicago, 2003), 7.

16. Quoted in Ruth A. Tucker, "John Calvin and the Princess," *Christian History* (September 3, 2009), http://www.christianitytoday.com/ch/bytopic/women/johncalvinandtheprincess.html?allcomments=true&start=4.

17. Ibid.

18. Ibid.

19. Ibid.

20. Ibid.

21. Ibid.

22. Ibid.

23. Quoted in Cornelius J. Dyck, "Elisabeth and Hadewijk of Friesland," in *Profiles of Anabaptist Women*, ed. C. Arnold Snyder and Linda A. Huebert Hecht, Studies in Women and Religion (Waterloo, ON: Wilfrid Laurier University Press, 1996), 361.

24. Bainton, *Women of the Reformation*, 106.

Chapter 5: Teresa of Ávila and Sectarian "Heretics"

1. Brooke Allen, review of Abraham Verghese, *Cutting for Stone*, Barnes & Noble website, http://www.barnesandnoble.com/w/cutting-for-stone-abraham-verghese/1100047420?ean=9780375714368.

2. Saint Teresa, *The Life of Teresa of Jesus* (New York: Doubleday, 1960), lxvii.

3. Quoted in Ruth A. Tucker and Walter L. Liefeld, *Daughters of the Church* (Grand Rapids: Zondervan, 1987), 202.

4. Teresa, *Saint Teresa of Avila*, "Art Humanities Primary Source Reading 28," http://www.learn.columbia.edu/monographs/bernmon/pdf/art_hum_reading_28.pdf.

5. Tucker and Liefeld, *Daughters of the Church*, 203.

6. Ibid., 204.

7. Deborah Kuhn McGregor, "Childbirth-Travells," in *Childbirth: Midwifery Theory and Practice*, ed. Philip K. Wilson (New York: Garland, 1996), 178.

8. Tucker and Liefeld, *Daughters of the Church*, 221.

9. Ibid., 223.

10. "Trial and Interrogation of Anne Hutchinson (1637)," available at http://www.swarthmore.edu/SocSci/bdorsey1/41docs/30-hut.html.

11. Paul Della Valle, *Massachusetts Troublemakers: Rebels, Reformers, and Radicals from the Bay State* (Guilford, CT: Globe Pequot Press, 2009), 12.

12. Tucker and Liefeld, *Daughters of the Church*, 223.

13. Ibid.

14. "Ballad of George Fox," available at Quakers, http://quakers.nu/George.

15. Quoted in "Life of Margaret Fell," http://www.ushistory.org/penn/margaret_fell.htm.

16. Ibid.

17. Tucker and Liefeld, *Daughters of the Church*, 230.

18. Margaret Fox, *The Life of Margaret Fox*, Part II, http://www.hallvworthington.com/Margaret_Fox_Selections/MargaretMemoir2.html.

19. Ibid.

20. Ibid.

21. Dr. Clark, quoted in John W. Lewis, *The Life, Labors and Travels of Elder Charles Bowles*, available at Documenting the American South, http://docsouth.unc.edu/neh/lewis jw/lewisjw.html.

Chapter 6: Susanna Wesley and Eighteenth-Century Evangelists

1. *Susanna Wesley: The Complete Writings*, ed. Charles Wallace Jr. (New York: Oxford University Press, 1997), 98.

2. Adam Clarke, *Memoirs of the Wesley Family* (New York: Bangs & Mason, 1824), 91.

3. Quoted in Charles Edward White, "What Wesley Practiced and Preached about Money," *Leadership Journal* (Winter 1987), http://www.christianitytoday.com/le/1987/winter/87l1027 .html.

4. John Kirk, *The Mother of the Wesleys: A Biography* (London: Henry James Tresidder, 1864), 189.

5. Ibid., 194.

6. Ibid., 186.

7. William Henry Fitchett, *Wesley and His Century: A Study in Spiritual Forces* (London: Smith, Elder, 1906), 23.

8. *Susanna Wesley*, 367.

9. Ibid., 80.

10. *Journal of John Wesley*, available at Christian Classics Ethereal Library, http://www .ccel.org/ccel/wesley/journal.vi.iv.xviii.html.

11. Ibid.

12. John Wesley, *The Works of Rev. John Wesley* (London: John Mason, 1829), 386.

13. *Journal of John Wesley*.

14. Luke Tyerman, *The Life and Times of Rev. Samuel Wesley* (London: Simpkin, Marshall, 1866), 125.

15. John R. Tyson, "Lady Huntingdon, Religion and Race" in *Methodist History* 50, no. 1 (October 2011), 29.

16. Selina Hastings, "Addressed to My Dear Friends," available at http://digitalcollections .smu.edu/cdm/ref/collection/hunt/id/11.

17. Aaron C. Seymour and Jacob Foster, *The Life and Times of Selina* (London: William Edward Painer, 1839), 315.

18. John R. Tyson, "A Poor, Vile Sinner," *Methodist History* 37, no. 2 (January 1999): 116.

19. Ibid., 108.

20. "An Account of Sarah Crosby," 18th Century Religion, Literature, and Culture, http:// 18thcenturyculture.wordpress.com/primary-sources/the-armenian-magazine/an-account -of-sarah-crosby/.

21. "Account of Mrs. Sarah Ryan," 18th Century Religion, Literature, and Culture, http://18thcenturyculture.wordpress.com/primary-sources/the-armenian-magazine/account -of-mrs-sarah-ryan/.

22. Ted A. Campbell, "John Wesley's Intimate Disconnections," *Methodist History* 51, no. 3 (April 2013): 191.

23. Ibid., 192.

24. Ibid.

25. Robert Southey, *The Life of John Wesley* (London: Longman, Hurst, Rees, 1820), 2:302ff.

26. Wesley, *The Journal of the Reverend John Wesley*, ed. John Emory (New York: Mason & Lane, 1837), 553.

27. Luke Tyerman, *The Life and Times of the Rev. John Wesley* (London: Hodder & Stoughton, 1870), 2:289.

28. Quoted in Henry Moore, *The Life of Mrs. Mary Fletcher* (New York: G. Lane and C. B. Tippett, 1818), available at https://archive.org/details/lifemrsmaryflet00moorgoog.

29. Lawrence W. Wood, *The Meaning of Pentecost in Early Methodism* (Lanham, MD: Scarecrow, 2002), 233.

30. Dorothy Graham, "Methodist Women Local Preachers," Wesley Historical Society (NZ) publication #68, http://www.methodist.org.nz/files/docs/wesley%20historical/68%20methodist%20women%20local.pdf.

31. Mary Fletcher, letter, the original can be viewed at Mullock's Specialist Auctioneers & Valuers website, auction lot 316, http://www.mullocksauctions.co.uk/lot-42714-method ists_-_mary_fletcher_important_group_of_four.html.

32. Henry Moore, *The Life of Mrs. Mary Fletcher* (London: J. Collord, 1840), 115.

33. Ibid., 271.

34. Quoted in James Boswell, *The Life of Samuel Johnson, Ll.D.*, vol. 1 (London: J. F. Dove, 1824), 405.

Chapter 7: Narcissa Prentiss Whitman and American Protestant Missionaries

1. Nard Jones, *The Great Command* (Boston: Little, Brown, 1959), 202, 229.

2. "The Letters and Journals of Narcissa Whitman, 1836–1847," *Archives of the West*, PBS.org, http://www.pbs.org/weta/thewest/resources/archives/two/whitman1.htm.

3. Ibid.

4. Julie Roy Jeffrey, *Converting the West: A Biography of Narcissa Whitman* (Norman: University of Oklahoma Press, 1991), 147.

5. "Letters and Journals of Narcissa Whitman."

6. Ibid.

7. Ibid.

8. Ibid.

9. Leonard Warren, *Adele Marion Fielde: Feminist, Social Activist, Scientist* (New York: Routledge, 2002), 19.

10. Ibid., 23.

11. Ibid., 41.

12. Ibid., 62.

13. Quoted in Irwin Hyatt, *Our Ordered Lives Confess* (Cambridge, MA: Harvard University Press, 1976), 104–6.

14. Quoted in ibid., 96.

15. Ibid., 99.

16. Ibid., 104–5.

17. Ibid., 115.

18. Ibid., 113.

19. Ibid., 114.

Chapter 8: Jarena Lee and African American Evangelists

1. Tyler Glodjo, "How the Church Resegregated Schools in the South," *Christ and Pop Culture* 1, no. 9, Patheos, http://www.patheos.com/blogs/christandpopculture/how-the -church-resegregated-schools-in-jackson-tn/.

2. Jarena Lee, *Religious Experience and Journal* (Philadelphia, 1849), 4.

3. Ibid., 6.

4. Ibid., 11.

5. Ibid., 17.

6. Ibid., 62.

7. J. M. Thoburn, introduction to Amanda Smith, *An Autobiography* (Chicago: Meyer & Brother, 1893), vi, available at http://docsouth.unc.edu/neh/smitham/smith.html.

8. Smith, *Autobiography*, 17–18.

9. Ibid., 25.

10. Ibid., 29.

11. Ibid., 30.

12. Ibid.

13. Ibid., 31–32.

14. Ibid., 142.

15. "Mary McLeod Bethune, Educator and Civil Rights Activist," January 4, 2012, IIP Digital (website), http://iipdigital.usembassy.gov/st/english/publication/2012/01/201201041 20546ael0.4446331.html#axzz3RwjLPVcR.

16. Mary McLeod Bethune, *Building a Better World*, ed. Audrey Thomas McCluskey and Elaine M. Smith (Bloomington: Indiana University Press, 2001), 276.

17. Robert Weaver, "Her Boys Remember," *Time*, July 10, 1974 (special publication of the National Council of Negro Women).

18. Joseph Jeter, quoted in "Eliza Davis George," The Malachi Project, http://www.iho pkc.org/malachiproject/biography/eliza-george.

Chapter 9: Elizabeth "Betsy" Fry and Women of the Social Gospel

1. "Elizabeth Fry," National Women's History Museum website, https://www.nwhm.org /education-resources/biography/biographies/elizabeth-fry/.

2. Quoted in Rich Nathan, *Who Is My Enemy? Welcoming People the Church Rejects* (Grand Rapids: Zondervan, 2002), 118.

3. Richard Wheatley, *The Life and Letters of Mrs. Phoebe Palmer* (New York: W. C. Palmer Jr., 1876), 26.

4. Ibid., 30.

5. "Phoebe Palmer (1807–1874) and Holiness Theology," TeachUSHistory.org, http://www .teachushistory.org/second-great-awakening-age-reform/approaches/phoebe-palmer-1807 -1874-holiness-theology.

6. Wheatley, *Life and Letters*, 39.

7. Quoted in "Phoebe Palmer: Revivalist and Social Activist," Bible Gateway, July 11, 2008, https://www.biblegateway.com/devotionals/faithful-through-the-ages/2008/07/11.

8. Melvin E. Dieter, *The Holiness Revival of the Nineteenth Century* (Lanham, MD: Scarecrow, 1996), 24.

9. F. de L. Booth, *The Life of Catherine Booth: The Mother of the Salvation Army* (Old Tappan, NJ: Fleming H. Revell, 1893), https://archive.org/stream/lifeofcatherineb01bootiala /lifeofcatherineb01bootiala_djvu.txt.

10. Ibid.

11. Ibid.

12. Catherine Mumford Booth, *Female Ministry: Or, Woman's Right to Preach the Gospel*, available at The Voice, http://www.crivoice.org/WT-cbooth.html.

13. "Catherine Booth," *Christian History*, http://www.christianitytoday.com/ch/131
christians/activists/catherinebooth.html.

14. Catherine Bramwell-Booth, *Catherine Booth* (London: Hodder & Stoughton, 1970),
341.

15. David Malcolm Bennett, *The General: William Booth* (Longwood, FL: Xulon Press,
2003), 2:272.

16. Carry A. Nation, *The Use and Need of the Life of Carry A. Nation* (Topeka, KS:
F. M. Steves & Sons, 1909), available at https://archive.org/stream/useandneedoflife00natirich
/useandneedoflife00natirich_djvu.txt.

17. Fran Grace, *Retelling the Life* (Bloomington: Indiana University Press, 2001), 101.

18. Catherine Booth, *Female Ministry; Or, Woman's Right to Preach* (London: Morgan
& Chase), available at http://webapp1.dlib.indiana.edu/vwwp/view?docId=VAB7105&doc
.view=print.

19. "Phoebe Palmer (1807–1874) and Holiness Theology," TeachUSHistory.org, accessed August 18, 2015, http://www.teachushistory.org/second-great-awakening-age-reform
/approaches/phoebe-palmer-1807-1874-holiness-theology.

Chapter 10: Anne-Marie Javouhey and British and European Missionaries

1. Quoted in F. Calvin Parker, *The Good Book Is Better Than It Used to Be* (Bloomington,
IN: iVerse, 2009), 119.

2. Glenn D. Kittler, *The Woman God Loved* (Garden City, NY: Hanover House, 1959), 58.

3. Dom Antoine Marie OSB, Spiritual Newsletter, Abbey of Saint-Joseph de Clairval
website, May 13, 2006, http://www.clairval.com/lettres/en/2006/05/13/2100506.htm.

4. Kittler, *Woman God Loved*, 225.

5. Sarah A. Curtis, *Civilizing Habits: Women Missionaries and the Revival of French
Empire* (New York: Oxford University Press, 2012), 236.

6. Kittler, *Woman God Loved*, 176.

7. Quoted in Michael Richardson, "The Adventurous Nun," e-Catholic 2000, http://www
.ecatholic2000.com/cts/untitled-479.shtml.

8. Kittler, *Woman God Loved*, 227.

9. David B. Calhoun, "Mary Slessor: 'Mother of All the Peoples,'" *Knowing & Doing*,
C. S. Lewis Institute website, http://www.cslewisinstitute.org/webfm_send/624.

10. James Buchan, *The Expendable Mary Slessor* (New York: Seabury, 1981), 91, 95.

11. Quoted in W. P. Livingstone, *Mary Slessor of Calabar* (London: Hodder & Stoughton, 1915), 142–43.

12. Ibid., 295.

13. Ibid., 278.

14. Ibid., 303.

15. Elisabeth Elliot, *A Chance to Die: The Life and Legacy of Amy Carmichael* (Old
Tappan, NJ: Fleming H. Revell, 1987), 142, 338.

16. Frank Houghton, *Amy Carmichael of Dohnavur* (London: SPCK, 1954), 73.

17. Elliot, *Chance to Die*, 119.

18. "Amy Carmichael," The Traveling Team, http://www.thetravelingteam.org/amy
carmichael.

19. Elliot, *Chance to Die*, 121–22.

20. Ibid., 155–56.

21. Amy Carmichael, *Gold Cord: The Story of a Fellowship* (London: SPCK, 1932),
37, 179, 182.

22. Elliot, *Chance to Die*, 268, 270.

23. Stephen Neill, *God's Apprentice: The Autobiography of Stephen Neill* (London: Hodder & Stoughton, 1991), 95.

24. Ibid., 45.

25. Alan Burgess, *The Small Woman* (New York: Dutton, 1957), 29.

26. Mary Brogi, "Gladys Aylward: The Small Woman with a Big Heart for China," http://washingtonubf.org/Resources/Leaders/GladysAylward.html.

27. Burgess, *Small Woman*, 166.

Chapter 11: Harriet Beecher Stowe and Nineteenth-Century Poets and Writers

1. Charles Edward Stowe, *Life of Harriet Beecher Stowe* (New York: Houghton Mifflin, 1889), available at https://archive.org/details/cu31924022183382.

2. Ibid.

3. Ibid.

4. Harriet Beecher Stowe, letter to Calvin Stowe, January 1, 1847, Romantic Love Letters, http://www.theromantic.com/LoveLetters/harrietbeecher.htm.

5. Mary Kelly, "At War with Herself: Harriet Beecher Stowe as Woman in Conflict within the Home," *American Studies* 26, no. 2 (Fall 1978), https://journals.ku.edu/index.php/amer stud/article/viewFile/2264/2223.

6. Ibid.

7. "Rewriting Uncle Tom," *Washington Post*, September 16, 1888, http://utc.iath.virginia .edu/articles/n2ar19cmt.html.

8. J. M. K., "Safe in the Arms of Jesus," Christian Biography Resources, http://www.whole somewords.org/biography/bcrosby3.html.

9. Ibid.

10. Edith L. Blumhofer, *Her Heart Can See: The Life and Hymns of Fanny J. Crosby* (Grand Rapids: Eerdmans, 2005), 93.

11. Ibid., 95.

12. Emily Dickinson, no. 49, in *The Poems of Emily Dickinson*, ed. Thomas H. Johnson (Cambridge, MA: Belknap, 1955), 38, available at https://archive.org/details/poemsofemily dick030097mbp.

13. Dickinson to Abiah Root, 31 January 1846, in *The Letters of Emily Dickinson*, ed. Thomas H. Johnson (Cambridge, MA: Belknap, 1986), 27; Dickinson to Jane, 3 April 1950, Genius (website), accessed August 20, 2015, http://genius.com/Emily-dickinson-35-annotated.

14. Emily Dickinson, no. 1581, in Helen Vendler, *Dickinson: Selected Poems and Commentaries* (Cambridge, MA: Belknap, 2010), 496.

15. Roger Lundin, *Emily Dickinson and the Art of Belief* (Grand Rapids: Eerdmans, 1998), 34.

16. Emily Dickinson, no. 338, in Johnson, *Poems*, 270.

17. Emily Dickinson, no. 564, ibid., 431.

18. Emily Dickinson, no. 1601, quoted in Roger Lundin, *Emily Dickinson and the Art of Belief*, 2nd ed. (Grand Rapids: Eerdmans, 2004), 29–30.

19. Emily Dickinson, no. 377, in Johnson, *Poems*, 299–300.

20. Emily Dickinson, no. 79, ibid., 64.

21. Hannah Whitall Smith, *The Christian's Secret of a Happy Life* (Old Tappan, NJ: Fleming H. Revell, 1883), 47.

22. Hannah Whitall Smith, *God of All Comfort* (New York: Anamchara Books, 1987), 11.

23. Eliza F. Kent, *Converting Women: Gender and Protestant Christianity* (New York: Oxford University Press, 2004), 100.

24. Marie Henry, *The Secret Life of Hannah Whitall Smith* (Grand Rapids: Zondervan, 1984), 119; italics in original.

25. Kerri Allen, "Representation and Self-Representation: Hannah Whitall Smith as Family Woman and Religious Guide," *Women's History Review* 7, no. 2 (1998), http://www .tandfonline.com/doi/pdf/10.1080/09612029800200167.

26. Henry, *Secret Life*, 159.

27. Ibid., 28.

28. Ibid., 33–34.

29. Emily Dickinson, no. 442, in Johnson, *Poems*, 341.

Chapter 12: Susannah Thompson Spurgeon and Ministers' Wives

1. Fox Butterfield, "At Wellesley, a Furor over Barbara Bush," May 4, 1990, NYTimes .com, http://www.nytimes.com/1990/05/04/us/at-wellesley-a-furor-over-barbara-bush.html.

2. Lewis A. Drummond, *Spurgeon: Prince of Preachers* (Grand Rapids: Kregel, 1992), 225.

3. C. H. Spurgeon, *The Autobiography of Charles H. Spurgeon: Compiled from His Diary, Letters, and Records* (1899; repr., London: Forgotten Books, 2013), 4–5, http://www .forgottenbooks.com/readbook_text/The_Autobiography_of_Charles_v2_1000040588/11.

4. Ibid., 10–11.

5. Arnold Dallimore, *Spurgeon* (Chicago: Moody Press, 1984), 71.

6. Ibid.

7. J. D. Fulton, *Spurgeon, Our Ally* (Chicago: H. J. Smith, 1892), 345.

8. Russell Herman Conwell, *Life of Charles Haddon Spurgeon* (Edgewood, 1892), 310.

9. Quoted in Mark Hopkins, "The Down-Grade Controversy," *Christian History*, https ://www.christianhistoryinstitute.org/magazine/article/down-grade-controversy/.

10. Susannah Spurgeon, "Postscript by Mrs. C. H. Spurgeon," in C. H. Spurgeon, *The Autobiography of Charles H. Spurgeon*, vol. 2, *1854–1860*, comp. by Susannah Spurgeon (Cincinnati: Curtis & Jennings, 1899), 61, available at https://archive.org/details/chspurgeon sauto01spurgoog.

11. Paxton Hibben, *Henry Ward Beecher: An American Portrait* (New York: George H. Doran, 1927), 149.

12. Ibid., 204.

13. Ibid., 229, 252.

14. Ibid., 232, 238, 244–45.

15. Clifford E. Clark Jr., *Henry Ward Beecher: Spokesman for Middle-Class America* (Urbana: University of Illinois Press, 1978), 244.

16. Eunice Beecher, "Mr. and Mrs. Beecher's Plans," *Ladies' Home Journal* 9 (February 1892): 12.

17. "Oswald J. Smith," Wikipedia, accessed February 17, 2015, http://en.wikipedia.org /wiki/Oswald_J._Smith.

18. Hope Evangeline, *Daisy* (Grand Rapids: Baker, 1978), 45–46.

19. Lois Neely, *Fire in His Bones* (Wheaton: Tyndale, 1982), 140–41.

20. Ibid.,161, 167.

21. Ibid., 238–39.

22. Quoted in Sheri Stritof, "Ruth and Norman Vincent Peale Marriage Profile," About .com, http://marriage.about.com/od/religious/p/normanvpeale.htm.

23. Ruth Peale, *The Adventure of Being a Wife* (Englewood Cliffs, NJ: Prentice-Hall, 1971), 55.

24. Norman Vincent Peale, *The True Joy of Positive Living* (New York: Ballentine, 1984), 130–31.

25. R. Peale, *Adventure*, 155.

Chapter 13: Aimee Semple McPherson and Pentecostal Preachers

1. "Foursquare," Wikipedia, accessed February 17, 2015, http://en.wikipedia.org/wiki/Foursquare.

2. Glenn Burris Jr., "Get Ready to Join a Town Hall Meeting," Foursquare Church website, http://www.foursquare.org/news/article/get_ready_to_join_a_town_hall_meeting.

3. Maria Woodworth-Etter, *Marvels and Miracles* (1922), 16.

4. Gary Kukis, "The Gift of Tongues," November 13, 2006, http://kukis.org/Tongues/Tongues.htm.

5. Wayne Warner, *Maria Woodworth-Etter: For Such a Time as This* (Gainesville, FL: Bridge-Logos, 2004), 92.

6. Woodworth-Etter, *Marvels and Miracles*, 78.

7. Warner, *Maria Woodworth-Etter*, 351.

8. Gastón Espinosa, *Latino Pentecostals in America* (Cambridge, MA: Harvard University Press, 2014), 286.

9. Allan Anderson, "To All Points of the Compass: The Azusa Street Revival and Global Pentecostalism," *Enrichment Journal*, http://enrichmentjournal.ag.org/200602/200602_164_allpoints.cfm.

10. Helen Dyer, "Pandita Ramabai: The Story of the Great Revival at Mukti, India, 1905," *Revival Library*, http://www.revival-library.org/catalogues/1904ff/dyer.html.

11. Helen S. Dyer, *Pandita Ramabai: Her Vision, Her Mission and Her Triumph of Faith* (London: Pickering & Inglis, n.d.), 71.

12. Pandita Ramabai, *The High-Caste Hindu Woman* (London: George Bell & Sons, 1888), xxi.

13. Shamsundar Manohar Adhav, *Pandita Ramabai* (Madras: Christian Literature Society, 1979), 131.

14. Ibid.

15. Ibid., 141–42.

16. Ibid., 142.

17. Matthew Avery Sutton, *Aimee Semple McPherson and the Resurrection of Christian America* (Cambridge, MA: Harvard University Press, 2009), 196.

Chapter 14: Corrie ten Boom and Celebrated Speakers and Missionaries

1. Anne Frank, *The Diary of Anne Frank*, rev. critical ed. (New York: Doubleday, 2003), 565.

2. Corrie ten Boom, *Tramp for the Lord* (Washington, PA: CLC Publications, 1974), 145.

3. Corrie ten Boom, *The Hiding Place* (Peabody, MA: Hendrickson, 2009), 223.

4. Ten Boom, *Tramp for the Lord*, 56.

5. Janet Maslin, film review of *Fargo* (1996), *New York Times*, March 8, 1996, http://www.nytimes.com/movie/review?res=9803e1da1f39f93ba35750c0a960958260.

6. Mother Teresa, *Come Be My Light* (New York: Random House, 2007), 210.

7. Sinclere Lee, "A Question of Faith: Letters Reveal Mother Teresa Questioned the Existence of God," http://www.blacknewsweekly.com/news396.html.

8. Anne Sebba, *Mother Teresa: Beyond the Image* (New York: Doubleday, 1998), 46.

9. Eileen Egan, *Such a Vision of the Street: Mother Teresa—the Spirit and the Work* (New York: Doubleday, 1985), 90–91.

10. Ibid., 357.

11. Elisabeth Elliot, *No Graven Image* (New York: Harper & Row, 1956), 237.

12. Elisabeth Elliot, *These Strange Ashes* (San Francisco: Harper & Row, 1979), 108–9.

13. Elisabeth Elliot, "Thirty Years Later: The Auca Massacre," *Christian Life* (April 1986), 28.

14. Alan Burgess, *Daylight Must Come: The Story of a Courageous Woman Doctor in the Congo* (New York: Dell, 1975), 45.

15. Helen Roseveare, "A HIS Interview with Helen Roseveare," *HIS* (January 1977), 19.

16. Ibid., 18.

17. Ibid., 19.

Epilogue

1. Thomas Cahill, *Mysteries of the Middle Ages* (New York: Random House, 2006), 3.

Index